Cornell Studies in Industrial and Labor Relations
Number 23

Administering the Taylor Law: Public Employee Relations in New York

Ronald Donovan

ILR PRESS
School of Industrial and Labor Relations
Cornell University

Cover design by Lorraine Heasley

Library of Congress Cataloging in Publication Data

Donovan, Ronald, 1924–
    Administering the Taylor Law : public employee relations in New
York / Ronald Donovan.
        p.   cm. — (Cornell studies in industrial and labor relations
    : no. 23)
    Includes bibliographical references.
    ISBN 0–87546–163–8 (alk. paper). — ISBN 0–87546–164–6
(pbk. : alk. paper)
    1. Collective labor agreements—Government employees—New
York (State)   I. Title.   II. Series.
KFN5562.P8D66   1990
344.747′01890413539—dc20
[347.47041890413539]   89–71717
                                                             CIP

Copies may be ordered through bookstores or from
ILR Press
School of Industrial and Labor Relations
Cornell University
Ithaca, NY 14851–0952

Printed on acid-free paper in the United States of America
5   4   3   2   1

CONTENTS

PREFACE

MORE THAN TWENTY YEARS have passed since 1967, when
New York enacted the Taylor Law, officially the Public
Employees' Fair Employment Act, and created the New
York State Public Employment Relations Board (PERB)
to see to its administration. New York was not the first
state to establish by statute the right of public employees
to engage in collective bargaining with their government
employers. Several other states—Wisconsin (1959), Connecticut (1965), Michigan (1965), and a handful of others—had accorded similar rights to segments of their
public workforce. Yet, for many reasons, events in New
York drew national attention.

Part of the reason for the attention was the genuine luster of the committee of experts, chaired by George W.
Taylor, whose recommendations were largely incorporated
into the legislation. The committee's 1966 report had
been widely disseminated and had evoked vigorous discussion and comment, both commendatory and critical, in
the labor relations community and beyond. Moreover, fea-
tures of the law set it apart from its precursors in other
states, such as its comprehensive coverage, its explicit
strike penalties, and its creation of a new administrative
agency charged exclusively with the regulation of public
sector labor relations.

But it was more than legislative innovation that attracted attention to what was happening in New York. The nation's largest city was the arena for a succession of huge work stoppages both before and after passage of the Taylor Law by welfare employees, subway workers, sanitation workers, and teachers. These disputes provided convincing evidence of a rising tide of discontent and militancy among public workers. The drama was further heightened by the presence of a cast of colorful players, including Nelson Rockefeller, John Lindsay, Michael Quill, Jerry Wurf, Albert Shanker, and Victor Gotbaum. (Edward Koch was still in the wings.) Finally, all of this action was taking place in the hometown of the *New York Times*, which added immeasurably to the visibility of the Taylor Law.

From the start the work of the New York State Public Employment Relations Board was more closely attended to than that of any other labor relations agency in the public sector. PERB was the first such agency to arrange for the publication of its decisions, with the result that agencies in other states often looked to New York for precedents. Also, PERB and its chairman, Robert Helsby, invested substantial time and effort in educational and public relations activities. A tireless and peripatetic promoter of the Taylor Law as a model of sound public policy, Helsby appeared at conferences throughout the country and consulted with representatives of states considering public sector labor legislation of their own. The priority Helsby gave to public relations is suggested by the early appointment to the small agency staff of two persons whose principal experience was in that field. PERB organized the first large national conference on public sector labor relations in 1968 and three years later held an international symposium on the subject. PERB's prominence has continued under the leadership of Harold Newman, so that the agency and the law it administers have been extremely influential in the development of public sector collective bargaining beyond the borders of the state.

The purpose of this book is to trace the development of public employment relations in New York from the post–World War II period to the present. The primary focus is on PERB and how it has administered the Taylor Law, which, despite several amendments, still bears the unmistakable imprint of George Taylor and his colleagues. In no sense is this book a legal analysis, although the legal evolution of the Taylor Law in a general way is identified. Instead, an effort has been made to convey how politics, active administration, and accumulating experience have shaped the law and led to the current state of labor-management relations in New York's public sector.

The first half of the book provides a more or less straightforward chronological account of events leading to the enactment and early testing of the law and of PERB. The heady excitement of this period eventually gave way to less contentious times of regularized procedures interrupted only rarely by crisis. The second half of the book is organized around topics that correspond to PERB's major functional activities: representation matters, improper practices, dispute resolution, strikes, and the like. The principal concern in this section is the administration of the law.

ACKNOWLEDGMENTS

THIS BOOK IS FIRST and foremost a study of a government agency, the New York State Public Employment Relations Board, and therefore the cooperation of the staff and board members of PERB, past and present, was essential to the undertaking. To all those people I am profoundly grateful. They have been unfailingly cooperative, forthcoming, and kind to me during the past five years, and indeed in the many years before that. In particular, I thank Harold Newman and Ralph Vatalaro, who strongly urged that a history of PERB and the Taylor Law be written. They also pledged financial support to underwrite some of the expense associated with the research. In early 1985 Harold and Ralph hoped that by the time of PERB's twentieth anniversary two years hence a book would be in hand. Thus, as the twenty-fifth anniversary approaches, I would especially like to thank the two of them for their continued civility toward me.

I have also received constant assistance and support from many colleagues in the School of Industrial and Labor Relations at Cornell University. Bob Doherty encouraged me to take on the project initially and read much of what I wrote. I also benefited greatly from Don Cullen's careful and critical reading of an early version of the manuscript.

I reserve for last my great thanks to Melissa Harrington, a long-time friend and co-worker. Missy did all the typing and retyping of the manuscript. She was in on the beginning of the project and continued even after she had moved to a new job within the school.

1
THE CONDON-
WADLIN ERA

WITH THE END OF World War II came a gradual lifting of many economic and political restraints. But as wage and price controls were relaxed, industrial disputes reached record levels. In the twelve months following V-J Day, more than 5 million workers, close to one-tenth of the nation's workforce, struck in 4,630 reported work stoppages, accounting for more than 120 million days of idleness. Every basic industry was afflicted: coal, steel, auto, railroads, maritime, oil refining, electrical, and meat packing. The extent and persistence of conflict threatened the entire process of conversion to a peacetime economy and caused President Harry Truman to take such drastic actions as seizing the coal mines and railroads and even proposing that railroad workers be drafted into the armed forces if necessary to maintain the operation of the railroads. This from a president generally sympathetic to the unions.[1]

Unrest also spread to the largely unorganized public sector. Strikes by public workers were not unheard of in earlier years—David Ziskind, writing in 1940, identified 1,116 "strikes" from the historical records—but the great majority were small and inconsequential.[2] The example of public school teachers illustrates well the change in the postwar years. Whereas teachers struck thirteen school districts in the nation between 1920 and 1943, some more than once, there were twenty-nine teachers strikes between February 1946 and May 1947.[3]

In early 1946 the New York City public was treated to what would become a recurring drama when a strike of the city's transit system was threatened. Faced with its perennial financial problems, the board of transportation was considering a proposal to sell off its power generation facilities to Consolidated Edison. Three plants, which employed fifteen hundred workers, many of whom were members of the Transport Workers Union, supplied the power required to run the system's trains. The president of the union, Michael Quill, also a member of the city council (American Labor party, Bronx), made clear that the union would strike if the board of transportation pursued the plan. On the verge of a total shutdown, Mayor William O'Dwyer announced that no sale of the plants would occur until a public referendum could be held on the issue. The idea of the sale was soon abandoned.[4]

A few months later public and private workers in upstate New York combined to stage a brief but dramatic general strike. The initial stirrings of union organization among these public works employees in Rochester was met with the abrupt dismissal of 489 workers and the announcement by the city manager of his intent to contract for services with private firms. The action of the city so offended notions of fairness that the labor movement coalesced, setting aside the intense rivalries of the AFL and CIO, to support the workers and their union, the American Federation of State, County and Municipal Employees (AFSCME). The lockout became a strike as other city workers refused to report for work. For one day, May 28, 1946, the dispute became a general strike as organized workers in transportation, newspaper handling, and other private employments, altogether some thirty thousand workers, joined in a show of solidarity. The demonstration was enough to bring intervention by Governor Thomas Dewey and a settlement calling for reinstatement of all who had been discharged plus a pledge from the city that it would recognize "the right of workers to organize into their own unions and to choose representatives to bargain with the city administration." But what seemed momentarily to be a great victory was by the end of the summer totally dissipated as the city of Rochester reasserted its intransigent position regarding recognition and bargaining. Soon after, the AFSCME local disintegrated.[5]

It was in this environment of intense labor-management conflict that a nationwide conservative reaction set in, typified by passage in 1947 of the Taft-Hartley amendments to the National Labor Relations Act, including section 305, which explicitly made strikes by federal employees unlawful. The law mandated immediate dismissal and a three-year bar to reemployment of any federal employee who went on strike.

Meanwhile, state and local governments were enacting laws declaring strikes by public employees illegal and restricting the right to organize. In 1946 the Virginia legislature passed such a law, and the following year eight other states, New York among them, adopted antistrike legislation. In so doing, these states reiterated with emphasis, and often with prescribed penalties, what was already the accepted legal interpretation in common law, that public employees had no right to strike.[6]

THE CONDON-WADLIN LAW

The proximate event that led to the enactment of New York's Condon-Wadlin law in March 1947 was a week-long strike by twenty-four hundred schoolteachers in Buffalo. Two weeks before the strike, one thousand teachers from around the state had gathered in Albany to demon-

strate on behalf of a higher salary schedule and greater
state aid to local school districts. According to the *New
York Times,* the rally revealed sharp divisions within the
ranks of teachers over the issue of tactics: whether they
should resort to a strike or instead rely on political pressure to achieve their goals.[7]

On the national level both the National Education Association (NEA) and the still-small American Federation
of Teachers (AFT) were officially on record as opposing
the strike as inappropriate conduct for teachers. The Buffalo group, however, composed predominantly of members of NEA, although several other teacher organizations
were involved, had already declared its intention to close
down the schools if substantial salary improvements were
not forthcoming. Buffalo teachers had not regained the
salary levels that had prevailed in 1932 until the year before, even though consumer price levels had risen 55 percent between August 1939 and December 1946. The scale
for grade school teachers was $1,775 to $2,575, and it
took eight years to achieve the top step. High school
teachers were doing slightly better; their salary scale
ranged from $2,175 to $2,975. A strike commenced on
February 24, and the teachers did not return to work until March 3, after having won some modest salary relief.[8]

Before the strike Senator William Condon (R) and Assemblyman John Wadlin (R) had introduced companion
bills to prohibit strikes by all state and local government
employees. Their measure would have provided as a minimum penalty that the compensation of a striking employee be reduced to the minimum salary applicable to the
position in which the striker was retained and that no further increases be granted for three years.

On February 12, reporters had asked a spokesman for
Governor Dewey whether the governor supported the
bill. The spokesman had answered no, that it was not part
of the governor's legislative program and further that the

governor had not been consulted. By March 4, however, the day after the teachers in Buffalo returned to their classrooms, the governor had changed his mind and had announced that he would insist on legislation outlawing strikes by public employees. He also stated that the pending bill would be amended to include "more teeth."[9]

As a serious presidential contender, Governor Dewey understood the desirability of staking out a strong position on strikes that were unpopular with the public. He could hardly ignore the events in Buffalo, which had commanded national attention.[10] The legislature quickly complied with his request. In his memorandum of approval for the bill, the governor wrote:

> Every liberty enjoyed in this Nation exists because it is protected by Government which functions uninterruptedly. . . . A strike against government would be successful only if it could produce paralysis of Government. This no people can permit, and survive.[11]

The governor elaborated on this point a few weeks later:

> It always has been the law that employees of government have no right to strike. Until recently it seemed that this was beyond argument. . . . But a series of recent events made it clear that unless the law was restated clearly and simply for all to understand, and with specific penalties for its violation, we should go on to an increasingly chaotic condition.[12]

The Condon-Wadlin Act was simple and straightforward in its purpose: to prevent strikes of public employees by making the cost of striking prohibitive. A strike was defined broadly as

> the failure to report for duty, the willful absence from one's position, the stopping of work, or the abstinence in whole or in part from the full, faithful and proper performance of the duties of employment, for the purpose of inducing, influencing, or coercing a change in the conditions or compensation or the rights, privileges or obligations of employment.[13]

An employee who engaged in a strike was regarded as having terminated employment and as having abandoned all rights as an employee. Should a striking employee be reinstated, however, the employee would be barred from any increase in compensation for three years and would be placed on probation without tenure for five years. Moreover, the law provided that an employee absent from work during a strike was deemed to be on strike, the burden of disproving the presumption resting with the employee, who could request a hearing.

THE RECORD OF ENFORCEMENT

Negative in thrust and severe in its penalties, the Condon-Wadlin Act proved difficult to implement. Stefan Rosenzweig, who has traced enforcement of the law from its inception through 1964, identified twenty-one strikes or job actions that presumptively were violations.[14] In seven instances the law was invoked, twice resulting in dismissal of the strikers (seven public works employees in Newark and eleven school bus drivers in Wappinger Falls). In the other five cases the strikers were reemployed. It is not clear, however, whether the full weight of the penalties was felt by those who were rehired. No penalty was assessed against five hundred workers in Yonkers who walked out for eight days in 1949 in support of fellow employees dismissed for striking. The appellate division held that the law did not apply because the sympathy strike was not for the purpose of changing the strikers' conditions of employment and thus not within the terms of the statute.

The law was explicitly applied in only two instances involving New York City workers. One of these occurred in connection with a ten-day stoppage by two thousand motor vehicle operators in November 1962. The city threatened to dismiss all the workers involved, but only Police

Commissioner Michael J. Murphy discharged any employees, sixteen civilian chauffeurs, which he did presumably without consulting Mayor Robert Wagner. The sixteen chauffeurs ended up being transferred and thus, like their fellow strikers, escaped the full impact of the law. The second instance involving New York City workers was a one-day wildcat strike by 648 ferryboat workers in 1964. The workers incurred a loss of three days' pay, but, contrary to law, they also received an immediate wage increase. Of the fourteen cases in which the law was not invoked, all but one—in Elmont, Long Island—occurred in New York City.[15]

Overall, the record on Condon-Wadlin enforcement reflects differences in geography (upstate versus downstate), political party (Republicans versus Democrats), and union strength (weak versus strong). Upstate Republicans tended to enforce the law against weak unions. When the offending employee organization was large and powerful, such as the Transport Workers Union (TWU) or the United Federation of Teachers (UFT), the statutory penalties could be ignored, and they were. Confronted by a determined union that proffered the choice of settlement and a speedy return to work, or alternatively the prospect of a prolonged and damaging work stoppage, even the most conscientious public official was likely to opt for quick resolution of the conflict over grand principle—and all the more so when the union possessed genuine political power.

That city political leaders could distinguish between powerful and less powerful unions is apparent in the case of the transit workers, who were involved in several stoppages and slowdowns. In none of these incidents was Condon-Wadlin directly invoked, although the city did act more vigorously when the offending group was the minority Motormen's Benevolent Association (MBA) rather than the majority TWU. On the occasion of a second MBA-led strike, the city went into court to seek enforcement of an earlier injunction. It also took disciplinary action, including dismissal and suspensions, against several of the strike leaders.[16]

The lesson was well stated in a *Times* editorial after Governor Rockefeller proposed granting amnesty to the transit workers following the 1966 strike.

> The inevitable effect will be to fortify the impression . . . that civil service unions can get what they want if they have enough economic muscle and the will to use it. . . .
>
> The moral is underscored by the contrast in the city's policy toward ferryboat captains who were punished under the law after their strike last summer. Their walkout stemmed from an interunion row, and the other union won. Seventeen of the officers are still out of jobs. Asked why they were penalized when TWU members were not, Les Brown, Commissioner of Marine and Aviation, had a simple answer: "The subway workers had," he said, "the numbers and the power."[17]

Amnesty for this group came later.

Clearly, the record of enforcement of Condon-Wadlin during its twenty-year life was not impressive. During its first dozen years its shortcomings were obscured, however, because the industrial unrest that had characterized the immediate postwar years and been mirrored in the public sector had subsided significantly. The passage of Condon-Wadlin, like Taft-Hartley, was a reaction to and reflection of public sentiment: a public disillusioned by the disorder in employee relations. The problems the law was designed to solve became much less acute as a period of relatively peaceful labor-management relations in both private and public sectors followed the turmoil of 1946. Through the 1950s the average number of days lost to work stoppages each year declined in the nation by about two-thirds from the high watermark of that earlier year.[18] It was this period of relative calm that enabled Condon-Wadlin to survive as long as it did, largely untested.

THE BEGINNING OF CHANGE

Time and events eventually caught up with Condon-Wadlin, exposing its shortcomings as credible public policy. From 1960 on, for instance, the state legislature began to pay attention to employee relations in the public service, a topic heretofore largely ignored. The Joint Legislative Committee on Industrial and Labor Conditions took the lead, and for a decade the subject was treated extensively in the committee's annual reports. One result was a variety of legislative proposals. One such proposal was the Ostrander-Pino bill of 1961 (recast as Pino-Drumm in 1962), which would have amended Condon-Wadlin by requiring governments to establish "appropriate and reasonable grievance and negotiation procedures for the orderly and effective settlement of differences with their public employees." It would have provided mediation services from the state board of mediation and in instances of serious (interest) disputes provided "advisory arbitration" at the mutual request of the parties before an "arbitration board" drawn from a fifteen-member permanent panel composed of five members each representing government officials, labor organizations, and the public. Although the arbitrators could not impose settlements, it was assumed that it would be difficult to ignore the public recommendations of such a prestigious group. The bill was not passed.[19]

The tempo picked up in 1962, spurred by a strike by twenty thousand New York City schoolteachers. Another contributing factor was the promulgation by President John Kennedy of Executive Order 10988 on Employee-Management Cooperation in the Federal Civil Service. Unable to agree on any replacement for Condon-Wadlin, the state legislature mandated a grievance procedure for public employees in all political subdivisions other than the city of New York having one hundred or more full-time employees. This requirement was not unlike the grievance procedure that applied to state employees under a series of gubernatorial executive orders since the Dewey administration.[20] Another measure, which would have provided dispute resolution procedures to uniformed firefighters, was vetoed by Governor Rockefeller on the ground that it applied to only one class of public employee.

The staff of the joint legislative committee undertook a detailed study of Condon-Wadlin. Summarizing its own work in December 1962, it concluded that the act was deficient in four basic respects:

> (1) the penalties called for are so harsh that public administrators have regularly ignored the Act altogether in order to get their men back to work; (2) the Act's procedures are unfair—as the Staff Report put it, "A public servant dismissed for engaging in a strike is in far worse shape procedurally than one dismissed for treason, subversion, murder or theft"; (3) the Act's definition of "strike" seriously overreaches: according to the Staff Report, the definition would, if literally applied, "require the dismissal of a worker who leaves his desk to ask the janitor to send up more heat, the worker who takes a few minutes of government time to write a letter to his assemblyman to urge repeal of Condon-Wadlin and even, apparently, the worker who presents a grievance to his supervisor"; and (4) the Act fails to make any provision for amelioration of the conditions that lead to strikes.[21]

The staff also drafted a bill to replace Condon-Wadlin. With relatively minor amendments, the draft was introduced in the 1963 session by Assemblyman Anthony Savarese (R), chairman of the committee. Because the Democrats refused to give their support, Savarese presented the bill as his own rather than as a committee bill.[22]

Under the Savarese bill, strikes by public employees would have still been prohibited, but they would have been dealt with as misconduct under section 75 of the

Civil Service Law and through the injunctive power of the courts. The right to organize and to bargain collectively was spelled out, and the New York State Labor Relations Board, the agency with private sector jurisdiction, was given responsibility for handling representation matters. In the event of a negotiation impasse, mediation and advisory arbitration under the auspices of the New York State Board of Mediation was available. Altogether, it was a bill that went a long way toward developing a private sector model of collective bargaining.

Because Savarese lacked support for his program, he agreed instead to recommend Governor Rockefeller's proposal to modify for a two-year trial period the penalties of Condon-Wadlin. In a joint announcement they said the proposal, "providing more realistic procedures while mitigating the present longer-term penalties, should go far toward insuring prompt and uniform application of the law." The governor went on to pledge that he would appoint a committee "to make an intensive study and recommendations for improving personnel policies and practices in the public service."[23] Three years were to pass before Rockefeller would fulfill his pledge.

The legislature adopted the governor's plan, and for two years, through June 30, 1965, a modified Condon-Wadlin Act was in effect. Instead of a three-year proscription on any increase in compensation for a reinstated striker, the period was reduced to six months. Further, the probationary period was cut from five years to one. A new, more direct penalty required the deduction of two days' compensation from the pay of a striker for each day on strike. Also, private citizens were empowered to initiate suit for enforcement of the penalties should public officials fail to act.

A year and a half passed without a test of the new law, although New York City teachers again threatened to strike in September 1964. The joint legislative committee expressed cautious optimism when it opined that the absence of stoppages "perhaps . . . may be taken as some evidence of the efficacy of the 1963 amendments."[24]

Matters changed quickly, however, in January 1965 when six thousand employees of the New York City Department of Welfare struck for twenty-eight days. Court orders to return to work were ignored, and nineteen leaders from the independent Social Service Employees Union and Local 371, AFSCME, were cited for contempt; three of the leaders were jailed. The mandatory penalties of the law became a major obstacle, with final settlement turning on agreement to suspend strike penalties pending a union challenge of the constitutionality of the law.

The welfare strike and the imminent expiration of the two-year trial period caused a flurry of legislative activity. Further affecting the atmosphere, the Democrats temporarily controlled both chambers during the 1965 legislative session because of a court-ordered redrawing of legislative districts. Although the governor supported continuation of the 1963 amendments, a variety of other bills were considered, and ultimately the so-called Lentol-Rosetti bill was adopted.

The Lentol-Rosetti bill endorsed the right of public employees to organize for the purpose of collective bargaining. It required a public employer to bargain with the majority representative of its employees, mandated binding arbitration of contract grievances, and provided for mediation and factfinding in the event of an impasse in negotiations. The prohibition of the strike was continued, with violations to be treated as misconduct under the Civil Service Law. Administration of the law was to be left to a "labor relations agency" established by the public employer or, should the employer not act, by the presiding justice in the appellate division. Leaving the decision on the administrative mechanism to local option accommodated existing arrangements fashioned by New York City and a few other public employers.[25]

Governor Rockefeller vetoed the bill. In his veto message he stated:

> The bill would set up an involved and ineffective procedure which would (1) undermine the deterrent to strikes by public employees; (2) be unworkable and probably unconstitutional in certain of its aspects; and (3) impair vital functions of State and local government.... This bill purports to allow a range of penalties from reprimand to discharge. In the light of experience in some areas of the State, the effect of such flexibility would be to guarantee that if a strike did occur, the foremost and most intransigent union demand would be that government waive these penalties. The consequence would be that no strike could be settled without public officials foregoing the very sanctions the bill purports to provide.... It is the certainty of a sanction, rather than its severity, that brings about compliance with a law barring strikes by public employees.[26]

The governor reiterated his request for making permanent the mitigated penalties of the 1963 version of Condon-Wadlin. The legislature balked, and as of July 1, 1965, the original penalties were restored. Everything was back to square one.

LABOR RELATIONS IN NEW YORK CITY

When Robert Wagner took office as mayor of New York City in 1954, the city had little that could be mistaken for a labor relations policy. To be sure there were unions among the city workforce, but they enrolled a minority of workers and devoted most of their time to intramural conflict and angling for political favors. The transit workers came closest of any to having a functioning union.

Gradually, Wagner moved to give a greater role to the unions, which, aside from its political benefits, was an ef-

fective way to gain a measure of mayoral control over the
city's fractured personnel system. In his first year in office,
he issued an interim order that guaranteed the right to
organize and required city agencies to establish grievance
procedures and joint union-management committees to
meet on matters of wages, hours, and working conditions
within departments. New departments of labor and of
personnel were created. Modest in its purposes, the interim order at least gave a boost to the unions, which
were further aided when the board of estimate authorized
union dues checkoff in 1956.[27]

Following Wagner's reelection in 1958, Executive Order 49 was introduced. Variously hailed as a "Little Wagner Act" or a "Magna Carta," the order became the
framework of a labor relations policy that was to last for
the next eight years. Although it seemed to promise more
than it delivered, it nonetheless represented a significant
move forward for the unions by providing them with an
opportunity to consolidate their positions. Executive Order 49 initially applied to less than half the city's employees, because it excluded the police department and all
nonmayoral agencies, such as the boards of education and
higher education, transit, and other authorities. Nonmayoral agencies had been given the option to come under the
procedures, but none chose to do so. By 1965, however,
150,000 employees, about half the city's workforce, were
covered by the terms of Executive Order 49.

The significant feature of the order was that it granted
exclusivity to those organizations certified as representative of a majority of employees in an appropriate unit,
customarily a cluster of job titles within a department. Altogether, almost eight hundred certificates of representation were issued by the commissioner of labor, who had
responsibility for representation matters. Once certified, a
union had exclusive right to process grievances, to repre-

sent its unit on department labor relations committees, and, where it had a citywide majority for a particular class, to bargain with the city on salaries and some fringe benefits. Only in those instances in which a job title was limited to a department, such as sanitationman, did the right to bargain with the city have much import.

For most of Wagner's time in office, city officials were able to retain political control over the labor relations program, in large measure because of the mayor's personal involvement and adroit management of the certification and negotiation processes. Wagner did not want a labor relations system to develop that was independent of his influence. Thus the strategy dictated that bargaining units be fragmented to prevent any union from becoming too strong and that bargaining procedures be sensitive to the mayor's concerns. Inevitably, as the unions grew, control over them became more difficult.

The welfare workers strike in January 1965 presaged the change. It forced enlargement of the hitherto constricted scope of bargaining and compelled acceptance of an impasse panel nominated not by the commissioner of labor, but by the disputants themselves. The final report of the factfinding panel, chaired by Charles Schottland, dean of Brandeis University School of Social Work, served as the basis of settlement. Its central recommendation was that there be a review of the entire status of collective bargaining by a committee of city officials, union representatives, and "impartial public representatives."

Acting on this idea, the parties created a tripartite panel under the auspices of the American Arbitration Association that was to propose a new labor relations policy for the city. The tripartite panel submitted its report on the same day as the Taylor committee, March 31, 1966, and the plan took effect, like the Taylor Law, on September 1 of the next year.

THE NEW YORK CITY TEACHERS

Concurrent with the ordered transition in labor relations policy under Executive Order 49 to something approaching collective bargaining, teachers in New York City public schools were experiencing difficulty in achieving similar gains. The principal impediments were a resistant employer in the board of education and a badly divided workforce, which was split into more than one hundred organizations. The creation of the United Federation of Teachers in March 1960 by the coming together of the AFT-affiliated Teachers' Guild and a dissident faction of high school teachers brought new energy to teacher demands for collective bargaining. A one-day strike in November 1960, though it was supported by only about 15 percent of the teachers, was pivotal in forcing the reluctant board of education to conduct a vote in June 1961 on whether the teachers wanted collective bargaining.[28]

The results of the balloting were a strong endorsement of collective bargaining by a margin of almost three to one. When a representation election was held in December 1961, the UFT, which still had only about five thousand members, handily won exclusive bargaining rights for a unit with more than forty thousand teachers.[29]

The union struck again for one day in April 1962 before a first contract was ultimately negotiated. On the occasion of this second strike Governor Rockefeller called upon the board of education to withhold "general action under the law" pending the findings of a citizens' committee that he intended to appoint to study problems of Condon-Wadlin.[30]

Public school teachers had hitherto been largely quiescent in their relations with employers. The prospect that they would prevail against the largest school district in the nation was indeed the stuff of high drama. The UFT victory thus had profound consequences not only for the city of New York but for the country at large, as teachers elsewhere, inspired by the example, pressed for collective bargaining rights.

ELSEWHERE IN THE STATE

New York City was not the only place in the state where public employee organizations had achieved bargaining rights by 1966, although the Taylor committee identified only eight formal agreements outside the city. In Kingston, firefighters and police had both negotiated their first contracts under a city ordinance that surprisingly called for binding interest arbitration should negotiation reach impasse.[31] And in Rochester, hardly regarded as a "union town," the Rochester Teachers Association had negotiated two agreements with the board of education, and among city employees there were contracts covering police, firefighters, and the other city workers. How the city had reached that accommodation illustrates some of the problems of operating within a highly charged political environment without benefit of a fixed legal framework for labor relations.

In November 1961 the Democrats won control of the Rochester City Council, long dominated by the Republicans. Shortly after the election, in the waning days of the retiring administration, a union organizing campaign was launched by three unions—the Teamsters, the Laborers, and the Operating Engineers—all closely identified with the Republican party. The lame duck council enacted ordinances to grant the right of union organization and to authorize union dues checkoff. The Democrats, who had earlier pledged support for collective bargaining, cried foul and, on taking office, repealed the earlier ordinances. They explained that additional time was needed to assess the situation.

By summer 1962 an AFSCME membership drive was under way. Department heads were instructed by the city manager to permit employees to be solicited during working hours. The county Democratic party chairman described AFSCME as "an intelligent, responsible union." In a matter of a few weeks, AFSCME had obtained signed authorization cards from a majority of employees and the council had authorized the city manager to recognize and bargain with any labor organization that provided satisfactory proof that it represented a majority within a unit. Though a number of legal challenges were interposed, AFSCME was eventually recognized for a citywide unit, and a first rudimentary collective agreement was negotiated the following year. The city also entered into agreements with the police and firefighters.[32]

THE TRANSIT STRIKE OF 1966

Until the appearance of the Transport Workers Union in 1934, the history of labor relations in the New York City transit industry was a litany of failed attempts to organize unions, of strikes and strikebreakers, of company spies (the notorious "beakies"), blacklists, and company unions. Private companies owned most of the industry, and they were tough employers indeed. A twelve-hour, seven-day workweek was not uncommon. Disregarding skill and craft distinctions that had characterized earlier union organizing efforts, TWU subscribed to the principle of industrial unionism. With the imaginative leadership of Michael Quill and the ready militance of its membership, TWU established itself in a few short years as a powerful presence on the city's subway and surface lines. The growth of the union coincided with the movement toward a publicly owned transportation system, which began with the 1940 takeover of two private subway lines.[33]

Frequently aided by political leaders who preferred a single union to a divided workforce, TWU was able over the years to defeat any rival organizations and to assert its supremacy as sole representative for most of the employees of the transit authority. This was achieved by the adroit use of the threat of or actual employment of strikes and slowdowns combined with considerable political acumen in dealing with mayors such as O'Dwyer and Wagner. Although the relationship was often stormy, the customary biennial negotiations between the parties had up to 1966 become sufficiently routinized that they were widely seen as being governed by a "script." As Albert Lincoln noted, "The scenario begins with exorbitant demands, declarations of impoverishment by management, and dire threats; and it ends with a peaceful settlement and the rescue of the fifteen-cent fare by the Mayor and Governor."[34]

For several reasons, the script did not get played out in the bargaining that occurred at the end of 1965. One reason was that newly elected Mayor John Lindsay was unwilling or unable to play the role assigned him. Consequently, the entire transit system was shut down on New Year's Day 1966 for what was to be a twelve-day strike, at an estimated cost of $100 million per day.[35]

Injunctions issued against the strikers were to no avail, and Mike Quill was jailed, though not without getting off one of his memorable lines: "Let the judge drop dead in his black robes!" Despite a heart attack and the efforts of some to get him released, Quill preferred his martyrdom, which he and the union exploited to achieve a hefty settlement.[36] That settlement was momentarily in jeopardy when, in response to a suit brought by a private citizen, Judge Irving Saypol ruled that payment of any increases in wages would be illegal. Renewal of the strike appeared imminent. In the face of that threat, the governor requested and obtained immediate passage of an amnesty bill waiving all Condon-Wadlin penalties against the transit strikers.[37]

The impact of the transit strike on public consciousness was manifest in President Lyndon Johnson's State of the Union Address on January 12 in which he stated his intent "to ask the Congress to consider measures which, without improperly invading state and local authority will enable us effectively to deal with strikes which threaten irreparable damage to the national interest."[38] Presumably, the president had in mind amendment of the Taft-Hartley definition of national emergency disputes. Except for an expression of anger that the transit settlement exceeded the administration's inflation guideposts, nothing further was heard from the president on the matter.

In twenty years public sector labor relations in New York had come full circle. The signs of worker militancy displayed by teachers in Buffalo and others elsewhere subsided during the 1950s only to revive and intensify in the 1960s. Just as the Buffalo teachers strike was the proximate cause of the enactment of the Condon-Wadlin Act, so too the New York City transit strike was the triggering event for enactment of the Taylor Law, but it would take some time to sort out the political obstacles to its passage.

NOTES

1. Dulles, *Labor in America*, 354–70.
2. Ziskind, *One Thousand Strikes of Government Employees*.
3. Eddison, "Teacher Strikes in the United States," 15–17, 47–50.
4. *New York Times*, 22 January 1946, l.
5. Hardisky, "The Rochester General Strike of 1946."
6. Spero, *The Government as Employer*, 32–33.
7. *New York Times*, 13 February 1947, 1.
8. Eddison, "Teacher Strikes in the United States," 86.
9. *New York Times*, 13 February 1947, 1; 5 March 1947, 1.
10. *Business Week*, 22 March 1947.

11. Public Papers of Thomas E. Dewey, 323–24.

12. Ibid., 620.

13. Chap. 391, L. 1947.

14. Rosenzweig, "The Condon-Wadlin Act Re-examined." Rosenzweig indicates that his tally of strikes may be incomplete, particularly regarding upstate events.

15. Ibid. See also Bellush and Bellush, *Union Power and New York*, 75–77.

16. *New York Times*, 9 December 1957, 1; 10 December 1957, 1; 11 December 1957, 1.

17. *New York Times*, 14 February 1966, 28.

18. U.S. Bureau of Labor Statistics, *Work Stoppages*.

19. *New York State Joint Legislative Committee on Industrial and Labor Conditions Report* (hereafter *Joint Legislative Committee Report*), 1960, 1961, 1962.

20. N.Y. General Municipal Law, art. 16, chap. 554, L. 1962.

21. *Joint Legislative Committee Report*, 1963, 41.

22. This political controversy marked the end of a twenty-five-year tradition of bipartisanship within the committee. It was engendered by differences over public sector and hospital labor legislation as well as, in the eyes of the Democrats, a Republican leadership decision to abandon the principle of party parity in membership on the committee.

23. *Joint Legislative Committee Report*, 1963, 58.

24. *Joint Legislative Committee Report*, 1964, 54.

25. Hanslowe, *The Emerging Law of Labor Relations in Public Employment*, 80–82. This monograph offers detail on the legislative deliberations.

26. *New York State Legislative Annual*, 1965, 556.

27. In writing about the Wagner period, I have relied heavily on Horton, *Municipal Labor Relations in New York City*.

28. *New York Times*, 8 November 1960, 1. Forty-six hundred strikers were suspended for the day under the board bylaws. Superintendent John Theobald explained that Condon-Wadlin was not invoked because the law presumed the guilt of those absent. The board defined collective bargaining in a fashion that reserved for it the right to terminate any negotiated contract at will, a definition at odds with one proposed by the board's own advisory committee of inquiry. The advisory committee, headed by George Taylor and on which David Cole also served, had made recommendations to the board that were in large measure ignored. The report itself was never publicly released.

29. Salz, "The Growth of Teacher Unionism in New York City," 224, 232.

30. *New York Times,* 16 April 1962, 1; 17 April 1962, 1.

31. Interview with Robert Gollnick, 25 June 1986.

32. New York State School of Industrial and Labor Relations, *Report and Findings,* 18–33.

33. Kheel and Turcott, *Transit and Arbitration.*

34. Lincoln, "The New York City Transit Strike," 271.

35. Interview with Theodore W. Kheel, 25 September 1985. Kheel attributed the length of the strike, if not the strike itself, to the part played by the editors of the *New York Times.* According to Kheel, Lindsay was a captive of the newspaper. He claims that union bargaining proposals made one day would immediately be addressed the next day on the editorial page without having been reported in the news columns of the paper.

36. Raskin, "Politics Up-Ends the Bargaining Table," 129–30.

37. *New York Times,* 17 February 1966, 1.

38. *New York Times,* 13 January 1966, 1.

2
ADOPTION OF THE TAYLOR LAW

IF THERE WAS ANY doubt before about the essential bankruptcy of Condon-Wadlin as a viable policy for regulating labor relations, the spectacle of New York City attempting to make do without a functioning mass transit system made it only too apparent. The final humiliation came soon after the strike when the legislature passed a bill waiving the penalties mandated by the law.[1] While the strike was still on, a group from within state government was convened by the counsel to the governor "to prepare legislation which might reasonably be expected to deter strikes in the public sector."[2] Before that group could complete its task, Governor Nelson Rockefeller decided to turn to the outside for advice, thus making good on his 1963 promise to Anthony Savarese, albeit three years late. On January 15, 1966, the governor announced the appointment of a Committee on Public Employee Relations charged "to make legislative proposals for protecting the public against the disruption of vital public services by illegal strikes, while at the same time protecting the rights of public employees."[3]

CREATION OF THE TAYLOR COMMITTEE

There was nothing novel in the idea of creating a committee to examine a complex and politically sensitive issue, particularly for Nelson Rockefeller, who made extensive use of outside experts. He was "enamored of experts and expertise." Others associated with his administration agree. William J. Ronan, who as secretary to the governor for many years was called upon to coordinate special "task forces," recalls having as many as forty-two in existence at one time. Referring to the Taylor committee, Sol Neil Corbin, former Rockefeller counsel, stated, "Rockefeller was accustomed to the use of outside experts and very receptive to an esteemed group like the Taylor committee." A more jaundiced view of the practice comes from another former member of the Rockefeller staff, Joseph Persico: "Nelson created Potemkin villages of objectivity. He appointed commissions, boards, panels, and task forces, heavy with respected names and recognized authorities. . . . Their purpose was not to advise him, but rather to give the appearance of detached judgment to what he had already decided to do."[4]

For the Committee on Public Employee Relations, the governor assembled a genuine blue-ribbon group. George W. Taylor, Harnwell Professor of Industry at the University of Pennsylvania, was appointed chairman. His choice was "natural" inasmuch as he was then the preeminent industrial relations authority in the country.[5] Taylor had served as vice-chairman and later chairman of the National War Labor Board and had chaired the National Wage Stabilization Board. His experience as an arbitrator and mediator in industrial disputes was extensive.

Taylor's committee colleagues were also nationally prominent in the field of industrial relations, and all possessed practical experience in government and arbitration. The one nonacademic in the group was a lawyer, David L.

Cole of Paterson, New Jersey, who made his living as a full-time labor relations neutral. Cole, in addition to other government service, had been director of the Federal Mediation and Conciliation Service. The other three members were professors of economics: John T. Dunlop of Harvard; E. Wight Bakke of Yale; and Frederick H. Harbison of Princeton.

All five members shared a characteristic apart from their wide knowledge of labor relations: none was from New York. The decision to appoint persons from outside the state was deliberate, the presumed advantage being to remove any possible taint that might arise from past links with the Condon-Wadlin law or too close association with the major actors on the New York scene.[6] But Cole, and to a lesser extent Taylor and Dunlop, were by no means strangers to New York public employment labor relations. Cole had been involved in New York City transit disputes going back to 1947. Soon after the election of John Lindsay as mayor in November of 1965, he resigned from the transit labor board (along with Taylor), a panel he had chaired since 1960. Both Taylor and Cole had also been members of a 1961 board of inquiry established by the city board of education to make recommendations regarding the dispute then raging over collective bargaining rights for teachers.

Putting the committee together was probably the work of Victor Borella and Taylor himself.[7] Borella, executive vice-president of Rockefeller Center and a former Dartmouth classmate of the governor, was well connected to the unions, especially the building trades, and he functioned as principal adviser to Rockefeller on labor matters. Dunlop's own recollection is that he learned of his appointment from Taylor.[8] Dunlop was acquainted with Borella, who was then serving on an advisory committee for a study project funded by Rockefeller Brothers Fund and directed by Dunlop and Derek C. Bok of the Harvard

Law School. The professional ties among Taylor, Cole, and Dunlop were numerous. In Dunlop's words the three of them "were a triangle with all three working on many projects and two sides of the triangle working separately on some projects."[9] It is clear from the testimony of Corbin and the papers of David Cole that Taylor, Cole, and Dunlop were the major figures on the committee. Dunlop said he did not know why Bakke and Harbison were appointed, adding that they played a less important role.[10]

THE COMMITTEE AT WORK

The committee staff consisted of Sol Neil Corbin as counsel and Melvin H. Osterman, Jr., as assistant counsel. Corbin had only a few months earlier returned to private practice following a period as counsel to the governor. Although he was not a labor law specialist, Corbin was nevertheless familiar with the history of Condon-Wadlin, having had a hand in drafting the temporary amendments of 1963, and he was especially knowledgeable about the structure and functioning of state and local government in New York. As counsel to a committee of out-of-staters, his main task was to offer advice on what could or could not be done under New York law. He also helped edit the final report.

Osterman too had worked in the governor's office when the 1963 legislation was prepared. Although committee members felt little need for assistance in framing the ideas that were to be subsequently expressed in their report, staff support was important in supplying the legal research necessary for the underpinning of any proposed law. Both Corbin and Osterman have made clear that this was by no means a situation in which staff did most of the work and the committee essentially endorsed the product. Corbin was lavish in his praise of committee members as "supreme rationalists" and of the committee as the best with which he had ever dealt.[11]

After meeting with Governor Rockefeller on January 21, committee members moved promptly to divide responsibility for initial drafts of what were to become the five parts of the final report. Taylor undertook the preparation of a broad summary statement setting forth the basic problems and issues; Bakke dealt with representation matters; Dunlop with dispute settlement procedures; Cole with the legal issues of strikes and strike penalties; and Harbison with organization for collective negotiations. The final report also included an appendix, largely the product of Dunlop, that compared association and union models of collective negotiations. In the meantime the staff was asked to prepare brief papers on fourteen topics such as public sector legislation in other states; New York law governing wages, hours, and working conditions; grievance procedures within the state; and court procedures in enforcing injunctions.

To obtain legislative proposals and explore points of view, the committee met informally and privately with a variety of interested groups and individuals. Discussions were held with labor and management representatives, including AFSCME president Jerry Wurf; top leadership of the Civil Service Employees Association; Raymond Cothran, executive director of the New York State Conference of Mayors; and Martin P. Catherwood, state industrial commissioner. The committee also met with members of the professional community of neutrals, such as Theodore Kheel and the public members of Mayor Lindsay's tripartite panel on labor relations, and with representatives of concerned groups, such as the influential Commerce and Industry Association and the city bar association. The range of interviews indicates that committee members were mindful of the political requirements of consultation, regardless of whether much of substance could be garnered from the exchanges.

Public hearings were held for one day, on March 4. The event was arranged primarily to fulfill a public relations purpose, in that some of the same witnesses at the public hearings had met earlier with the committee in private. The relative value of private exchange versus public testimony is illustrated by the public and private statements of Victor Gotbaum of District Council 37 of AFSCME. Meeting in February with Harbison and Corbin, Gotbaum indicated "he wouldn't be concerned with a statute barring strikes, so long as it was combined with [impartial factfinding on a voluntary basis with recommendations] and is not preoccupied with penalties." In contrast, Gotbaum's public testimony urged that the law be silent on the strike, leaving the matter to the courts.[12]

Another source of ideas the committee members drew upon was their vast personal network of acquaintance among labor relations practitioners who, through correspondence and conversation, proffered suggestions. One example was an eight-page letter to David Cole from friend and prominent labor attorney Frederick Livingston. In it Livingston proposed the creation of a public employment relations board that among other functions would determine minimum employment standards and, in the event of a continuing bargaining impasse, be empowered to set terms of employment. A legal strike could occur if a legislature refused to fund a negotiated settlement.[13]

This was a hard-working committee, and a measure of the time it devoted to the task in two and one-half months can be observed in Cole's personal records. Altogether, he worked for twenty-eight days on the assignment, the bulk of these in meetings in New York City.[14]

THE COMMITTEE ON THE RIGHT TO STRIKE

On March 2 the committee submitted an interim report to the governor summarizing its activities and identifying five groups of questions that it deemed crucial to its inquiry. The committee hoped to receive comment on these questions at the public hearing scheduled two days hence. Slightly paraphrased, the questions were as follows:

1. What forms of representation best serve the public interest and the interest of employees?

2. What arrangements should be followed to resolve problems that may arise concerning questions of employee representation?

3. What procedures should be developed for facilitating the process of agreement?

4. In the event of deadlock, what additional procedures should be available?

5. What should be the penalties for striking, and how should they be administered?[15]

Noteworthy is the absence of any question concerning whether public employees should have a right to strike. The language of the governor's charge to the committee did not explicitly foreclose that option, although the implication seemed plain; the charge referred only to "illegal strikes." For the committee, however, the issue quickly became a nonissue as there was almost instant agreement among its members that strikes in public employment were clearly inappropriate. The interview testimony of Dunlop and Corbin affirms the point, as do the detailed notes that Cole maintained of many committee discussions.

It is surprising that this collection of experts, intimately familiar with private sector bargaining and the use of the strike, should so easily reach that conclusion. After all, only five years earlier Taylor, Cole, and Dunlop had been members of the study group that produced *The Public Interest in National Labor Policy,* a report published by the Committee for Economic Development, which stated:

> Another set of special problems is raised by the possibility of disputes involving public employees, whether at the federal, state, or local level. In all these cases, the strike is a questionable weapon and heavy emphasis must be placed on seeking

other means for resolving disputes. Some services, police and fire protection, for example, must not be interrupted. While others are less essential, they still involve employment by government and a test of strength between a group of citizens and the community at large has disturbing connotations. *Nevertheless, we would not favor a blanket prohibition on strikes for all employees, many of whom perform work identical with that in private industry and any of whom could conceivably be subjected to extreme provocation.*[16]

Later, in speaking of the Taylor committee, Cole observed:

Our committee quickly agreed that the unqualified prohibition of the strike in the public service should continue. This represented a partial change in the thinking of most of us. We had at earlier times separately expressed the view that in the non-essential functions public employees should be free to strike. In our report we recommended that at this stage no public employee in New York State should have this right.[17]

The committee's report explained why its members believed the strike was inapplicable in government employment; it did not explain the "partial change in the thinking" about the issue by some members. It would seem that as pragmatic men of affairs, "supreme rationalists" to use Corbin's phrase, the committee members placed great weight on practical political considerations. In the report they make the argument that "in order to spur the legislative bodies and the administrative agencies to accord more effective participation rights to public employees, doubts should not be raised about the firmness of the well-established principle that the strike... is not available."[18] Therefore, when it came time to recommend legislation, fine distinctions between essential and nonessential government services, abstractly appealing perhaps, were in fact "administratively impossible." Realistically, the achievement of the goal of genuine employee participation required a measure of cooperation from government officials, the price of which was the unequivocal rejection of any right to strike. Furthermore, the near debacle of the subway strike and other jarring work stoppages were too recent to disregard.

Convinced then that any new law had to make clear the "inapplicability of strikes," Taylor and his colleagues set forth the arguments. Beyond references to the politics of the matter and to the longstanding U.S. legal tradition barring public employee strikes, the members based their position on two major points. The first was the familiar argument that the marketplace constraints that customarily play a disciplining role in private industry bargaining are either wholly absent or severely attenuated in the government setting.

A second and equally fundamental reason for concluding that the strike was totally inappropriate related to ideas about governance in a democratic society. The claim is made that a strike in the public sector is essentially a contest of relative political power and as such is in conflict with the orderly functioning of democratic political processes, whereby elected officials exercise executive and legislative authority on behalf of the electorate. According to the committee, a strike "introduces an alien force in the legislative processes."[19] This insistence on the ultimate supremacy of the legislature as representative of the people is reiterated throughout the report and informs many of the committee's recommendations.

COLLECTIVE NEGOTIATIONS, NOT COLLECTIVE BARGAINING

To underscore the distinction between private and public employee relations, the report adopted the term *collective negotiations* "to signify the participation of public employees in the determination of at least some of their conditions of employment on an occupational or functional basis."[20] This notion is in contrast to the joint determination of terms of employment by union and management that occurs in private sector collective bargaining. Although the report did not offer a detailed explanation for the preference of the phrase *collective negotiations,* it was clearly related to the committee's belief that the scope of negotiations would perforce be more restricted by the presence of a civil service system and the nature of representative government that does not recognize a right to strike.

Martin P. Catherwood, the state industrial commissioner and former dean of the New York State School of Industrial and Labor Relations at Cornell University, expressed the same general idea to the committee:

> Collective bargaining is probably not the best term to cover the necessary steps to insure fairness to the employees and to the public as employer within the framework as suggested in these observations. The use of the term collective bargaining has the effect of encouraging the uncritical assumption that practices and policies which have emerged in the field of private employment with respect to bargaining, the determination of the bargaining unit, etc. will appropriately apply in the public service. Some such term as collective representation is probably more nearly accurate. Isn't this really what has been provided for federal employees?[21]

In choosing to use the phrase *collective negotiations,* the committee was calling attention to the fact that the scheme it envisioned was fundamentally different from customary private sector bargaining.[22]

The committee's reading of the political realities led to the same conclusion:

> Unions [or] Associations can move, however, to ... allegedly *real* collective bargaining with the executives of political entities only if the public, through the action of its legislatures is ready to delegate to a bargaining "team" composed of the executives of government agencies and the negotiators for em-

ployee organizations the virtual determination of its budget, the allocation of public revenues to alternative uses, and the setting of the tax rate necessary to balance that budget. The delegation of those powers is not likely in the foreseeable future.[23]

Several years later George Taylor was to observe with some disappointment: "The proposed term has not 'caught on' perhaps to some extent because the significance has not been fully understood and to some extent because it was."[24]

THE PUBLIC EMPLOYMENT RELATIONS BOARD

The committee recommended that a new agency, the New York State Public Employment Relations Board, be created to administer the proposed law—to resolve representation matters, to provide mediation and factfinding services, to administer strike penalties, and to collect and disseminate information and undertake studies. It opted for a new agency rather than utilizing the well-established state labor relations board and state board of mediation. As Jean McKelvey put it, "The proposed board was thus to be a labor relations agency, a mediation board, a court, and a research institute—all wrapped into one package!"[25]

The report offers no explanation of why or how it chose this alternative. At the time there was nothing in the experience of the handful of other states with statutes that suggested the desirability of establishing a multipurpose agency devoted exclusively to public sector labor relations. On the contrary, states such as Wisconsin, Michigan, Connecticut, and Massachusetts had elected to assign jurisdiction to existing agencies that also served the private sector. A few states had turned to nonlabor agencies of government such as education departments where teachers were involved or to civil service commissions. Furthermore, earlier bills considered by the legislature would have used the existing agencies or, in the case of the Lentol-Rosetti bill vetoed in 1965, would have decentralized administration completely.

The committee retained a degree of decentralization in its recommendation that local governments be empowered to establish procedures for handling representation matters in consultation with interested employee organizations and public administrators. To that extent at least, the committee acknowledged the distrust of state authority shared by some local governments and unions. New York City was, of course, the prime example.

The idea of a public employment relations board was not original with the committee. A similar idea appeared in a bill introduced early in the 1966 legislative session under the sponsorship of Senator Whitney North Seymour, Jr., (R) and Assemblyman Paul Curran (R).[26] Theirs differed in that all three board members would have been part time and appointed by the governor for five-year terms.

Although the report is silent as to reasons for recommending a new agency, the explanation undoubtedly lies in the committee's firm belief that the differences between the public and private sectors outweigh any similarities, the same outlook that prompted the adoption of the term *collective negotiations* instead of *collective bargaining*. McKelvey provides an explanation:

> An emphasis on the dissimilarities between public and private employment creates an implicit recognition of the need for keeping jurisdiction out of the hands of those bodies which regulate the private sector. In addition, the fact that the proposed legislation covers state employees, as well as those of subordinate units of state government, adds even greater impetus to the proposal for new agencies, given the distaste expressed by employee professional organizations operating at

the state level, such as the Civil Service Employees Association, New York State Teachers Association, and New York Nurses Association, for being lumped together with trade unions in matters involving recognition and negotiation.[27]

McKelvey also notes that the board of mediation had made clear its own disinterest in expanding jurisdiction into the public sector. She also suggests that the state labor relations board lacked strong support from the labor movement. Thus, given the committee's philosophical predilections, the lively suspicion of the traditional agencies, and the absence of bureaucratic competition, the choice of a new agency, a public employment relations board, seemed logical.

DETERMINATION OF REPRESENTATION STATUS

Committed to the proposition that the best way to protect the public from strikes was to fashion methods whereby public employees could participate in affecting their terms and conditions of employment, the committee had to confront its most troublesome issue, namely, how to structure that participation. It had to develop a framework that would fit a mixture of government units with widely varying powers and internal authority structures. It also had to accommodate to a body of law and regulation, including a civil service system, that defined many of the employment conditions that mattered to government workers. And finally, it had to take into account the diversity in outlook and objectives among the contending employee organizations. Avoidance of open conflict and strikes would in substantial part depend on success in structuring employee participation.

The critical threshold question of how to define negotiating units was treated at length. The report suggests why in important respects the practice in private industry

was not a reliable guide. The great weight customarily assigned to community of interest indicia in the private sector may yield quite different results in the public sector
because the assumption cannot be made that all employees
seek to negotiate over the same range of issues. Nor can it
be assumed that the interests of supervisors and professional employees necessarily separate them from their co-
workers.

> Employees have, in the past and present, carried on their col-
> lective participation and joint negotiations in a great variety
> of ways and have chosen various types of employee organiza-
> tions to represent them. There is no *a priori* reason to assume,
> therefore, that their future choices would not also be diverse.
> We cannot assume that employees, if given free choice, would
> support the development of any *single pattern* of participation
> or any *single type* of employee organization utilizing any *single
> model* of collective negotiations. Indeed the opposite assump-
> tion would appear more reasonable.[28]

Moreover, the locus of decision making on the employer
side will vary depending on the matters to be negotiated.
Finally, some weight needs to be given to administrative
convenience and efficiency in determining units if the obligations of officials and employees alike to serve the public interest are to be observed. Therefore the committee
recommended that three statutory criteria be considered
in defining negotiating units:

(a)   That the definition of the unit corresponds with a community of interest among the employees to be included in the
unit.

(b)   That the conditions of employment upon which the employees desire to negotiate are those with respect to which
the agency has discretion to determine or recommend to
other administrative authority or the legislative body.

(c)   That the unit is compatible with the effective fulfillment
by administrators and employees of their joint responsibilities
to serve the public.[29]

The committee drew no distinction among managerial, supervisory, or nonsupervisory employees in prescribing the reach of the proposed statute. The rights of organization and collective negotiations were to be extended to all public employees. One important reason presumably for recommending all-inclusive coverage was that the committee wished to leave open the possibility for new modes of representation quite different from private sector practice. Perhaps an even more compelling reason was the presence of the Civil Service Employees Association (CSEA) and of a few other organizations that did not trouble themselves with neat distinctions between bosses and bossed. CSEA in particular was very much a power to be reckoned with if any new legislation was to be adopted.

The tone of caution, of tentativeness, exhibited throughout the report is pronounced in the discussion of unit determination. It is apparent also in its handling of exclusive representation. The committee enumerated the many advantages of granting exclusive status to the negotiating representative chosen by employees in a unit and proposed that such status be permitted by agreement, but it withheld recommending exclusivity pending "prior solution of the unit problem." Instead the committee proposed that PERB study the matter. Likewise, the committee was offhand in treating the representation election as a method of ascertaining employee choice, observing merely that it was "frequently employed."

RESOLUTION OF DEADLOCKS IN COLLECTIVE NEGOTIATIONS

"The avoidance of the strike is substantially the perfection of procedures and policies to provide an effective alternative to conflict."[30] Thus begins part three of the report, dealing with the resolution of deadlocks in collective negotiations. The statement is at once a profession of faith and an expression of hope. Distrustful of third-party intervention, the committee members believed that the parties as they acquired experience and became accustomed to dealing with one another should be able to settle differences with little or no outside assistance. Further, the committee recommended that parties develop procedures of their own more attuned to their particular circumstances than the statutory procedures could be. John Dunlop, who drafted this section of the report, would have gone further and required the establishment of a negotiated impasse procedure as a precondition to recognition or certification.[31]

The report mentioned several procedures the parties might consider, including arbitration, at the same time assuming that "varied and perceptive experience" would yield still other possibilities.[32] Realistic enough to know that the parties would not always be able to agree upon procedures of their own devising, the committee recommended a statutory impasse procedure of mediation, factfinding with recommendations, and ultimately legislative determination after a form of "show cause hearing." Under the show cause scheme, the legislature would hear the parties to negotiations on why the factfinding recommendations should not be adopted. The presumption was that in most instances the legislature would endorse the report of the factfinding panel.

The committee's fundamental philosophical commitment to the principle of legislative supremacy is manifest in its recommendations on impasse resolution. It is a constant theme throughout the report. Impasse procedures are tied to the budget-making process on grounds that the results of collective negotiations need to be in hand before a budget can be adopted. Further, because allocation of public resources is being determined, the final say has to reside with the legislative body. The idea of compulsory arbitration, in contrast to arbitration that is entered into voluntarily, was rejected as an improper and possibly illegal infringement on legislative authority and, more pragmatically, because of its potential chilling effect on negotiations. On this point as on others dealing with dispute resolution, John Dunlop differed from his colleagues. His March 23 draft made provision for compulsory arbitration one element in a flexible "arsenal of weapons" approach to bargaining impasses. This view was totally unacceptable to George Taylor.[33] Likewise, Dunlop's preference for tripartite factfinding lacked support from the other committee members.

STRIKE PENALTIES

Given the premise that strikes must be prohibited, the committee had to address the question of penalties in the event that some might yield to the "temptation to follow the old course and test the law." It recommended that the injunctive power of the courts be used to assess fines as necessary for criminal contempt of court orders. It recommended further that the existing limit on fines of $250 per day be removed to enlarge the area of the court's discretion and that the law obligate law officers to initiate court action for injunctive relief. Individual strikers would continue to be subject to discipline for misconduct under section 75 of the Civil Service Law, with penalties ranging from a letter of reprimand to dismissal.

Borrowing from the policies followed by the federal government, the committee recommended that as a precondition of recognition, an employee organization be required to affirm that it did not assert a right to strike against government. Additionally, a violation of the strike prohibition would subject the employee organization to the loss of dues deduction privileges and possibly to the revocation of its representation rights. PERB would be authorized to determine the nature of the penalty after a hearing and would take into account the efforts of the employee organization to prevent or end the strike as well as allegations that the employer had engaged in acts of extreme provocation so as to detract from the fault of the organization for the strike.

THE REPORT: A CONCLUDING COMMENT

The sixty-three-page report delivered to Governor Rockefeller on March 31, 1966, is notable in its style and tone. It reads more like a scholarly piece than a lawyer's brief, and in that sense it is consonant with the background of the men who wrote it. It could also be argued, however, that the report reflects less the academic background of the authors than their real-world experience in employee-employer relations, where enormous variety in practice is the norm. In either case the report often approaches an issue by providing judicious examination of the alternatives before reaching a conclusion, and frequently the conclusion is that further study or experimentation is required. At times, as in the appendix in which union and association models are compared, one is reminded of the explication found in labor relations textbooks. The cautionary approach, a willingness to suspend judgment and to proceed slowly, could and did provoke exasperation (and a measure of hyperbole), as in this opening paragraph of a monograph written by Walter Oberer, Kurt Hanslowe, and Robert Doherty:

> The one thing clear about the Taylor Act is that little is clear about it. Unlike its predecessors in other states, the act is not so much an effort to define and establish principles and procedures to formalize employment relationships in the public sector as it is, paradoxically, an effort *not* to define and establish such principles and procedures. Its purpose is to provide for flexibility and diversity in public employment relationships—to provide, that is, a kind of state-wide laboratory for the conduct of experiments and research in such relationships.[34]

The tone of the report conveys unmistakably an unspoken assumption that the pace of development of public sector labor relations in New York would be gradual enough to permit study and thought. Dunlop acknowledged much later that the growth of organization following the law was faster and greater than he expected.[35]

PUBLIC REACTIONS, LEGISLATIVE INACTION

Not surprisingly, the report drew mixed reactions. The governor expressed confidence that the recommendations "will furnish valuable assistance to the legislature, as it will to me, in deciding upon fair and effective legislation." The *New York Times* hailed it as a "trail-blazing contribution"; "their white paper rips aside cliches and provides an exemplary balance between rights and responsibilities." And in a personal letter to members of the committee, Peter Seitz, an arbitrator and a member of the tripartite panel that had just issued its own recommendations for New York City's labor relations, called the report a "landmark." Seitz continued, "You should have a satisfying sense of accomplishment in having mapped out so large an area of terra incognita with such care and clarity."[36]

Less generous in their appraisal were union officials Jerry Wurf and Victor Gotbaum, who in a press conference referred to the committee's work as a "Mad Hatter idea." They further stated that it was essentially the same as Condon-Wadlin except that "Condon-Wadlin tried to bludgeon unions to death and failed: the report would try to bleed them to death to make sure they don't function."[37] A major concern to AFSCME was that the report would jeopardize the tripartite agreement on collective bargaining worked out with Mayor Lindsay and signed on March 31, 1966. On every important point, from the perspective of AFSCME leadership, the two plans were at odds. The absence in the tripartite agreement of any explicit prohibition of strikes was taken to mean that strikes were allowed.[38]

A highly charged debate over the report and whether to adopt legislation incorporating its recommendations continued for the next three months. Early on, Anthony Travia, Speaker of the Assembly, declared, "I don't like it [the report] at all. I feel it's very stringent. . . . Labor will never go for it."[39]

Governor Rockefeller, despite his first kind words, seemed in the estimation of the *New York Times* to be slow in forcefully pressing for action. In early May, however, as a bill was finally introduced, the *Times* reported, "Mr. Rockefeller's position in the negotiations has been that his final bill must hew as closely as possible to the Taylor report. His reasoning, he has told those close to him, is that if he strays too far from the report and fails to put anti-strike teeth into the legislation, he will 'get clobbered by the newspapers,' meaning the editorial writers."[40] Richard N. Winfield, who as assistant counsel in the governor's office was primarily responsible for drafting the bill, confirms the point. Winfield recalled, "For political purposes I slavishly tried to follow the report. Since the administration was relying on an outside panel of experts and since the report was so complete and so comprehensive, to the extent that the draft departed from the report, anyone with half a mind would say, 'What is the administration up to?' "[41]

Throughout the state newspapers were full of praise for the report. The *Times* in particular ran frequent editorials urging passage of the governor's bill. To counter claims of "union-busting" from critics such as Raymond Corbett, president of the state AFL-CIO, its editorials invoked the credentials of the Taylor panel as impartial experts of national reputation. On only one aspect of the committee's recommendations did the *Times* editors express reservation, that regarding the practicality of the decertification penalty against a striking union. The editors believed the purposes of the law would be better served by the loss of dues checkoff.[42]

The draft bill differed from the committee's blueprint in one respect. It did not incorporate the idea of a show cause hearing by the legislative body in the event that fact-finding could not resolve a negotiation impasse. As Winfield recalls, "The omission was advertent"; the executive department believed that it had the constitutional responsibility for employee relations and ought not to delegate it to the legislature. "This was a balance of powers, a constitutional turf, issue. When they [the governor's office] spoke of the legislative body they had in mind the people upstairs, the third floor. They were not thinking of local government."[43]

Each legislative chamber followed its separate path. The Republican Senate went with the governor's measure, while the Democrats, in control of the Assembly, preferred a version of the Lentol-Rosetti bill vetoed the previous year. That bill had been highly decentralized on the matter of administration and had dealt leniently with strikes through the regular civil service disciplinary processes.

Amid talk of possible compromise, Earl Brydges, majority leader of the Senate, produced an amended bill that among other things discarded the penalty of decertification and established an upper limit on fines against striking unions of one year's dues.[44] Brydges stated that he had consulted with the Taylor committee and, although it had not given its "formal approval," the intimation plainly was that the members supported the changes.[45]

Brydges's reading did not completely square with a letter George Taylor had written on May 31 to John J. Phelan, counsel to Senator Brydges. Taylor said, "May I suggest that it is not entirely in accord with our telephone conversation of May 24 categorically to state that, in my judgment, 'these amendments are in accordance with the

Report of the Governor's Committee on Public Employee Relations and do embody the principles thereof.' "[46] In tactful language, Taylor suggested that proposals to lighten strike penalties and to move partially in the direction of unfair labor practice language were not fully in line with the committee's report. For the Democrats and Speaker Travia, the penalties of the Senate version were still too stiff; thus in early June each body passed its own bill.

According to newspaper accounts, Brydges, despairing of an acceptable compromise, at one point toyed with the idea of adopting the Assembly bill on the ground that some legislation was better than nothing. There were also political considerations for such a tack. At the time it seemed possible that the city's sanitation workers would strike on July 1. If that happened, it would strengthen the GOP call for a strong law and would also provide the governor with a good political issue for the fall campaign.[47]

During these months Travia repeatedly expressed his wish to work a compromise even though it was clear that it would have to entail some increase in penalties. Responding to the notion of placing no limit on union fines, he said, "When you take the lid off the top, you're putting the whole world out of business."[48] Even as the legislature adjourned, Travia, mindful of the number of negotiations then stalemated in the city, suggested that a special session might be required to address public sector legislation.[49] But it was too late. Although the sense of real crisis engendered by the transit strike had passed, there was evidence of disarray all around, not only in New York City (Plainview teachers had struck for four days, for instance, and Buffalo teachers had threatened a walkout), and a substantial public clamor for effective legislation.

For New York City public employee unions and their Democratic allies, the stiff penalties of the Senate bill and a public employment relations board appointed by an un-friendly governor were especially distasteful. Moreover, because the bill threatened the new labor relations policy based on the tripartite Office of Collective Bargaining, the unions saw no advantage to be derived from state leg-islation that did not meet their expectations. Thus the governor's bill was vigorously opposed by the state AFL-CIO and by George Meany, president of the national AFL-CIO, as well.

The ranks of labor were far from united, however, in opposition to the Taylor report or its translation into leg-islative form. From the beginning two major labor figures in the state, Harry Van Arsdale, president of the New York City Central Labor Council, and Peter J. Brennan, president of the New York City Building Trades Council, had endorsed the report and sought to line up support for it.[50] The reasons for their positions were probably a mixture of personal, philosophical, and political consider-ations. Van Arsdale and Brennan, among others in the city labor establishment, heartily disliked Jerry Wurf and by extension the rest of AFSCME. Besides finding him personally obnoxious, Van Arsdale and Brennan found Wurf and his kind too radical and thus too threatening to a conservative established leadership concerned with pre-serving its own hegemony. As Wurf once said of the labor council, they "like AFSCME about as much as a bone in the throat."[51]

Moreover, a number of private sector unions, epito-mized by the building trades, had little enthusiasm for public employee unionism. Alton Marshall, secretary to the governor, observed that "the established unions were probably more reluctant to have unionization in govern-ment than some of us who had spent all our lives in government."[52] Finally, Van Arsdale and Brennan were close political friends of Rockefeller, who had lavished

large sums of state money on numerous construction un-
dertakings and had generally been supportive of labor on
issues such as minimum wage, unemployment insurance,
and workers' compensation. Both endorsed Rockefeller's
reelection bid in the fall of 1966, and they succeeded in
persuading the state AFL-CIO to remain neutral in that
election.[53]

For many public employee organizations outside New
York City, nearly any legislation that established a right to
negotiate was far preferable to Condon-Wadlin. A president of an AFSCME local of state employees in a letter to
the *Times* disputed Speaker Travia's criticism of the Taylor
report, saying that many state employees welcomed it.[54]
Support came as well from the Civil Service Employees
Association and from the New York State Teachers Association, an NEA affiliate and the predominant teacher organization in the state.

Why was political leadership unable to reach accord on
a bill in 1966 but could a year later under much the same
circumstances? According to Alton Marshall, the administration decided not to press the issue. This was a "period
of aging," he said, a time municipalities could use to ad-
just to the new approach to employee relations, but even
more important, it was a period in which CSEA could get
"psychologically and organizationally" prepared for the
change. In Marshall's recollection, an understanding was
reached with CSEA whereby the administration would
submit a bill, feeling obliged to act on the committee's
report, but not push for enactment in the 1966 legislative
session. Harry Albright, CSEA's counsel at the time, did
not recall the event, although he did not dispute Marshall's version.[55]

Another reason for the legislative inaction had to be the
concern of the governor and the legislature with the fall
1966 elections. For Rockefeller a third term was at stake.
In the case of the legislators, they would be running in

redrawn districts, a consequence of the implementation of a court-ordered redistricting plan. Under these circumstances a controversial topic like public sector bargaining meant added political risks.

CIVIL SERVICE EMPLOYEES ASSOCIATION

The Civil Service Employees Association was a major force in state employee relations. Against its objections, no labor relations bill was likely to pass in either the Assembly or Senate.[56] In 1966 it had a membership of approximately 140,000, more than two-thirds of whom were state employees. Since its founding in 1910, CSEA had through its lobbying activities sought to strengthen and extend the civil service system. It had had considerable success in obtaining greater job protections for state workers, as well as improved pensions, salaries, and other employment benefits. Over the years CSEA had developed valuable political connections with governors and legislators. Indicative of its status its headquarters had for years been in the basement of the state capitol, an arrangement that was ended when Council 50, AFSCME, arrived on the scene in the early 1950s and claimed similar privileges. Also, according to legend, CSEA's decision in 1948 to accept local government workers into what heretofore had been an organization exclusively of state employees was taken at the urging of Governor Dewey. True or not, there was no doubt that relations between CSEA and the Dewey and Rockefeller administrations were especially cordial.

The success of CSEA in attracting members was due to a combination of low dues, a low-cost insurance program available to members, and a record of legislative achievement. Its influence was further enhanced by the large pool of talented members within its ranks—professional and managerial employees from the middle and upper

reaches of the state bureaucracy—many of whom occupied leadership positions within the organization. For
example, both the superintendent of the state police and
Alton Marshall, who was to head the first state negotiating committee, were members at the time the Taylor
Law was passed. Each resigned soon after.

In its internal organization and its operations, the influence of the law firm representing CSEA was pervasive.
The firm, DeGraff, Foy, Conway and Holt-Harris, was
one of Albany's most prestigious, and it had a reputation
as an effective lobbyist for its clients, which included
among others the state medical society. Authority within
CSEA was diffuse. It had no paid full-time officers, and
the paid staff lacked real authority. The lawyers assigned
by the firm to act as day-to-day counsel thus exercised
great influence in shaping the direction and policy of the
organization. Harry Albright occupied that post until he
joined Rockefeller's staff in 1967 and was succeeded by
John Carter Rice.

The use of outside counsel and the role of higher-level
state employees in its leadership made CSEA a more
conservative organization and more accommodative in
its dealings with the state than unions such as AFSCME.
Albright recalled how in 1961 he personally persuaded
CSEA convention delegates to accept, albeit reluctantly,
the recommendations of a McKinsey Company report
that revised the state salary structure and resulted in a 5
percent increase for the lowest paid grade 1 employees and
a 17 percent raise for persons at grade 38.[57]

Soon after Theodore Wenzl became president of CSEA
in 1968, the position became a paid full-time office, followed later by even more substantial structural changes.
The lawyers retained great influence nonetheless, whether
Rice of the DeGraff firm or later the firm of Roemer and
Featherstonhaugh. (In 1987, CSEA abandoned its relationship with Roemer and Featherstonhaugh in favor of

employing house counsel, but only after a prolonged and bitter struggle.)

THE LAW IS PASSED

When yet another politically divided legislature convened in January 1967, labor relations was again a major agenda item, there having been no letup in the signs of unrest. The New York City welfare workers, having received legislative forgiveness for their 1965 strike, once again went on strike, as did employees of the city housing authority. Even CSEA exhibited unusual militance when in its March 1967 convention it took the first step toward eliminating the no-strike clause in its constitution as a gesture of displeasure with the failure of the legislature to act and, not incidentally, as a signal of its unhappiness with the governor's budget, which did not provide a general salary increase for state workers. (Two months later the constitutional change was confirmed at a special convention.) This time around adoption of the governor's bill was a priority legislative aim of CSEA, which viewed it as a vehicle for protecting and enhancing its own status vis-à-vis state government and for further extending its penetration into local government.

At stages during the legislative process, the advice of the Taylor committee was sought on whether a proposed revision was or was not in keeping with the principles and recommendations of its report. Reference was made earlier to the query from Senator Brydges. In February 1967 Robert R. Douglass, counsel to the governor, wrote Taylor to solicit the committee's advice about certain revisions designed to meet some of the criticism of opponents.[58] In both instances George Taylor responded with circumspection yet left little doubt about his own opinion. Meanwhile, the full committee avoided taking what might be called an official position on the questions. In a note to his colleagues the day after passage of the Taylor Law, George Taylor reported:

> There were occasions, during the negotiations, when I was importuned to get our committee to say that a proposed concession would not do violence to the recommendations of our committee. This seemed unwise in view of our feeling that we were doing a "White Paper" and not attempting to substitute our judgment for that of the legislative body. I am now assured that this attitude was exactly right.[59]

These exchanges indicate the great respect accorded the committee on the one hand and the committee's own political astuteness on the other. These exchanges are also a mark of wisdom on the part of the political leaders, who were prepared to trade on the good reputation of the Taylor committee in order to obtain legislation.

A state constitutional convention was scheduled to convene on April 4, which limited the amount of time the legislature had to act. Still divided over the same key elements, strike penalties and administration, the pace of negotiations among Rockefeller, Travia, and Brydges picked up in the closing days of the session. Rumblings among New York City police and firefighters provided fresh incentives as these groups, frustrated in the ongoing negotiations with the city, spoke of militant actions—mass picketing of City Hall by the police and a possible work slowdown by the firefighters. On March 31 the three leaders came close to resolving their differences only to falter over the issue of exempting New York City from PERB's jurisdiction.[60] Nonetheless, negotiations continued and a final compromise was fashioned and brought to the floor of the respective chambers for a vote in the early hours of Sunday, April 2.

The compromise bill placed limits on the amount an employee organization could be fined for contempt of court. Rather than leaving full discretion to the courts, the bill established a maximum daily fine equal to one week's dues or ten thousand dollars, whichever was the lesser amount, and a minimum fine of one thousand dollars per day. The other central ingredient in the compromise was the addition of section 212, dealing with local government procedures. It gave local governments the option of creating their own agencies, what came to be known as mini-PERBs, to function in place of the state public employment relations board, so long as their procedures were substantially equivalent to the state law and had prior approval from PERB. This feature was attractive to the many upstate government officials who were not keen on allowing Albany to run the show.

To make the legislation more palatable to New York City interests, a proviso was added that eliminated the need for PERB to approve New York City procedures. Instead, there was a presumption of substantial equivalence with the state law that, if challenged, would be decided by the courts rather than by PERB. A final element in the compromise package was the adoption in separate legislation of amnesty provisions to excuse recent strikes by housing authority and welfare department employees in New York City.

The Senate adopted the compromise bill by a vote of thirty-eight to eighteen, with Joseph Zaretsky, Democratic minority leader, joining the majority and declaring that this was "not a union busting bill." A few hours later the Assembly followed suit by a margin of ninety-three to fifty-one (seventy-five votes were required) as Travia produced a score of Democratic votes in favor of the measure, including his own. That he voted was a departure from customary practice of the Speaker, which was to abstain unless his vote was needed. The outcome, according to the *New York Times,* "marked the first time in recent memory that the Democrats had broken with organized labor on a major issue."[61]

Anthony Travia's conversion was critical in winning

enactment of the Taylor Law. His support represented a turnaround from the position he had so vigorously defended in the past. Some cynical political observers suggested the switch was motivated by dark personal motives—a federal judgeship that was to come a year later or the repayment of a political debt to Rockefeller for his support in a bruising intramural Democratic fight for the speakership in 1965. Neither explanation is persuasive.[62] A far more plausible explanation is that Travia accurately read the strong public sentiment for legislation and responded accordingly. This is a view shared by former senator Thomas Laverne, who was close to the legislative negotiations at the time, and by Jack Rice of CSEA.[63] Travia had been able to extract some concessions that made the bill easier to accept, as did the divisions within union ranks on the issue.

It was only in the last few hours of the session that the final version of the bill was put together by the leadership and presented for a vote. Reportedly, members of the Assembly received printed copies just moments before the debate began, but such is the workings of the legislative process. While the measure was still awaiting gubernatorial approval, Raymond Cothran on behalf of the Conference of Mayors urged a veto. His principal objection had less to do with the content of the bill than with the fact that no local government officials had had the opportunity to participate in preparing it. He went on to complain that as of April 13 his organization had still been unable to obtain copies of the bill from the legislative document room.[64]

Richard Winfield, assistant counsel to the governor, remembered the night the bill passed:

We were standing in a hallway on the second floor. Nelson Rockefeller was there and Happy [his wife] was there. . . . We had worked thirty-six to forty-eight hours without stop and so had the governor. It was four o'clock in the morning. Nel-

son was full of beans. We got word that the Assembly had
passed the bill. The governor said, 'Get George Taylor on the
phone.' I said, 'Governor, it's four in the morning.' 'Oh, get
him up, he'll be glad.' The call was made. To Taylor's suggestion that the law should be called the Rockefeller law, the
governor, uncertain how it would be received politically, responded that it would be known as the Taylor Law. Taylor
was delighted.[65]

Supporters of the Public Employees' Fair Employment
Act, its official title, could feel some sense of achievement
in having finally replaced Condon-Wadlin after several
years of effort. The *Times* called the legislature's action "a
significant and overdue accomplishment."[66] But for legislators and editors alike the enthusiasm was tempered by a
degree of skepticism. Would the Taylor Law fare any better than Condon-Wadlin? Were political leaders, government administrators, and unionists prepared to accept the
strictures of the new law and accommodate to a system of
collective negotiations?

To judge from the comments of John DeLury, Victor
Gotbaum, Barry Feinstein, Matthew Guinan, and other
New York City union leaders, there was not much reason
for optimism. Gotbaum declared, "He [Rockefeller] is not
going to have peace; we're going to give him war."[67] De-
Lury called the bill "infamous" as the sanitationmen announced their intention to establish a strike fund for the
first time.[68] The same attitude, stated with more restraint,
was voiced by the editor of the *Chief,* the city civil service
newspaper, under the heading "Serious Setback":

> Democrats at Albany gave their friends in labor a slap in the
> face when they agreed to a new anti-strike bill to replace the
> 20-year old Condon-Wadlin law. One quid pro quo was pas-
> sage of exemption bills for Housing Authority and welfare
> workers but the price is too high.[69]

Condemnation of the new law reached a crescendo at a
mass rally in Madison Square Garden on May 23, staged

by the city's public employee unions. The Transport Workers and the United Federation of Teachers joined District Council 37, AFSCME, in sponsoring the event and in denouncing "the RAT Law" (Rockefeller and Travia) as "this illegitimate offspring of diseased bipartisanship." The union leaders pledged "to stand together in defense of one another until this evil law and its promoters are left in the dust of history."[70]

NOTES

1. Chap. 6, L. 1966. The same session granted legislative amnesty to New York City welfare workers and ferryboat captains for their 1965 strikes.

2. Lefkowitz, *The Legal Basis of Employee Relations of New York State Employees*, 6. Lefkowitz, later deputy chairman of PERB and at that time counsel to the state labor department, was a member of that group.

3. *New York State Governor's Committee on Public Employee Relations, Final Report*, 31 March 1966 (hereafter *Final Report*), 9.

4. Benjamin and Hurd, *Rockefeller in Retrospect*, 292, 265; interview with Sol Neil Corbin, 29 April 1985; Persico, *The Imperial Rockefeller*, 209. Persico's characterization obviously did not fit this case.

5. Interview with John T. Dunlop, 29 July 1985. This according to Dunlop.

6. Interview with Corbin.

7. Interviews with Corbin; with T. Norman Hurd, 9 July 1985; with Alton G. Marshall, 30 April 1985.

8. Interview with Dunlop.

9. 1980 interview with Dunlop cited by Mackell, "David L. Cole," 146.

10. Interview with Dunlop.

11. Interviews with Corbin; with Melvin H. Osterman, Jr., 2 April 1985.

12. Memorandum, Corbin to committee, 4 February 1966, Cole Papers; transcript, public hearing of governor's committee, 4 March 1966, Cole Papers.

13. Letter from Frederick R. Livingston to David Cole, 8 February 1966, Cole Papers.

14. Cole Papers.

15. "Governor's Committee on Public Employee Relations, Interim Report," 2 March 1966, Cole Papers.

16. Committee for Economic Development, *The Public Interest in National Labor Policy,* 75–76, cited by Mackell, "David L. Cole," 122; emphasis added.

17. Mackell, "David L. Cole," 155.

18. *Final Report,* 18.

19. Ibid., 15.

20. Ibid., 11.

21. Catherwood, notes for discussion with governor's committee, 18 March 1966, Cole Papers.

22. The origin of the term *collective negotiations* has generated speculation. Thomas Mackell, Jr., (page 178) credits Michael Moskow and Myron Lieberman with having coined it in their book *Collective Negotiations for Teachers.* That volume did not appear until 1966, however, and the authors' use of the term was intended to bridge the competitive vocabularies of the NEA and AFT, between professional negotiation and collective bargaining.

Philip J. Ruffo has pointed out that *collective negotiation* was used as a term of art by an advisory committee appointed by Mayor O'Dwyer in 1946 to head off an earlier strike threat to the New York City transit system by Michael Quill. The committee, chaired by Arthur S. Meyer, recommended "the greatest degree of collective negotiation should be provided in public employ that is compatible with the maintenance of the essential attributes of the civil service system." Rather than exclusive representation by a single organization for all board of transportation employees, it endorsed "sole negotiation" in a multiunit system.

On the right to strike, it said: "Every strike of public employees challenges the authority of government and thus tends to endanger the safety and welfare of the people. . . . Such a strike would be morally indefensible under the system of collective negotiation we have recommended.—It may be argued that effective collective negotiation is not possible without either the right to strike or the right to secure legally binding arbitration. The integrated demands of 33,000 men, however, represent a considerable force. When to this force is added the persuasion of advisory review with its impact on public opinion, collective negotiation will, in our judgment, operate effectively even though the final step of trial by combat is denied." New York City, *Report of the Mayor's Advisory Transit Committee.*

There is a striking congruence between the position staked out by the transit panel and the Taylor committee report twenty years later.

Whether there was any direct link is open to conjecture. A final irony, however, is worth noting. One member of the transit panel was Theodore Kheel, who in 1968 was to criticize the Taylor committee's concept of collective negotiations as nothing other than unilateral determination by the employer. *Report to Speaker Anthony J. Travia*, 3.

23. *Final Report*, 60–61.

24. Industrial Relations Research Association, *The Next Twenty-Five Years of Industrial Relations*, 35.

25. McKelvey, "State Agencies in Public Employee Labor Relations," 193.

26. S. Int. no. 874, Pr. no. 877 (1966); A. Int. no. 1609, Pr. no. 1619 (1966).

27. McKelvey, "State Agencies in Public Employee Labor Relations," 193.

28. *Final Report*, 21.

29. Ibid., 32.

30. Ibid., 33.

31. Draft chapter on procedures for dispute settlement, 23 March 1966, Cole Papers.

32. McKelvey, "State Agencies in Public Employee Labor Relations," 190. That voluntary arbitration was not farfetched as a possibility was demonstrated by its use by the Rochester schools and its teachers in 1965. Having reached impasse, the parties submitted the dispute to a factfinding panel that obtained advance consent that its recommendations would be binding.

33. Interview with Dunlop.

34. Oberer, Hanslowe, and Doherty, *The Taylor Act*, 1.

35. Interview with Dunlop.

36. *Government Employee Relations Report*, no. 135, 11 April 1966, B-2; *New York Times*, 8 April 1966, 30; letter of Peter Seitz, 18 April 1966, Cole Papers.

37. *Government Employee Relations Report*, no. 135, 11 April 1966, B-2.

38. The perceptions among the public members of the tripartite panel were at odds on that score, as became apparent through an exchange of letters to the editor of the *Times*. In their report to Mayor Lindsay, the public members had included a statement to the effect that the problem of the strike by public employees was a matter of legislative policy best left to other forums.

While the legislature was considering a bill modeled on the Taylor report, members Peter Seitz and Saul Wallen in a joint letter declared their belief that the issue "was a statewide problem requiring a solution at the state level. We did not intend to, nor did we offer the 'agreement' as a substitute for either the Condon-Wadlin Act or for a more sensible regulation of the right of public employees to strike. Those who assert that the 'agreement' was intended to do so mistake our purpose." They further asserted that there is a difference between the public and private sector and "a separate code of rights and duties for them is in order." *New York Times,* 20 June 1966, 32.

Another public member of the committee saw the issue quite differently. Vern Countryman responded to Seitz and Wallen: "This public member, at least, proceeded in the hope that the Governor's task force would recommend abandonment of efforts to penalize strikes by public employees." *New York Times,* 27 June 1966, 34. The Reverend Phillip Carey, the fourth public member, associated himself with Countryman's position. *New York Times,* 26 July 1966, 34.

39. *New York Times,* 13 April 1966, 33.

40. *New York Times,* 28 April 1966, 42; 5 May 1966, 1.

41. Interview with Richard N. Winfield, 29 April 1985.

42. *New York Times,* 25 May 1966, 46.

43. Interview with Winfield. The legislative chambers are located on the third floor of the capitol building; the governor's office is on the second floor.

44. S. Int. no. 4784, Pr. no. 5689.

45. *New York Times,* 27 May 1966, 1.

46. Letter from Taylor to John J. Phelan, 31 May 1966, Cole Papers.

47. *New York Times,* 14 June 1966, 1.

48. *New York Times,* 10 June 1966, 30.

49. *New York Times,* 13 July 1966, 22.

50. *New York Times,* 5 May 1966, 1.

51. Goulden, *Jerry Wurf,* 132.

52. Interview with Marshall.

53. *New York Times,* 29 September 1966, 41.

54. Letter from Herbert Levine, Local 382, AFSCME, to *New York Times,* 28 April 1966, 42.

55. Interviews with Marshall; with Harry Albright, 20 November 1985.

56. Interview with John Carter Rice, 20 June 1985.

57. Interview with Albright.

58. Letters from Robert R. Douglass to George W. Taylor, 2 February 1967, and from Taylor to committee members and to Douglass, 9 February 1967, Cole Papers.

59. Memorandum from Taylor, 3 April 1967, Cole Papers.

60. *New York Times,* 1 April 1967, 1.

61. *New York Times,* 3 April 1967, 1.

62. Travia was appointed to the U.S. District Court by President Johnson in April and confirmed in June 1968; he joined the bench after the legislature adjourned. Travia had in fact been nominated a year earlier, but the nomination was withdrawn because of divisions within the state party over who would succeed him as Speaker.

During the first five weeks of the 1965 legislature, Assembly Democrats were locked in battle as Travia and Stanley Steingut vied for the post of Speaker. The stalemate was ended when the Republicans intervened on the side of Travia. See Kramer and Roberts, *I Never Wanted to Be Vice President of Anything!* 90. Rockefeller's favor was presumably repaid later in the 1965 session when Travia supporters gave the governor the votes he needed to carry an unpopular 2 percent sales tax.

Travia's negotiating position was not helped by the revelation that his counsel, Harold L. Fisher, was receiving a retainer from AFSCME Councils 50 and 37 for assistance on legislative matters or with litigation, depending on whose testimony one believed. In any event, the newspaper story was enough to cause Fisher to refund $750 he had received from Council 50 for three months and to terminate his seven-year association with District Council 37. *New York Times,* 17 March 1967, 46; 23 March 1967, 34.

63. Interviews with Thomas Laverne, 16 April 1985, and with Rice.

64. Letter from Raymond Cothran to Robert R. Douglass, 21 April 1967, governor's bill jacket.

65. Interview with Winfield.

66. *New York Times,* 3 April 1967, 32.

67. Ibid., 32.

68. *New York Times,* 4 April 1967, 28.

69. *Chief,* 7 April 1967, 4.

70. *New York Times,* 24 May 1967, 31.

3
TRIAL BY FIRE:
PERB IS LAUNCHED

IT TOOK ONE YEAR for the recommendations of the Governor's Committee on Public Employee Relations to be transformed into the Public Employees' Fair Employment Act or Taylor Law. In the few months between enactment of the law and its effective date of September 1, 1967, a new agency to administer it needed to be established. That agency, PERB, was quickly put to a critical test in a multidimensional dispute over representation rights for state employees, a contest that more than any other would determine the overall effectiveness of the law.

AN AGENCY IS PUT TOGETHER

On June 21, 1967, Governor Rockefeller announced his nominations for the three-member public employment relations board. He chose as chairman and head of the new agency Robert D. Helsby, then dean of continuing education for the State University of New York (SUNY). The other nominees, who would serve as per diem members of the board, were Professor of Law Joseph R. Crowley of Fordham University and George H. Fowler, chairman of the New York State Commission for Human Rights.

The selection of Helsby was something of a surprise, at least within the labor relations community. A more conventional choice would have been Jay Kramer, chairman of the state labor relations board and someone thoroughly conversant with labor relations law. Indeed Kramer had been approached at one stage despite misgivings among some close to the governor who saw him as too much the maverick and also too closely identified with the private sector model of collective bargaining. Kramer had declined, in part because he was concerned that his good relations with unions would be jeopardized.

Nonetheless, Helsby possessed many of the right credentials. A Republican, he had extensive administrative experience, which he had gained as executive deputy industrial commissioner, the post he held before moving to SUNY a year and one half earlier. In addition, he held a doctorate from the School of Industrial and Labor Relations at Cornell University. That the degree was in industrial education and his familiarity with labor relations was admittedly scant were less important. Finally, Helsby had the respect and trust of influential figures in the administration, including T. Norman Hurd in the budget division; Martin P. Catherwood, the industrial commissioner, who had originally brought Helsby to Albany; Robert Stone, the governor's appointments secretary; and Alton Marshall, secretary to the governor. It was Marshall who could probably claim major credit for the choice.[1]

When the post at PERB was first offered, Helsby turned it down on the grounds that he lacked the necessary qualifications. He also believed that the job would sidetrack him from what appeared to be a promising career in educational administration. A month later, however, Nelson Rockefeller personally renewed the offer. Speaking to Sam Gould, chancellor of SUNY, who was present at the meeting, the governor said, "I want to borrow this guy for a year and a half." To Helsby that meant

Rockefeller had his presidential campaign in mind. When the governor turned to him and said, "You are the guy to do the job. Are you going to do it?" Helsby felt he had no choice but to accept. At the same time he believed that it was essentially a temporary assignment and that he would be able to return to SUNY.[2]

What Helsby may have lacked in knowledge about labor relations, he more than compensated for in personal leadership qualities. Beyond knowing his way about the state bureaucracy, he brought strong personal integrity, total dedication, and enormous enthusiasm and energy to the task at hand. He possessed confidence not only in himself but in the importance of the undertaking on which he was embarked, and he instilled in others much of his enthusiasm for the mission.

The son of a minister, Bob Helsby had grown up in a small town in upstate Oswego County. He had been a naval officer and a teacher in a rural school, and he embodied many of the old-fashioned virtues we commonly associate with such a background. While some observers might on occasion mockingly refer to him as an Eagle Scout, few questioned his genuineness. It was his passionate belief in the rightness of the Taylor Law, leavened by a feel for political realities, rather than intellectual leadership, that made Bob Helsby an extraordinarily effective leader of PERB.

The intellectual leadership in that first board was supplied by Joseph Crowley. Because the law required that no more than two members could be from the same political party, Crowley, former party chairman in Yonkers, was the Democratic appointment. Coming from the conservative wing of the party, he had cordial relations with another Westchester politician, Lieutenant Governor Malcolm Wilson, as he did with most people. Crowley had both practiced and taught labor law, making him the only member of the new board with substantial background in the field. Because of his knowledge, natural modesty, wit, and easygoing style, Crowley became an influential member during his ten-year tenure. He and Bob Helsby developed a warm friendship and worked easily together.

The appointment of George Fowler was much more of a calculated political maneuver. Fowler was a black who at one time had served as a deputy industrial commissioner. By appointing him to PERB, the administration was partially able to deflect sharp criticism from civil rights groups that the human rights commission was not sufficiently vigorous in enforcing the law.[3]

GATHERING STAFF

In assembling a staff for the new agency, Helsby looked to old associates from his days at the labor department. His first two recruits were Jerome Lefkowitz and Thomas E. Joyner. Lefkowitz, then counsel in the labor department, was initially invited to assume the same post at PERB, but because that would not have allowed for any adjustment in salary, a new title of deputy chairman was devised for him. In fact, he was the chief lawyer, a forceful intellect on whom Helsby heavily relied. Joyner, a political scientist by training, had been associated with Helsby in both the labor department and in SUNY. Officially listed as PERB's director of research, he functioned as a personal sounding board, trusted adviser, and speech writer to the chairman and particularly in the early period was also involved in shaping policy. Together the ebullient Lefkowitz and the slow-paced Joyner put in place an organizational plan for the agency.

Relations between Helsby and two other early staff appointments—that of his secretary Ellen Zimmerman and Ralph Vatalaro—also went back to labor department days. Vatalaro joined the staff as director of information and education, an area of importance for the fledgling agency, especially while Helsby was its head. Later Vatalaro was to become executive director of the agency.

The original staff also included Frank J. Higgins as counsel, John F. Hans as director of conciliation, and Paul E. Klein as director of representation. The first two did not stay long; each returned to his old agency within a year or so, and they were replaced by Martin L. Barr and Harold R. Newman, respectively. Although PERB was relatively free of patronage pressures, the appointment of Paul Klein, formerly an attorney with the National Labor Relations Board, presented something of a political problem. Klein was a Democrat, and approval of his appointment was made contingent on PERB hiring two staffers recommended by the Republican organization.[4]

Likewise, the hiring of Newman to head the New York City office called for deft handling because of his prominent, long-time association with AFSCME. Newman had been a leader in Local 1412 while he was employed by the state labor department's Division of Employment and for a time had been a vice-president and staff member of the national union. Anticipating CSEA's opposition to Newman, Helsby obtained a pledge from Theodore Wenzl, president of CSEA, that he would not crucify PERB for the appointment. To play it safe, the appointment was also discussed with Jerry Wurf because Newman had been in the opposition camp during the bitter internecine AFSCME wars of the early 1960s.[5]

In the fall of 1968 when Newman became director of conciliation, CSEA interpreted the appointment as further evidence of PERB's prejudice toward it, coming as it did when CSEA was also calling for the dismissal of Jerry Lefkowitz and Paul Klein for their roles as architects of PERB's state unit determination. The CSEA denunciation was loud, but by then PERB was better able to withstand outside pressures.[6]

Political interference in staff appointments at PERB has been minimal overall. Harold Newman tells of an amusing and minor political flap that occurred almost ten years after the agency's founding when he, as the new chairman, recommended that Erwin Kelly succeed him as director of conciliation. Kelly, the assistant director for several years, was respected and well liked by the agency's clients. Since the position of division director was an exempt one with appointment subject to the approval of the governor's office, Kelly's status as a registered Republican became an obstacle. Newman's pleas on behalf of the appointment were unavailing until finally word came back that objections would be withdrawn if Kelly, who lived in the town of Latham, would telephone the town Democratic party leader to thank him for his support. Apprised of this, Kelly told Newman that he could not in good conscience make the call even if it meant forgoing the promotion; after all, he did not know the man, and it just did not seem right. Utterly failing to persuade Kelly to change his mind, an exasperated Newman dismissed Kelly, picked up the telephone, dialed, and said, "This is Erwin Kelly. I want to thank you. . . . " The appointment came through.[7]

Tension between the Agency and the Committee

Jerry Lefkowitz took the lead in preparing PERB's rules of procedure with the help of a distinguished advisory committee consisting of Michael I. Sovern of Columbia University Law School, Walter E. Oberer and Kurt L. Hanslowe of Cornell University Law School, and Melvin H. Osterman, who had served as a counsel to the Taylor committee. Public hearings were held, and a final version was adopted in November 1967. Included in the rules was a section (part 204) that stated that PERB would hear charges brought by a public employee who alleged that his employer had engaged in reprisals for his having exercised rights guaranteed by section 202 of the act. The reasoning, of course, was that if the guarantee of rights in the act were to be meaningful, there needed to be an expeditious way to protect them and to achieve compliance with the law. By adopting this procedure, PERB was in effect arming itself via the rule-making process with limited unfair labor practice authority, even though the statute was silent with respect to the matter. This issue was to provoke an interesting episode in relations between the agency and the authors of the act.

Just a few days after PERB opened its doors for business on September 1, 1967, Bob Helsby arranged a meeting in Princeton, New Jersey, between key PERB staff and the members of the Taylor committee. John Dunlop was unable to attend, but the others including counsel Sol Corbin were there. Here was an opportunity to obtain advice and insights (perhaps blessings as well) from the progenitors of the law. That may have been the intent; it certainly was not the outcome.

PERB staff vividly recall heated exchanges with Cole, Taylor, and Corbin on the draft rule for reprisals. Corbin attacked the idea as politically impractical, asking whether PERB was prepared to take on Mayor Erastus Corning of Albany, who headed the most powerful political machine in the state. Corbin's argument seemed to be that since PERB already had inherited the displeasure of the unions, it ought not to go out of its way to provoke the opposition of the management community as well.

In the opinion of members of the committee, government employers were less likely to impose reprisals than were private employers, and besides, most employees had some protection through civil service law. But central to their thinking about the entire matter of unfair labor practices was a conviction that any effort directed toward preventing unfair practices would divert the energy and attention of the parties and of the brand-new board from the fundamental goal of developing sound habits of labor-management relations. Taylor had expressed the essential position in an earlier letter to his colleagues when he had commented on a proposal to incorporate a provision regarding unfair labor practices in the governor's bill.

> We discussed at considerable length whether or not to recommend inclusion in the law of an "unfair labor practices" section relating to actions of an employing agency. There are valid reasons for doing so. We did not so recommend, as I recall the reasons, because so much "litigation" would doubtless result as to submerge the Public Employment Relations Board with an impossible task when a likely host of unfair labor practices charges have to be dealt with along with problems in the many new areas in which its pioneering efforts were called for. As I remember our discussions, we conceived of the two-way hearing on strikes—where the employing agency could be called to task for any provocative acts—as serving, at least to some extent, to deter the employing agency from engaging in unfair labor practices.[8]

Eighteen years later John Dunlop reflected the same point of view, roundly condemning "labor relations bureaucracies," PERB included, that wish to regulate in detail when the real need is to get the parties accustomed to dealing with one another. It was for this reason, he said, that the committee refused to propose unfair labor practice language; it wanted to avoid what members believed was the disastrous precedent of the NLRB. The committee was "preoccupied with getting it started," one reason for its emphasis on training inexperienced labor and management. Getting swamped in litigation would defeat that purpose.[9]

But more than differences over substantive issues separated the two groups, making the Princeton meeting indelible in the memories of Joyner, Klein, and Lefkowitz.

The scolding, patronizing tone with which Cole and Taylor seemed to deliver their opinions irritated the PERB folk. Paul Klein remembers Cole as "bristling" at the notion that the neophyte PERB staff would dare challenge the accumulated wisdom of the committee. When the meeting broke up for the night, Joyner and Lefkowitz walked the town in an effort to soothe their bruised feelings. The emotions of the night before were revived the next morning when Taylor remarked to Joyner, "You know, you're not in the private sector."[10]

Any feelings of deference the PERB staff had toward the founders were gone after Princeton. The committee was reconvened two more times for additional reports and its members were feted and accorded public homage at the large Governor's Conference the following year, but its influence had been reduced to that of a political totem and its counsel was largely ignored.

THE LAW TAKES EFFECT

Some 900,000 employees of state and local government came under the terms of the Taylor Law when it took effect on September 1, 1967. Of these, perhaps 340,000, the bulk of them in New York City, were already represented by organizations for collective dealings with their public employers. One year later an estimated 360,000 additional employees had gained recognition and were engaging in collective negotiations for the first time.

During its first year PERB established a staff (it totaled fifty-three by year's end) and the administrative mechanisms necessary to perform the multiple functions assigned it by statute. At the same time it faced a rush of activity, representation matters being foremost. It received 309 petitions from employee organizations seeking certification, 56 of which were for various units of state employees, and it conducted 42 representation elections involving nearly 20,000 workers.

Most matters of representation were handled without
direct PERB involvement as municipalities and school districts voluntarily extended recognition or, less frequently,
when there was a dispute, used local procedures under
section 206 of the act to resolve the matter. More often
than not only one employee organization claimed to represent a unit of teachers, police, firefighters, or other
grouping of public employees. PERB reported in its first
annual summary that more than two hundred local governments outside New York City and some six hundred
school districts had extended recognition to some or all of
their employees. Thus, with the exception of the festering
dispute over representation rights for the bulk of state employees, which was to continue for another year, PERB's
conclusion that "the representation machinery provided
under the Taylor Law appears to be working well" seemed
justified.[11]

Almost immediately after the law's effective date, PERB
was confronted with a major strike when New York City's
teachers refused to report for the scheduled opening day
of school. Negotiations between the board of education
and the United Federation of Teachers were deadlocked
despite mediation and factfinding arranged for by the parties themselves. The strike began while the PERB staff
was meeting in Princeton. When that meeting broke up,
Chairman Helsby dispatched John Hans, Tom Joyner,
and Ralph Vatalaro to the city, believing that PERB
should be on the scene. Helsby himself left for an affair at
the Rockefeller estate at Pocantico Hills. An hour after his
dutiful staff had checked into their hotel, Helsby phoned
to tell them to pack up and go home. Members of the
governor's staff had persuaded him that PERB should stay
clear of the dispute.[12] It was seventeen days before the
strike was settled; Al Shanker was sentenced to fifteen
days in jail for contempt of court, and the UFT was fined
$150,000.

Such was PERB's inglorious introduction to dispute settlement in New York City. But it learned from that and from the experiences to come that labor relations as practiced in the Big Apple was different. The parties had developed their own methods for settling differences. When third parties were needed, the negotiators preferred familiar faces rather than mediators assigned by a distant, somewhat suspect agency in Albany. Thus PERB had to curb its impulse to intervene, which was not easy given the media attention accorded New York City disputes. It did show restraint and flexibility, however, in connection with the transit authority–TWU negotiations in late 1967, which promised to be troublesome. Helsby met early with the parties but was persuaded that strict adherence to the procedures of the law would be disruptive; therefore, PERB stayed on the sidelines as a new agreement was negotiated in another cliff-hanger.[13]

Summing up the experience during the first twelve months, PERB reported nine strikes, including the dramatic and consequential sanitation workers strike in February 1968. On a more positive note, it reported handling in excess of three hundred impasses; school districts accounted for approximately 80 percent of these, and more than half were settled through mediation. Moreover, in a case challenging the authority of PERB to enter a contract dispute, the court endorsed a broad reading of the term *impasse* as opposed to the restrictive reading urged by the employer.[14]

The Contest for State Employees Begins

More than any other matter to come before the agency, how and by whom state employees were to be represented was to be the crucial test of PERB's capacity to act effectively and independently. Failure would have seriously undercut whatever moral authority the agency possessed and confirmed the misgivings of its original critics. Here the board was called upon to deal with the governor as employer, the same person to whom its members owed their appointments. The case was also of critical importance for the employee organizations contesting for the grand prize of the right to represent upwards of 160,000 state employees. Given the stakes involved for unions, employer, and agency alike, it is not surprising that the battle was long and embittered.

In February 1967, even before the Taylor Law was enacted, the Civil Service Employees Association, clearly the predominant organization in terms of membership among state employees, wrote the governor seeking designation as sole bargaining agent for all state employees. The request was denied, for reasons Alton Marshall explained in a subsequent letter to Alfred Wurf, executive director of AFSCME Council 50: "In the absence of legal authorization which provides a method for the designation of any organization to act for any group of public employees in collective negotiations with the State, the Governor has advised the Civil Service Employees Association that he is unable to grant the request."[15] CSEA's request was renewed in August. It submitted affidavits claiming a membership of 101,300 among state employees, 97,726 of whom were on dues checkoff.[16]

The governor established a three-member negotiating committee to represent the state on all matters related to employee relations under the Taylor Law. It consisted of Alton Marshall as its chairman, T. Norman Hurd, director of the budget, and Ersa Poston, president of the civil service commission. In the weeks following, a parade of organizations filed requests with the state negotiating committee for recognition in units of varying size and description, some for a single job title or cluster of titles, others for a grouping of employees in a particular department or location. Among the many claimants were the Police Benevolent Association, the Operating Engineers, the Teamsters, the Building Service Employees, the Safety Officers Benevolent Association, the New York State Nurses' Association, and the Civil Service Attorneys Association. One petition was from a group calling itself the Association of New York Highway Employees, which asked only that it be allowed the right to process grievances for its members.

The state negotiating committee met with several of these organizations to hear their views, all of which shared a common theme: they opposed CSEA's claim to a statewide unit. When it came to stating a position on what constituted an appropriate unit, however, some of the recognition requests were vague to an extreme. The unions' strategy was first to stop CSEA; the task of defining units could be left for later.

Clearly this was the tack taken by Council 50, AFSCME, CSEA's most serious competitor with 13,341 members on payroll dues deduction.[17] Writing the governor, Alfred Wurf maintained that "the Public Employment Relations Board should establish bargaining units on a departmental job title basis ... [and] that appropriate representation rights should be granted minority organizations in all bargaining units."[18] That Council 50 argued against the concept of exclusive recognition at this stage indicates its pessimistic assessment of how it would fare in any head-to-head contest with CSEA. Although Council 50 sought recognition and certification for two specific units, one of nonsupervisory correction officers and another of nonsupervisory state troopers, its basic position was that all matters of representation should be deferred until PERB had an opportunity to act. Answering Wurf on November 2, Marshall stated that "a hearing before the Public Employment Relations Board prior to action by the State would be inappropriate in view of the Board's power to review actions by the State."[19]

At the request of the state negotiating committee, the state comptroller assembled data on employment and organization membership as reflected in dues deduction authorizations for each department and agency of state government. According to his figures, there were 124,000 employees in what the state called the general unit, that is, the unit composed of all employees except state police and professionals of the state university system. Of these, 88,300 had authorized the checkoff of CSEA dues and an additional 3,500 paid dues directly to the association. Thus 74 percent of employees in the general unit were CSEA members. In all but five departments—civil service, conservation, labor, law, and state—CSEA had majority membership, and in these it held a substantial plurality over rival organizations. Taken together, the other organizations had less than 23 percent of general unit employees on dues deduction.[20]

CSEA is Recognized in a General Unit

Accepting the recommendation of Marshall and his colleagues on the state negotiating committee, Governor Rockefeller announced on November 15, 1967, his determination that there would be three negotiating units:

1) professional employees of the State University;

2) members of the State Police; and

3) a general unit made up of all other State employees, most of whom are covered under Section 130 of the Civil Service Law. Excluded from these units are members of the organized militia who are exempt by law, and those employees determined to be management.

The governor explained his action in these terms:

1. With only a few exceptions (such as the State Police and State University professional employees) State employees have more common interests than differences. Such major negotiable items as salaries, retirement, health insurance, and other fringe benefits are provided under plans that cover all employees in the general unit. Almost all of these employees are subject to the provisions of the Civil Service Law governing appointment, retention, promotion, classification and compensation, attendance rules, and job security.

2. In the past the State has "negotiated" statewide issues on a statewide basis. There is a tradition and a workable and successful pattern of determining these issues on a statewide basis.

3. Because the Governor is the only executive official with authority to agree to terms and conditions of employment and to make effective recommendations to the Legislature, a general unit is administratively more realistic.[21]

On the same day, the governor said that the state would recognize CSEA as representative of employees in the general unit for a period of one year. No recognition of an employee organization was granted in the other two units because both CSEA and the independent Police Benevolent Association could claim majority membership in the state police unit (dual membership was not uncommon) and no organization had asserted a claim to majority membership among university professionals.

The reasons for the state's preference for a large general unit went beyond considerations of administrative convenience. Marshall expressed it this way: "We did as little unitizing as we could initially in order to give CSEA the edge, just as simple as that." Aside from his long personal ties to CSEA, Marshall and other high officials regarded CSEA as a known quantity and as an organization that over the years had demonstrated a reasonableness and a willingness to reach accommodation in its dealings with the administration. The governor himself, according to Marshall, "felt some obligation to CSEA; he owed CSEA." Moreover, the "wall-to-wall" unit was a way to prevent the mercurial and militant Wurf brothers from establishing a toehold.[22]

The policy contained in the November 15 pronouncement did not have the enthusiastic endorsement of all the governor's advisers. Some like Victor Borella whose major concern was the handling of Rockefeller's national political interests were worried about the effect the decision would have on relations with the trade unions that were precluded from a piece of the action. Often during this period there was disagreement and tension on labor relations strategy between the political managers and those like Al Marshall, whose central mission was running state government. In the opinion of Tom Joyner, part of Helsby's success as chairman of PERB was his ability to maintain good relations with both camps most of the time. Events of the next year would place a serious strain on Helsby's relations with Marshall, but at that point Borella proved to be an especially valuable ally in protecting Helsby from Marshall's displeasure.[23]

From the perspective of CSEA, the governor's recognition was nothing more than what was justly deserved. Jack Rice stated, "We didn't have an agreement with the administration that we would be recognized in a statewide unit, but we knew what the law said." For comparison he cited the history of private industries such as steel and auto where large units were established by employer recognition. When at one stage in the proceedings the state suggested that CSEA ought to abandon its litigation and instead consent to letting PERB decide matters, CSEA rejected the proposition, confident in the correctness of its own position.[24]

PERB Acts to Stay Negotiations

CSEA's rivals reacted immediately to the governor's decision to recognize a general unit. Several organizations filed petitions with PERB contesting the appropriateness of the unit and asking that the board order the state to cease and desist from negotiating with CSEA. In a parallel action Council 50 applied to the court for a preliminary injunction and temporary restraining order against negotiations with CSEA scheduled for November 27. Refusing the request, Supreme Court Judge John Pennock held that the governor had "done exactly what the statute had authorized him to do, i.e. 'ascertain the public employees choice of employee organization as their representative . . . on the basis of dues deduction authorization and other evidence.' "[25]

PERB meanwhile continued its hearing on the petitions from the competing organizations, and on November 30 it rendered a decision of its own. PERB ordered the state negotiating committee to refrain from negotiations with CSEA on an exclusive basis until the board had resolved the representation dispute. It further ordered the state to be neutral in its treatment of employee organizations. PERB's concern, of course, was that the state's recognition would ultimately prejudice the claims of the rival organizations. Simultaneously, it was mindful that to order cessation of all negotiations would injure the interests of state workers when the budget for the next fiscal year was being formulated. The decision of the board acknowledged that the state possessed statutory authority for its initial determination, but it asserted that primary overriding responsibility lay with PERB when there was a dispute concerning representation. To justify its grant of provisional relief, PERB cited its general authority under the law, the absence of a statutory requirement of exclusivity in representation, and private sector analogies under the National Labor Relations Act and the Railway Labor Act, even as it acknowledged that these precedents were not controlling.[26]

PERB's decision was not an easy one; nor was the board confident of its legal position insofar as the Taylor Law lacked specific authority for the board to regulate unfair labor practices. Nonetheless, the board plunged ahead. Jerry Lefkowitz, who was the principal proponent of the action, later explained: "Responding to the realization that excessive zeal might be remedied by the court, whereas excessive timorousness would be unremedied, the Board decided upon the more aggressive course."[27]

To preserve maximum confidentiality, Helsby gathered the board and a few top staff for a two-day retreat at the Gideon-Putnam Hotel at Saratoga Spa to act on the state case and another important agenda item, the question of whether to revoke the dues deduction privileges of the United Federation of Teachers for its September strike. On the latter, in its first application of the strike penalty, the board imposed a twelve-month forfeiture of checkoff rights, dismissing the UFT's allegation that what had occurred was a mass resignation of teachers, not a strike.[28] With respect to the state case, Lefkowitz eventually persuaded the board members that a stay of negotiations should be issued. Helsby, initially dubious, became so convinced of the correctness of their position once it was sustained by the Supreme Court that he was unable to understand how the Court of Appeals could see it otherwise several months later.[29]

Helsby suggested that he should probably advise Al Marshall that the board was intending to issue a stay of negotiations, to which Tom Joyner responded, "If you do, you won't issue the decision." Joyner observed that Helsby was reacting out of habit developed during his years at the labor department when it was customary for agencies to clear any public pronouncements with the governor's office. According to Joyner, "Helsby had to work to overcome those instincts."[30]

The state reacted to PERB's decision with shock and anger. Recalling that time, Osterman said that PERB was "rocking the boat" just as things "were going along nice and easy." The state representatives never really took the unions seriously; Council 50 was seen as "an unstructured, fairly motley group . . . and the remainder of the unions were all special-interest groups . . . put together to cash in on the new field."[31]

Marshall was furious, a feeling that was not lost on the people at PERB. With the board members conveniently unreachable at the time, Lefkowitz was the recipient of a phone call from Marshall and the torrent of abuse that came with it. The ex-Marine, who was capable of memorable outbursts of temper and profanity, later hurled similar abuse at Helsby during the representation proceedings.[32] Marshall attacked Helsby as "a Goddamned Benedict Arnold" and as someone suffering from "the black robe syndrome," and he accused Helsby of being a captive of Jerry Lefkowitz. As a sign of Marshall's displeasure, Lefkowitz reputedly was the only state employee not to receive a salary increase in 1968.[33]

Despite its unhappiness with PERB's order, the state negotiating committee halted exclusive negotiations while it awaited the outcome of CSEA's challenge in the courts. PERB was sustained by Judge DeForest Pitt in the Supreme Court, but that decision was soon unanimously reversed at the appellate division.[34] The Court of Appeals affirmed the appellate division on March 7, 1968, by a five to two margin.[35] The majority opinion held that the board had no authority to issue its order, stressing the absence of statutory provisions concerning unfair labor practices and cease and desist orders. It referred as well to the practical consideration of an April 1 deadline for adoption of the state budget. In dissent, Chief Judge Stanley H.

Fuld found the majority view "unreasonable and unfair."
He summarized his opinion as follows:

> In sum, if the Board be held powerless to issue the sort of
> provisional order which it has issued in this case, then, the
> function of the Board, insofar as it was set up to assure a fair
> election and a true collective bargaining agreement, may be
> frustrated and the design of the statute undermined.... Un-
> less the Board has the power to issue such a provisional or-
> der, the rights given public employees by Section 203 may be
> violated with impunity. Nor will the rendition of a *final*
> Board determination as to the bargaining unit repair the
> harm done by permitting the organization (selected by the
> employer) to negotiate and enter into an agreement on behalf
> of persons it may not actually represent.[36]

Although PERB lost this particular engagement, the
fight served a more important purpose. Melvin Osterman
made the point well: "I think from [PERB's] point of
view this was an opportunity to establish the credibility of
the agency. This was tangible proof to the unions that it
was not beholden either to the state or to CSEA."[37] Following on the heels of the Court of Appeals decision,
CSEA and the state were back at the negotiating table,
and within three days they reached an agreement that
dealt with wages and pension improvements only. No
written contract was produced, but state employees were
to get a 10 percent salary increase.

THE REPRESENTATION HEARING

As litigation of the stay order made its way through the
courts, PERB went forward with hearings on the petitions of Council 50 and of more than a dozen other organizations that were attempting to decertify CSEA and
in turn certify themselves as representing various negotiating units. The petitioners claimed that, altogether, there
were more than thirty appropriate units, several of them

overlapping. The hearings began in December 1967 and continued for seven months. When they concluded on June 21, 1968, the record contained in excess of five thousand eight hundred pages of testimony and more than three hundred exhibits. Additional hearings were required in early 1969 to define the precise boundaries of who was to be included and who excluded from the five broad units that PERB finally established.

The hearings got under way at the PERB offices on Central Avenue in Albany, where mysteriously the inscription on the front door, "Nelson A. Rockefeller, Governor," vanished overnight.[38] Jerome Lefkowitz, deputy chairman of PERB, presided as the hearing officer. The other major players were Julius Topol representing Council 50, Jack Rice for CSEA, and Melvin Osterman, who midway through the proceedings took over as representative for the state, replacing attorneys from the attorney general's office. The office of the attorney general wanted out because it did not feel competent in the area of labor relations law and, according to Jerry Lefkowitz, because the attorney general felt strongly that it was demeaning to his office to argue a case before a state administrative agency. For that reason it had earlier declined to handle prosecution of the United Federation of Teachers for violation of section 210.[39] Osterman, recalled from private practice and designated assistant special counsel to the governor, was knowledgeable in both labor law and state government.

Also participating in the proceedings were representatives from three locals of the Building Service Employees (BSEU); Local 30D of the Operating Engineers; Local 456 of the Teamsters; the Safety Officers Benevolent Association; District 15 of the Machinists; the Police Conference of New York; the New York State Nurses' Association; the New York State Council of Carpenters; the Association of New York State Civil Service Attorneys; the New

York State Correction Officers Association; and the American Physical Therapists Association. Along the way the Carpenters and Local 200, BSEU, withdrew, and PERB ultimately dismissed the petitions of the civil service attorneys and the physical therapists on the grounds that their organizations did not qualify as employee organizations under the act.

The challenging organizations sought to have CSEA disqualified on the grounds that it was not an employee organization within the meaning of the act. Their major argument was that CSEA was employer dominated insofar as large numbers of managerial and other high-level personnel—commissioners, judges, the attorney general himself—were members and that as a consequence it was accorded preferential treatment. At the outset of the hearing much was made of the fact that the two assistant attorneys general representing the state were themselves members of CSEA. The hearing officer rejected the argument, however, on the grounds that it was predicated on practice under the National Labor Relations Act, which specifically prohibits employer interference with or domination of a labor organization.

Nonetheless, the entire issue of who was management continued to be troublesome in that the employer was ill prepared to declare and defend a position about which it had given little thought beyond a vague notion that some individuals would be excluded. When quizzed about who within the corrections department were managerial employees, for example, Julius L. Sackman, assistant attorney general, mentioned the commissioner, deputy commissioners, department counsel, and the personnel director and his deputy. He continued, "The wardens are employees just like everyone else. They are not managerial help." Nor in his estimation were a whole array of division directors. Alton Marshall recalled that "the state did not have any clear idea about management exclusions beyond

exempt employees." Other considerations were also involved. Marshall said, "They [managers] could not only
vote but they would be very influential on people down
the line."[40] It was only later under the pressure of draw-
ing lines for impending representation elections that the
state developed anything like a coherent position on managerial exclusions.

The petitioners' main thrust was to establish through
witnesses and argument that the units they sought reflected a strong community of interest that set a particular
group of employees apart from others. Not surprisingly,
the units they identified as appropriate corresponded to
their extent of organization or to what they perceived to
be winnable in an election. For example, the Union of
Operating Engineers first petitioned for two units of nonsupervisory employees in power plants, one in metropolitan New York City and one upstate, but seeing that
that configuration was unlikely to prevail, it changed
its proposal to a unit of all skilled craftsmen employed by
the state. Council 50 sought to justify a separate unit
for employees of the Division of Employment, part of
the labor department, on the basis that its funding came
from the federal government and its employees were under the special strictures of the Hatch Act. Council 50
also proposed a very large unit composed of all mental
hygiene attendants. And finally, the Safety Officers Benevolent Association petitioned for an interdepartmental unit
of safety officers whose presumed common interest in
achieving peace officer status warranted that they get separate treatment.

CSEA and the state, both intent on avoiding fragmentation of the workforce into multiple units, stressed the
common interests of employees working under a comprehensive civil service system. Through a parade of witnesses, they sought to demonstrate that the community of
interest shared by most employees within the general unit,

with respect to wages, retirement, health insurance, time and attendance regulations, transfers, and tenure, far exceeded any potential for conflict. It was suggested that multiunit negotiations might place in jeopardy the financial integrity of the state retirement system. The example of New York City with hundreds of units was emphasized to underscore the grave problems of multiple bargaining units. Both the state and CSEA argued further that the interest of the public at large in addition to that of the employees would best be served by the broad unit proposed by the governor.

The contending attorneys approached the issue from opposite legal frameworks. Hearing officer Lefkowitz wrote later:

> The representatives of most of the unions which were challenging the recognition of CSEA were attorneys with experience under the National Labor Relations Act. They assumed that the course of events under the Taylor Law would be determined by thirty years of labor relations experience in the private sector. Paying little heed to the Civil Service Law and to civil service procedures, they sought units which were similar to those found appropriate in the private sector and, in advocacy of their positions, they used the private sector arguments with which they were familiar and comfortable. CSEA, on the other hand, assumed the almost complete irrelevancy of experience under the National Labor Relations Act and presented its case as if the Taylor Law had effected only a procedural change, with the substance of civil service concepts unaffected. The hearing officer found the principles of both labor relations and civil service to be relevant.[41]

Units Nobody Wants

A voluminous record and briefs from the parties in hand, Jerry Lefkowitz struggled with the task of preparing his decision. He wrote of the thought processes he went through (referring to himself in the third person):

[The hearing officer] did not anticipate the extent to which he would feel compelled to innovate a solution to the problem of appropriate units. Expecting that he would determine to be appropriate those units which its advocates had "sold", and a residual unit of the rest of the general unit, he announced that in the receipt of both evidence and arguments, the parties would be bound by the formal positions specified in their petitions and alternative units would not be considered. This posture was to plague him when the time came to write his decision and he found neither the general unit nor any of the alternative proposals attractive.[42]

Reviewing the evidence, Lefkowitz was convinced that "an attempt to join all the diverse groups in a single unit denied effective representation to large numbers of employees."[43] Moreover, he found a measure of merit in some of the alternatives proposed. The state in its brief, while seeming to concede that the nurses' association had made a persuasive case for separation, went on to caution that granting this one exception would open the door to any number of other exceptions. As Lefkowitz thought about it, he came to believe that adopting the nurses' claim would offer a "road map" that other organizations would follow, ultimately leading to total dissolution of the general unit.[44] Faced with that unattractive prospect and yet believing that a single unit would not do, he cast about for some middle ground. Again Lefkowitz:

He began to think of a limited number of units, each of which would be cohesive and each of which would encompass a large number of occupations; there would be a substantial conflict of interest between the employees of any one of these units and the employees in any other unit, and the aggregate of these several units would be the totality of State employment in the classified civil service. The intention of the hearing officer was that a small number of units, perhaps no more than eight, could be identified, which units would

be sufficiently large to protect the labor relations procedures
of the State and sufficiently stable so that further fragmentation would not be invited.[45]

Tom Joyner, director of research for PERB, proved
helpful in the process. Together the two discussed various
formulations, Joyner the more knowledgeable about civil
service structure, procedures, and job titles, Lefkowitz
steeped in the testimony and argument from the hearings.
Joyner visited Washington to examine bargaining arrangements in the U.S. Post Office and also Canada, where a
new labor relations program had been adopted by the federal government.[46]

The Canadian trip was fruitful, and the imprint of the
Canadian experience is apparent in the state units PERB
established. Canada's statute, the Public Service Staff Relations Act of 1967, contained guidelines to assist the staff
relations board in determining bargaining units. It identified five broad occupational categories to which occupational groups were assigned, and it specifically prohibited
combining employees from different categories in the
same unit. The designated occupational categories were
(1) scientific and professional, (2) technical, (3) administrative and foreign service, (4) administrative support, and
(5) operational. The general concept as well as some of
the terminology were to appear in PERB's decision. One
unique proviso in the Canadian law, had it been included
in the Taylor Law, would have spared Lefkowitz and
PERB considerable anguish; namely, that in determining
appropriate units, the staff relations board is not bound
by the unit configurations proposed in the applications
received.[47]

The recommendations of the hearing officer on appropriate units were endorsed and issued as the decision of
Paul Klein, the director of representation, on August 28,
1968. Six negotiating units were proposed:

1. operational services—blue-collar titles, skilled and unskilled;
2. inspection and security services—occupations engaged in protection and security functions including correction officers and park police;
3. health services and support—nonprofessional personnel engaged in recreational, educational, vocational, and social programs for the physically or mentally ill or handicapped;
4. administrative services—white-collar clerical occupations;
5. professional, scientific, and technical services—occupations requiring specialized or advanced education and training;
6. all seasonal employees of the Long Island Park Commission—other seasonal employees were left unplaced, at least temporarily.

The matter of exclusions from the units based on managerial or confidential status was deferred for further hearings.[48]

The decision came as a huge surprise to the parties. The outraged CSEA denounced the decision as "stupid and ridiculous." President Wenzl stated, "We are shocked that the Public Employment Relations Board's three member board could allow such a document to be issued by anyone under their supervision. The decision reeks of ineptness and reflects gross inability and lack of foresight on the part of those responsible."[49] The association's state executive committee followed with a long statement attacking the decision and demanding that the governor ask for the resignation of Lefkowitz and Klein, sarcastically labeled "Labor Messiahs" by the editor of the *Civil Service Leader*. The governor was also called upon to order an investigation of PERB and its activities.[50]

Employers were no less surprised, although public criticism was muted. Based on conversations with Lefkowitz before the decision, Osterman had told his client, Alton Marshall, that it was his impression that Lefkowitz was going to sustain essentially the general unit with some minor tinkering in the way of carving out the nurses and perhaps the attorneys. Thus, when Lefkowitz changed his mind "without warning" and came up with six units, "Al reacted very badly."[51] Marshall's anger was made plain to everyone in the governor's office and at PERB. The story circulated that had it not been for the public demand from CSEA for the firing of Lefkowitz and Klein, Marshall himself might very well have taken such action. Reflecting on the period many years later, Lefkowitz observed, "It was like reliving Henry II and Beckett."[52]

Like CSEA, most of the other employee organizations were unhappy with Klein's decision, even if they were less strident in expressing it. Council 50 of AFSCME was an exception. In the subsequent appeal to the board, it was alone in not challenging PERB's authority to find appropriate units other than those proposed by the employer or the petitioners. The reason was clear enough. Council 50 saw in the proposed health services and support unit enough correspondence to its own proposed unit of mental hygiene attendants to warrant hope that it could prevail in an election. Similarly, the inspection and security services unit was a realistic target.

CSEA Explores a Merger

Concurrent with the state representation proceedings, probably in early 1968, the governor attempted to broker a marriage between CSEA and an AFL-CIO affiliate. Although Alton Marshall and Jack Rice have somewhat different versions of events and their timing, their recollections are essentially consistent and provide further evidence of the degree to which the Rockefeller administration saw its interests closely allied to those of CSEA. According to Marshall, the governor suggested the idea of finding a place for CSEA within the ranks of the AFL-CIO and for that purpose dispatched Victor Borella and Peter Brennan to Washington. If an affiliation could have been arranged, it would have strengthened Rockefeller's standing with the trade unions and also rescued him from the awkward position vis-à-vis the labor movement of seeming to favor an independent association (a company union in the eyes of many).[53]

As Marshall put it, the governor's emissaries "found a moribund AFL-CIO union that CSEA could take over." The union was the Office and Professional Employees International Union (OPEIU), then headed by Howard Coughlin and considerably smaller than CSEA.[54] According to Rice, Lieutenant Governor Malcolm Wilson arranged a meeting for Rice and George Foy, a senior partner in CSEA's law firm, with his personal friend Coughlin.[55] Wilson told them that "it's the unions' company union," a reference to the fact that OPEIU represented the employees of a number of unions. A meeting took place with John DeGraff, Sr., substituting for Foy. Rice was impressed by Coughlin as an "urbane, sophisticated guy," and the two of them met alone on a few other occasions. But nothing was to come of these negotiations. Neither Wenzl, Joseph Lochner, executive director of CSEA, nor the board of directors could be sold on the idea. Rice said, "They had spent too much time selling the fact that CSEA was different. 'We're unique. Let's not sell out.'"[56]

The flirtation with OPEIU was not the only instance during those early years in which CSEA explored possible merger partners. Talks were held at one time or another with Victor Gotbaum, Al Shanker, George Hardy, president of the Service Employees' International Union, and others. Any proponents of affiliation had to overcome deeply held convictions on the part of many in CSEA's leadership that their organization was different from a trade union and that the difference was well worth preserving. Ironically, many of the same people who bristled at references to CSEA as a union would within a couple of years pridefully adopt the slogan "New York's Largest Public Employee Union."[57]

THE MENTAL HYGIENE STRIKE

As PERB entertained appeals resulting from the decision of its director of representation, the state resumed negotiations with CSEA for the 1969–70 fiscal year, provoking charges from AFSCME that this constituted a "gross breach of faith" and a disavowal by the governor of his public promise a year earlier that CSEA would be recognized for only one year. Jerry Wurf warned on October 24, 1968, in a telegram to Governor Rockefeller, "If recognition is renewed before the employees have the opportunity to exercise their right to elect the bargaining agent of their own choice in reasonably designated bargaining units, our local unions in New York will have no choice but to take the most drastic action to protect the interests of our membership."[58]

Two weeks passed before Alton Marshall replied. In a letter dated November 7, Marshall explained that PERB was taking longer than expected in part because AFSCME's own legal challenges had been rejected by the Court of Appeals and in the meantime the negotiating committee was keeping in contact with various employee organizations, including AFSCME. In no way did he hint that he was willing to suspend talks with CSEA, though he did suggest meeting on November 12. The meeting between Wurf and Marshall took place, but neither side was prepared to back off from its position.[59]

The "drastic action" Jerry Wurf threatened was made explicit in a *New York Times* ad appearing on November 8. The caption read, "INDECENT: Governor's High-Handed Action Forcing Strike November 18th at Mental Health Institutions." Council 50 had built a strong base among attendants in the Department of Mental Hygiene, especially in downstate hospitals, where there were many black and Hispanic workers. Attendants were by far the largest occupational grouping in the hospitals, were poorly paid, and generally had few prospects for job advancement. They were also a militant faction; months earlier they had pressed for strike action but been dissuaded by the union leadership. This group and the other non-professional employees in the mental hygiene department became the focus of AFSCME's organizing efforts and the union's principal hope for success in establishing a formidable base among state workers. To this end the national union had committed huge resources, including more than one hundred full-time organizers, and Jerry Wurf had assumed overall direction of the campaign, shunting to the side his brother Al, executive director of Council 50.[60]

The previous year Jerry Wurf had appointed Lillian Roberts of District Council 37 to serve as the director of organization for Council 50's campaign in the Department of Mental Hygiene. Roberts, who was black and had been a nurse's aide in Chicago, had earned a reputation as a dynamic and effective organizer there and in New York City, where she worked with Victor Gotbaum. She played a major role in District Council 37's key victory in 1965 against Local 237 of the Teamsters for representation rights for nineteen thousand aides and clerical workers in the New York City hospital system.[61]

As forecast, the strike commenced on November 18, 1968, when more than one thousand employees failed to report for work at Creedmoor State Hospital in Queens.

Three days later the strike spread to state hospitals in the Bronx (about six hundred strikers) and Manhattan (about two thousand). On the 25th another 150 workers at Buffalo State Hospital walked out. The strike was effective in disrupting service and causing the state to evacuate thousands of patients from struck hospitals and from facilities where a strike was anticipated.

Both before and during the stoppage, the union made it clear what was required to keep employees on the job. Wurf reiterated the position in a telegram to the governor on the first day of the strike:

> If you agree to carry out your specific promise of November 1967 by ending your unilateral negotiations with the Civil Service Employees Association, and if a date is set at which time the employees can choose which organization they wish to have represent them, I am confident the employees will return to work.

The governor responded with a call to return to work and to await the PERB decision.[62]

At the request of the state, Judge J. Irwin Shapiro issued a temporary injunction. He also proposed a plan for settlement, namely, that the governor agree to halt negotiations with CSEA and pledge to abide by PERB's decision. The union accepted, but the state rejected the proposal. As the strike continued, Judge Shapiro sentenced Lillian Roberts and the local union president from Creedmoor to jail for contempt, thirty and twenty days respectively.[63] (Each eventually served twelve days in December.)

PERB DECIDES ON STATE UNITS

The strike ended on November 27, 1968, when PERB issued its unit determination, affirming in the main the conclusions of the director of representation. The determination was accompanied by an order directing "the State Negotiating Committee to be neutral in its treatment of all employee organizations which are parties herein until this Public Employment Relations Board certifies employee organizations in the units determined to be appropriate."[64] Thus, in an ironic fashion, the principal objective of the union in striking—the cessation of preferred status for CSEA—was achieved not by the strike but by the action of PERB.

The decision identified as the "most basic question . . . whether this Board, in a representation proceeding, may devise a unit that it deems to be most appropriate although such a unit is not sought by any of the parties."[65] The state had argued in its brief that

> Having found the general unit inappropriate the Director had the choice of (a) remitting the matter to the employer to permit it to make a further unit determination, or (b) directing further hearings at which the employer and all other affected groups could introduce testimony concerning possible alternative configurations. He could not proceed on his own to devise his own units, without regard to the issues tried or the desires of the parties.[66]

The board rejected that view citing the statutory criterion of section 207(c) that "the unit shall be compatible with the joint responsibilities of the public employer and public employees to serve the public." It also argued that logic dictated the result: "If the Board's power herein were so restricted, a representation dispute might be interminable, in that it would continue until a party to the proceeding petitioned for a unit which the Board found to be appropriate in the light of statutory criteria."[67] Redrawing the boundaries to some extent, the board sustained in general five of the six broad units found by the director of representation. It postponed decision on the proposed sixth unit for seasonal workers as unripe for resolution.

Whether the strike made a difference in PERB's decision is problematic. Helsby says no. He says he might have prevented the strike a few hours before it began had he not declined Jerry Wurf's request for a commitment that the board uphold the recommended units.[68] Jerry Lefkowitz suggested that marginally the strike might have influenced the board to the extent that it dispelled any possibility that the case would be remanded for additional hearings, a "remote likelihood to begin with" but an approach advanced by the state as one alternative the board could adopt.[69]

On the other hand, it seems that the strike had an effect on the attitude and behavior of the state. Council 50 had proven that it could inflict real damage on the state with potential political costs for the governor. The editorial writers of the *New York Times,* while reserving their sharpest condemnation for the union, did over the course of the strike extend their criticism to the state (and governor) for "consistent partiality" toward CSEA and for having spurned Judge Shapiro's plan for resolving the dispute.[70] Gradually but perceptively, the state altered its relations with CSEA, distancing itself from an earlier stance that suggested an identity of interests. It did not join CSEA in the protracted legal challenge of the board's decision; it parted company from CSEA on the matter of managerial exclusions; and it eventually complied with the board's order to be neutral in its treatment of the contending organizations. The pragmatists had prevailed over the partisans.

FURTHER COURT CHALLENGES

Although CSEA lost the battle before PERB on the general unit, it was by no means ready to concede defeat. It therefore initiated a series of legal moves that proved long and complex in order to obtain judicial review of the unit determination, to overturn the board's neutrality order, and to stay further proceedings on the conduct of representation elections.

CSEA reached the end of the trail on July 1, 1969, when the Court of Appeals ruled against it, affirming the lower court without opinion. One member of the court, Judge Francis Bergan, dissented, agreeing with CSEA that PERB had been arbitrary. Bergan sharply challenged the presumed expertise of the three members of the board, in part by seizing on words member Crowley had used in a law review article in which he had suggested that PERB was still in the process of learning through experience. Bergan seemed to be saying, albeit in finer judicial language, "What expertise? You've got to be kidding!"[71] By the time the Court of Appeals decision came down, PERB had already commenced the huge mail balloting among employees in the five units.

Lefkowitz tells an interesting story relative to the final litigation before the appellate division in late May as CSEA in a last desperate effort sought to stay elections. As PERB's attorney in the case, Lefkowitz was called suddenly to meet in chambers with the full court. Also present was John DeGraff, chief counsel for CSEA. The members of the court hoped that Lefkowitz and PERB would consent to continuation of a stay granted earlier by the court, thereby sparing them from having to make an uncomfortable decision that could very well result in a strike if the stay were continued. Calling Lefkowitz by his first name and offering him coffee and danish, the members of the court reminded him that the term was coming to a close and that they were ready for vacation. Lefkowitz did not yield to the blandishments. Thus the court heard argument on the issue on May 28 and it declined to grant a further stay. Instead, it scheduled a hearing on the merits of the unit determination for early June.[72]

Appearing on behalf of AFSCME, which had filed an amicus brief in support of PERB, was Simon Rifkind, distinguished Wall Street lawyer, former general counsel to Senator Robert Wagner, and law partner to Arthur Goldberg. Because Rifkind knew relatively little about the complexities of the case, it was agreed that he would deal with broad, general legal principles, leaving Lefkowitz to argue the "nuts and bolts." According to Lefkowitz, Rifkind was absolutely brilliant, the best he had ever witnessed, as he dwelt on the link between labor law principles and the common law, appealing to the conservative instincts of the jurists. At the end of the day, the court unanimously confirmed PERB's unit determination. In the opinion of Lefkowitz, his case was aided further because DeGraff rather than Jack Rice represented CSEA. The former took over presumably because of his greater prestige and close personal acquaintance with the members of the court. He lacked an understanding of the case, however, which Rice had acquired in a year and a half of argument and litigation.[73]

THE VOTE

The votes from the balloting in the five units were tallied the week of July 28. The results are shown in table 3.1. On September 22, 1969, PERB officially certified CSEA as representative for four of the units and AFSCME for the security services unit. Thus, after two years of bruising controversy, the agency emerged from the sternest test it would ever encounter with its processes vindicated and its reputation significantly enhanced.

AFSCME's defeat among workers in the institutional unit, particularly the margin of defeat, was a surprise to many. Voter turnout in the unit was by far the poorest of any; the total vote (valid plus challenged ballots) represented only 56 percent of the eligibles. Downstate

TABLE 3.1. Results of Representation Election by New York State Employees, 1969

Security Services Unit—eligible voters 5,236	
AFSCME[a]	2,733
CSEA	1,825
Teamsters Local 456	328
No representative	24
Institutional Services Unit—eligible voters 45,499	
CSEA	14,828
AFSCME	7,396
No representative	120
Operational Services Unit—eligible voters 20,150	
CSEA	10,074
AFSCME	1,847
Operating Engineers Local 30-D	486
SEIU Local 223	13
No representative	69
Administrative Services Unit—eligible voters 35,946	
CSEA	18,643
AFSCME	2,428
SEIU Local 223	28
No representative	230
Professional, Scientific, and Technical Services Unit— eligible voters 30,712	
CSEA	15,290
AFSCME	3,282
Nurses' Association	597
SEIU Local 223	115
No representative	570

Source: PERB Files.

[a]Security Unit Employees Council, AFSCME, was the organization on the ballot. It brought together Council 50 and two independents, the Safety Officers Benevolent Association and the Correction Officers Association. It was to become District Council 82, AFSCME.

minority workers did not vote in the numbers AFSCME had hoped for, and there was some evidence of an anti-black backlash among white employees.[74] In the opinion of Victor Gotbaum, the loss was attributable more to the union's militant behavior, the strike, and the antics of Jerry and Al Wurf, which scared off many upstate workers.[75]

OFFICE OF EMPLOYEE RELATIONS ESTABLISHED

The difficulty of conducting multiunion negotiations in the absence of any employee organization having exclusive representation rights was illustrated during the spring of 1969, before the elections. Acquiescing to PERB's neutrality order, the state negotiating committee announced that it would hold parallel negotiations with CSEA and AFSCME regarding employment terms for the coming fiscal year while CSEA's appeal was making its way through the courts. The resulting spectacle had the elements of farce as the rival unions sought to upstage one another.

In the middle of the negotiations, the governor's negotiating committee decided that it no longer wished to be responsible for day-to-day labor relations. A new Office of Employee Relations (OER) was therefore created with Abe Lavine as its director. With the assistance of Melvin Osterman, Lavine acted as the state's chief negotiator. Osterman has provided a colorful description of those negotiations.

—In one of the dumber decisions that has ever been made, the State decided to negotiate simultaneously with everyone.—These negotiations were a nightmare. Since the election was then imminent, each of the unions was anxious to trumpet each new State offer as something it had wrested from the State only as the result of superhuman negotiating skills. We were negotiating with Council 50 at the Tom Sawyer Inn on Western Avenue with television cameras in the lobby. The union representatives could barely wait for an offer to be handed to them before they turned, dashed to the door, and read the offer aloud to the television cameras.

—It was critical to the State to conclude negotiations simultaneously with both unions. Unfortunately we reached an agreement with CSEA at 2:00 on a Friday morning and had no negotiations scheduled with Council 50 until the next Monday morning. We enjoined upon CSEA absolute secrecy.

On Monday morning we returned . . . to conclude the negotiations. At that point, perhaps not surprisingly, Abe decided that it was more important to finish up the final details of the agreement with CSEA and that I . . . should finish up with Council 50.

I entered the ballroom [of the hotel] with some real trepidation. My fears increased when I found, not the field representative who had been representing Council 50, but instead Jerry Wurf, AFSCME's International President. . . . He was among our most effective and most militant labor leaders. Unfortunately he was also crazy.

Wurf opened the meeting . . . with the suggestion that Council 50 had heard rumors that we had settled with CSEA. He inquired whether that was true. I told him accurately, if not completely honestly, that we had made great progress with CSEA and that Abe was back in the office working with CSEA. I stated what was only a literal truth, that to my knowledge we had not *completely* finished with CSEA. I persisted in these denials until about 10:00 when a member of the union negotiating team brought in a copy of that day's edition of the *Albany Knickerbocker News*. Emblazoned as its headline was "State Settles With CSEA." Needless to say, my credibility was somewhat impaired.

At some point during this morning which seemed almost interminable, Abe appeared, having completed his negotiations with CSEA. Abe was able to confirm to Wurf that in fact an agreement had been reached. Wurf, seeking to salvage something from the process, suggested that he would be

satisfied by the same terms we had offered to CSEA if we
gave him something more. Wurf did not much care what the
something was, as long as it was something more than CSEA
had agreed to take. We agreed on a modified form of life
insurance for members of the negotiating unit. Again we
urged upon Wurf that he keep this quiet until we were able
to get back to CSEA.

When we returned to CSEA it stated that it did not want
the benefit. What then to do? Was the benefit to be included
or not? CSEA simplified our problem by going public and
announcing to the press that they had won this benefit on
Friday night and that Wurf's truthful statement that his team
had got it on Monday simply was a lie. Never believe what
you read in the newspaper.[76]

Another participant also had vivid memories of these
negotiations. T. Norman Hurd, director of the budget, recalled that for years in the past he had met regularly with
CSEA for informal annual negotiations and that these had
always been congenial and reasonable even when CSEA
might have been pressing for more than the state was able
to give. On this occasion, however, he remembered a Sunday after church when he was asked to attend an after-
noon meeting at CSEA headquarters, the implication
being that a breakthrough in negotiations was possible.
He and Abe Lavine arrived to find not the small CSEA
negotiating committee, but a room full of sixty to seventy
angry CSEA members who proceeded to heap abuse upon
him and Lavine in some of the worst language he had
ever heard. Hurd resolved then that this was the last time
he would personally take part in negotiations.[77]

It was more than unpleasant personal adventures at
the bargaining table, however, that convinced Marshall,
Hurd, and Poston that the state required a structure other
than the patched-together governor's negotiating committee to represent effectively the employer's interest in labor
relations. The job could not be performed adequately as a

sideline for officials with other important duties even with the aid of a small staff drawn from budget and civil service. The establishment of the Office of Employee Relations within the governor's office was a way to make the labor relations function an integral part of the administrative network. At the outset with the Lavine appointment, OER was still a one-person operation, and Lavine continued to rely on staff assistance from outside. As time passed, however, and negotiating relationships were defined and stabilized, OER grew both in size and influence.

The choice of Abe Lavine as OER director was Alton Marshall's. The two of them were long-time friends who had entered state service on the same day as public administration interns. Lavine was an able, if somewhat colorless, career administrator who knew nothing of labor relations. Marshall explained the choice in these terms: "It was much better to work with someone who knew state government and have him introduce the new thing than to get someone from outside who was familiar with labor and who would perhaps superimpose on government the private sector model."[78] Marshall's remark fairly well reflects the state's orientation toward collective bargaining during the remainder of the Rockefeller period.

THE STATE POLICE

The representation issue was less complex in the Division of State Police, one of the three original units proposed by the governor, and the PERB processes were allowed to operate without recourse to the courts. Not that there was any absence of competition. On the contrary, three organizations vied for representation rights—CSEA, the Police Benevolent Association (PBA), and Council 50, AFSCME. Delineation of negotiating units was again the major point of contention. The board ultimately found two units to be appropriate, a rank-and-file unit of personnel below the rank of lieutenant and a supervisory unit composed of lieutenants, captains, and majors. Elections were held in August 1968, and PBA won in the supervisory unit. In the nonsupervisory unit AFSCME narrowly failed to obtain a majority in the first balloting, so a runoff election was held between AFSCME and PBA. PBA won and was certified in March 1969 but not until PERB disposed of a challenge by AFSCME to the conduct of the election. CSEA's poor showing in the balloting—it garnered less than 10 percent of the vote in the large unit even though 92 percent of the state police were members—was exploited by Council 50 as convincing evidence of the shallowness of support for CSEA among "insurance memberships" in the continuing dispute within the general unit.[79]

CONCLUSION

PERB's handling of the representation contest involving state employees was absolutely critical in determining the future of the agency. Had PERB failed to demonstrate genuine independence of the governor, the agency might very well have had no future at all. Certainly its reputation would have been severely injured, probably to the degree that its capacity to perform its duties would have been gravely impaired. The result would have confirmed the allegations of the law's sharpest critics. But these events did not occur, and instead PERB came through a difficult period with its independence and integrity secured. A good deal of the credit for this success belongs to PERB's chairman, Robert Helsby.

Meanwhile, the law was undergoing other tests, especially in New York City. The spotlight shifts to that locale.

Notes

1. Interviews with Alton G. Marshall, 30 April 1985, and with Robert D. Helsby, 2 June 1985.

2. Interview with Helsby; remarks of Helsby in Benjamin and Hurd, *Rockefeller in Retrospect,* 166.

3. Interviews with Joseph R. Crowley, 23 July 1985, and with Marshall; *New York Times,* 22 June 1967, 26.

4. Interview with Thomas E. Joyner, 9 July 1985.

5. Interviews with Helsby and with Joyner.

6. *Civil Service Leader,* 1 October 1968, 1.

7. Interview with Harold R. Newman, 16 April 1987.

8. Letter from George W. Taylor to members of governor's committee, 9 February 1967, Cole Papers.

9. Interview with John T. Dunlop, 29 July 1985.

10. Interviews with Jerome Lefkowitz, 9 July 1985; with Paul E. Klein, 27 October 1986; with Joyner.

11. New York State Public Employment Relations Board, *Year One of the Taylor Law,* 11.

12. Interview with Joyner.

13. Memorandum from Joyner to Helsby, 16 October 1967, PERB Files; Kheel, *Report to Speaker Anthony J. Travia.* Even Kheel praised the agency. Of course, Kheel was himself the chief mediator in the negotiation.

14. *City of Schenectady,* 1 PERB 704.

15. Letter from Alton Marshall to Alfred Wurf, 10 March 1967, Cole Papers.

16. Cole Papers.

17. Report of state comptroller to state negotiating committee, Cole Papers.

18. Letter of 30 August 1967 cited in affidavit of Alton Marshall, 22 November 1967, Cole Papers.

19. Marshall affidavit, Cole Papers.

20. Report of comptroller to negotiating committee, Cole Papers. When representation elections were held in July 1969, the total number of eligible voters in what had been the general unit, excluding several thousand managerial or confidential employees, was 137,543, a measure of growth in state employment during the period.

21. Governor's press release, 15 November 1967, Cole Papers.

22. Interview with Marshall.

23. Interviews with Marshall; with Joyner; with Ralph Vatalaro, 18 November 1986.

24. Interview with John Carter Rice, 20 June 1985.

25. *Council 50, AFSCME v. Rockefeller,* 55 NY 2d 250 (1967).

26. *Council 50, AFSCME et al.,* 1 PERB 301.

27. Lefkowitz, *The Legal Basis of Employee Relations of New York State Employees,* 8. This short piece provides an excellent account of the legal complexities of the state representation case.

28. *United Federation of Teachers,* 1 PERB 300. To the chagrin of Helsby and others, the decision in the UFT case made the front page of the *New York Daily News* before it was officially announced. The source of the leak was never identified. Interview with Vatalaro.

29. Interview with Lefkowitz, 26 February 1985.

30. Interview with Joyner.

31. Interview with Melvin H. Osterman, Jr., 2 April 1985.

32. There was no consensus among interviewees as to whether Marshall or Mayor Corning took the prize for vile, abusive language directed toward PERB. Helsby gave the nod to the mayor; mildmannered Hurd found it difficult to believe that anyone could outdo Al Marshall.

33. Interview with Osterman.

34. 1 PERB 701.

35. 1 PERB 702.

36. Ibid.

37. Interview with Osterman.

38. Interview with Joyner.

39. Interview with Lefkowitz.

40. New York State, *Record of Proceedings, Matter of New York State and AFSCME Council 50, et al. and CSEA,* 181–86; interview with Marshall.

41. Lefkowitz, *The Legal Basis of Employee Relations,* 10.

42. Ibid., 10.

43. Ibid., 11.

44. Telephone interview with Jerome Lefkowitz, 15 August 1986.

45. Lefkowitz, *The Legal Basis of Employee Relations,* 11.

46. Interview with Jacob Finkelman, 26 July 1985. Joyner was not the first person from PERB to visit Ottawa. Earlier, board member George Fowler had met briefly with Jacob Finkelman, chairman of the Public Service Staff Relations Board, and his staff.

47. Finkelman and Goldenberg, *Collective Bargaining in the Public Service,* 99–116.

48. *New York State,* 1 PERB 424.

49. *Civil Service Leader,* 3 September 1968, 1.

50. *Civil Service Leader,* 10 September 1968, 1, 6.

51. Interview with Osterman.

52. Interview with Lefkowitz.

53. Interviews with Marshall and with Rice.

54. Interview with Marshall.

55. Later as governor, Wilson appointed Coughlin to the state banking board.

56. Interview with Rice.

57. For a fleeting moment in 1973, affiliation with the independent National Federation of Federal Employees loomed as a possibility, but Wenzl's tentative agreement was rejected by the board of directors. That Wenzl should have even considered a merger with a relatively ineffectual independent union suggests his innocence of the trade union world. Interviews with Gotbaum, 26 September 1985; with Wenzl, 20 June 1985; with Rice.

58. *Locals 69, 318, 1567 and 1069, AFSCME et al.*, 3 PERB 8009.

59. Ibid.

60. Ibid.

61. Bellush and Bellush, *Union Power and New York*, 141–58.

62. *Locals 69, 318, 1567 and 1069, AFSCME et al.*, 3 PERB 8009.

63. *New York Times*, 27 November 1968, 1.

64. *State of New York*, 1 PERB 399.85, 3227.

65. Ibid., 3231.

66. Lefkowitz, *The Legal Basis of Employee Relations*, 12.

67. *State of New York*, 1 PERB 399.85, 3231.

68. Interview with Helsby. PERB did announce on November 20 that a decision would be forthcoming the following week.

69. Lefkowitz, *The Legal Basis of Employee Relations*, 13.

70. *New York Times*, 21 November 1968, 46; 25 November 1968, 46.

71. *CSEA v. Helsby et al.*, 2 PERB 7013, 7042–43.

72. Interview with Lefkowitz.

73. Ibid.

74. Interviews with Lefkowitz and with Osterman.

75. Interview with Gotbaum.

76. Osterman, "Two Strikes and You're Out" (unpublished speech).

77. Interview with T. Norman Hurd, 9 July 1985.

78. Interview with Marshall.

79. Lefkowitz, *The Legal Basis of Employee Relations*, 17; *New York Division of State Police*, 2 PERB 3019; letter from Council 50 to Governor Rockefeller, 23 October 1968, Cole Papers.

4
NEW YORK CITY, OCB, AND THE 1969 AMENDMENTS

THE STRIKE BY NEW York City sanitation workers in February 1968 was a pivotal event in the early history of the Taylor Law in much the way the concurrent struggle for state representation rights was. The latter established PERB on firm footing; the former prompted a reexamination of the relationship of the state law and PERB to the labor relations structure of the city as represented in the Office of Collective Bargaining (OCB). The strike was also instrumental in bringing about substantial revisions in the law the following year.

NEW YORK CITY OFFICE OF COLLECTIVE BARGAINING

New York City enacted its own collective bargaining law, effective September 1, 1967, an option available under section 212 of the Taylor Law, which allowed local governments to establish their own procedures for the regulation of labor relations so long as the procedures were substantially equivalent to those of the state act. In the case of New York City, prior approval of PERB was not required because of the statutory presumption of substantial equivalence. The city law was based on the recommendations of a tripartite panel initially appointed by Mayor Robert Wagner and continued by Mayor John Lindsay. Its central feature was, and is, the Office of Collective Bargaining, a tripartite agency charged with administering the labor relations program. The costs of OCB are shared by the city and the Municipal Labor Committee, which is composed of and open to any certified employee organization. OCB's major functions are performed by the board of collective bargaining and the board of certification. The chairman of these two bodies also serves as the director of the Office of Collective Bargaining. Until 1988 that person was Arvid Anderson, who prior to his selection had been a member of the Wisconsin Employment Relations Commission.

The board of collective bargaining is composed of seven members: two each are designated by the city and by the labor committee; the other three are impartial members who are jointly chosen by the city and the unions. The board has final say on the scope of collective bargaining, on matters subject to grievance and arbitration procedures, and on approval of individuals to serve as mediators and members of impasse panels. Subsequent changes in the law enlarged its authority to remedy improper practices and to impose finality in negotiation impasses.

The three impartial members of OCB constitute the board of certification, which decides representation questions, including the determination of appropriate bargaining units. Having inherited a system that had spawned upwards of nine hundred units, much of the activity of the board of certification has been directed toward reducing the number of units through consolidations. By 1986 the number had been reduced to about eighty.

OCB's jurisdiction extended to city departments and agencies under the control of the mayor, initially some fifty in all, with the proviso that nonmayoral agencies could elect to come under its coverage. Over time many have done so. Remaining outside OCB jurisdiction were a number of government entities, most prominently the board of education and the transit authority. The issue of jurisdiction was a major concern in 1968 as it seemed to present a sharp conflict between the principle of voluntarism, fundamental to the conception of OCB, and a public policy stressing peaceful, strike-free labor relations. The sanitation strike offered a dramatic example of city employees who clearly came within the jurisdiction of OCB but who for their own purposes declined to join the Municipal Labor Committee or to observe the procedures of OCB. The Uniformed Sanitationmen's Association (Local 831, Teamsters) was but one of thirty-one employee organizations that initially remained outside the labor committee; some seventy-six other organizations were affiliated.[1]

THE SANITATION STRIKE

Like the transit strike of two years earlier, the repercussions of the sanitation walkout were profound. More than any other single event, it led to the 1969 amendments in the Taylor Law, and for a time it jeopardized the consensual arrangements of OCB.

Ten thousand sanitation workers stayed away from their jobs for ten days at the beginning of February 1968 as garbage piled up in the streets of New York City. Throughout negotiations, which had dragged on for many months, the union had rejected the use of OCB impasse procedures, acceding only a few days before the strike to mediation by Arvid Anderson and Walter Eisenberg of Hunter College.

The union called for a mass rally on the doorstep of City Hall at 7:00 A.M. on February 2 to receive a report from the negotiating committee. Some seven thousand members showed up. Believing that he had the basis for a settlement in hand, John DeLury, president of the union, proposed a mail ballot by the membership on whether to ratify or to strike. He had misjudged the temper of the crowd, however, which hooted and jeered, and DeLury was compelled to retreat under police protection. Unable to extract further concessions from the city, DeLury returned two hours later to announce that he would lead his members on strike.[2]

Amid accumulating garbage and a growing fear of a serious public health emergency, conflict between John Lindsay and Nelson Rockefeller occupied center stage. Here were two of the leading politicians in the state, both Republicans, both with national political ambitions, at odds with each other in the middle of a public crisis. The veteran governor, relaxed, self-assured, and pragmatic; the mayor, still relatively new, the principled reformer, seemingly rigid in style and in policy. Richard Winfield said it put him in mind of "Rome versus the tribal chieftains of Connemara."[3]

Responding to rumors that the mayor would ask for the assistance of the National Guard, Rockefeller stated that the mayor "will have to say that he's lost control and ask the state to come in."[4] A formal request came from the mayor asking the state "to provide whatever assistance may be available under the law, including the use of organized militia, if necessary." Rockefeller rejected the idea of employing the National Guard and instead appointed, with Lindsay's concurrence, an expanded five-member mediation panel chaired by Vincent McDonnell of the state board of mediation. The panel quickly formulated new recommendations slightly more generous than those first suggested.[5] An incensed Lindsay attacked the proposal as "capitulation" to "extortionist demands," as "a little bit of blackmail" to which the city would never agree.[6]

With the city's rejection of the mediator's proposal, the governor announced that he would ask the state to take over sanitation services. That declaration was enough to send the workers back to their jobs in a matter of hours. The announcement was made in the presence of John De-Lury, who had briefly been released from jail, where he was serving a fifteen-day sentence for contempt of court.[7]

There was little enthusiasm in the legislature for the takeover plan, and the matter never came to a vote. Indeed the Assembly in an unprecedented action turned down the governor's request to address a joint session of the legislature. Ultimately the city and union agreed to arbitration by Vincent McDonnell, whose award was essentially a reworking of the package recommended weeks earlier by the mediation panel he had headed.[8]

The fallout from the strike was great in terms of Rockefeller's political prospects. Many of his close political advisers thought it cost him the presidency. He was almost universally condemned in the press for knuckling under to the union, for violating principles of home rule, and for ignoring and perhaps severely damaging the Taylor Law. The following comments typify the press's harsh treatment:

New York Daily News: "He might as well just stand on the front steps of the Executive Mansion shouting 'come and get it' for every gravy-hungry boss of a public employees union."

New York Times: "The Governor sees nothing wrong with undermining his own no-strike law or court orders issued to enforce it, so long as he can argue that it didn't cost much to buy peace."

New York Times: "Governor Rockefeller's crassly political abandonment of Mayor Lindsay in his resistance to flagrant law defiance by the striking sanitation union has confronted New York with a crisis worse than the one that currently engulfs it in filth."

In contrast, Lindsay emerged in the short run at least with an enhanced reputation as a valiant defender of the public interest. A *New York Times* poll showed 59 percent support for the mayor's position, as opposed to 15 percent for Rockefeller, even as a majority of respondents said they disapproved of using the National Guard.[9] One person who defended the governor was the chairman of the state labor relations board, Jay Kramer, who in a long letter to the *Times* praised Rockefeller for "keeping his cool" and asserted he had "strengthened and preserved" the Taylor Law.[10]

Lest the public erroneously believe that PERB had somehow failed in the sanitation dispute, a statement by Chairman Helsby was released a week after the strike disclaiming responsibility. PERB correctly, if not magnanimously, pointed the finger at OCB. The press release called attention to differences between the local ordinance and the Taylor Law with respect to the strike and impasse procedures and ended with a cautionary note that PERB would "give continuing thought and study . . . to the relationships between the State PERB and local boards."[11]

Presumably as a step to control further political damage, on February 19 Governor Rockefeller reconvened the Taylor committee, the group that had won him wide praise not so long ago. Before the committee could begin its assessment of the law (its so-called interim report was not completed until June 17), Theodore Kheel weighed in with his own evaluation, a report commissioned by Assembly Speaker Travia before the sanitation strike.[12] In his customary provocative fashion, Kheel declared,

> Obviously the Taylor Law has not worked. The law has not prevented strikes, its procedures are cumbersome and indecisive, and its system of penalties has proved not only ineffective but in some respects an impediment to the settlement of disputes through negotiation.[13]

For Kheel, collective negotiation as envisioned by the Taylor Law was nothing other than unilateral determination by the employer, whereas the promise of joint determination could be achieved only through "true collective bargaining," which carried with it the prospect of a strike. Thus he counseled legalizing the strike and, for those limited instances when a strike might threaten public health and safety, making use of cooling-off periods and, if necessary, arbitration.

Kheel's judgment of the Taylor Law could be criticized on the grounds that it was too hasty—after a mere six months—and that it focused exclusively on New York City; not a single mention was made of how the law had fared elsewhere in the state. The report caused hardly a ripple in the policy debate, but it obviously provoked one member of the Taylor committee, David Cole. Cole wrote in the margin of his copy observations such as "What gall!" "God has spoken!" "*Ad nauseum*," "Nuts."[14] Kheel's view regarding the centrality of the right to strike was to receive a more hospitable reception in Pennsylvania, where a few months later an advisory commission appointed by Governor Raymond Shafer recommended a limited right to strike. This idea eventually became part of Act 195, adopted in 1970.[15]

Taylor Committee Reconvened

Since the Taylor committee had performed so well before, the Rockefeller administration presumably hoped that it might again be able to come up with concrete proposals for avoiding future debacles. Counsel to the governor Robert R. Douglass submitted twelve specific questions to the committee with the suggestion that it might entertain these in its deliberations.[16] The first question asked "whether local government units with procedures 'substantially equivalent' to the Taylor Law provisions should continue to be exempt from general jurisdiction of the state Public Employment Relations Board." Others were similarly framed to evoke a response in specific terms. Instead of answers, however, the committee in its interim report of June 17 delivered more questions. Taylor stated in his cover letter to the governor, "The limited experience to date does not, in our judgment provide an adequate basis for now recommending changes in the Act. The experience has been sufficient, however, to point up the questions and issues to which intensive study and discussion should be directed."[17]

The report offered few surprises. It declared that the law was working well. The considerable attention given to New York City's special problems was mostly a reprise of discussion from the first report. The committee did use the occasion, however, to respond to "observers," Kheel obviously in mind, "who expound the view that agreements between governmental agencies and their employees cannot be 'satisfactorily' consummated unless the threat of an illegal work stoppage is everpresent." In the opinion of the committee, the problems that needed to be dealt with were "gravely obstructed" by those "observers."[18] It dismissed the proposition that the law encouraged unilateral determination by public employers, asserting that the reverse was more likely when strikes by strong unions were countenanced. Indeed, the committee went so far as to suggest that closer scrutiny of the quality of settlements might be warranted, noting that some recent settlements might have been excessive. Although this latter point was not carried forward into the committee's final report of January 1969, its expression here and in internal committee discussion reveals the very high value George Taylor for one placed on retaining ultimate say for the legislative body as the responsible representative of the public. The notes of Richard Winfield, then serving as a counsel to the committee, summarized a meeting between the committee and Robert Helsby in which Taylor was reported as saying:

> He [Taylor] also raised the question about the necessity for show cause hearings in the local legislative body, not only where a fact-finding board has made its recommendations, *but also in settlements agreed upon between the chief executive and the employee organization.* It is necessary Dr. Taylor said, to give a greater presumption of validity to agreements entered into between the chief executive and the employee organization; a show cause hearing before the legislative body should recognize and be bound by the presumption.[19]

That this concept of the legislative role was not pursued suggests that not all members of the committee shared Taylor's view.

One reader of the report, Tom Joyner of PERB, thought he detected a split within the committee. In a memorandum to Helsby, he said, "From the way most of the punches are pulled, it is fairly clear that there was either— some kind of basic disagreement within the Committee itself, or else that the Governor's office did a censorship job because of the current political situation. Both, of course, may be correct."[20] Or neither, it could be added.

What seemed apparent to Joyner is not readily so to other readers. This was an "interim" report and the time was hardly propitious for presenting recommendations for action even supposing the committee felt prepared to do so. The divided legislature was winding up its business and a new one would take over in January. Moreover, the national political conventions were in the immediate offing. Perhaps the main purpose of a report at this time was to signal the public that the administration had not forgotten its unfinished business.

Rockefeller met with the committee after the fall elections to discuss its interim report and asked that it submit recommendations for legislative changes. Thus, on January 23, 1969, the committee transmitted what was to be its final report.[21] It limited its recommendations to four areas—finality in impasses, New York City procedures, strike deterrents, and the establishment of an advisory council. Several other issues examined in the interim report were left unmentioned. Overall, the report was moderate in its recommendations, and many reiterated positions initially staked out in 1966.

The committee maintained that to have an effective substitute for the strike there needed to be finality in the impasse procedure and that any final judgment must necessarily reside with the legislative body. It therefore urged once more that when factfinding recommendations were rejected and the impasse continued, the legislature hold a show cause hearing on the factfinding report and render a final judgment on the matters in dispute. It also proposed that factfinding reports not be made public until five days after their issuance, thereby allowing additional time for negotiation and mediation.

"It is in New York City where the failure of the Taylor Law to protect vital public interests have been so manifest," the report stated. The committee believed that New York City should not be accorded the presumption of substantial equivalency unless it acted to remedy matters of coverage and finality in the impasse procedure.[22] With respect to the former, it suggested that jurisdiction of OCB be extended to all agencies and employee organizations fiscally dependent, entirely or largely, on the city. Concerning finality, the committee observed that current OCB procedures neither required that factfinding recommendations be made public nor action by the city council when recommendations were rejected. It also noted with disapproval the exemption of New York City from the requirement that impasse procedures be related to the budget submission date. It concluded by recommending that both OCB and PERB submit reports indicating what steps would be taken to bring OCB procedures into substantial equivalence with the state law.

To strengthen deterrents to illegal strikes, the committee recommended removing the limit on the amount an employee organization could be fined in a contempt proceeding; full discretion was left to the court. Similarly, it recommended doing away with the eighteen-month limit on the loss of dues deduction privileges. At the same time it opposed as ineffective jailing of union officials for disobeying injunctions. (So-called antimartyrdom bills were introduced but failed to win passage.) Noting that public employers had avoided bringing misconduct charges against individual strikers under the Civil Service Law, the committee recommended that chief executive officers be required to make public written reports on the action they had taken to carry out their responsibilities to enforce disciplinary penalties.

Finally, the committee recommended establishment at the state level of a public employment relations advisory council composed of representatives of labor and management from both the public and private sectors as well as representatives of the public at large. The council would meet periodically with the governor to review developments in the public sector and to advise him: "It should be concerned with such matters as the relationships between the levels of compensation and benefits in the public and private sectors and, perhaps, the exploration of criteria which could be used in the setting of equitable compensation in the public sector."[23] The committee hoped that similar councils would be established locally.

A comparison of the original Taylor committee report and its reports in 1968 and 1969 makes it abundantly clear that the committee saw nothing in the events during the intervening period that justified altering its original analysis. On the essential points of the inapplicability of the strike, on the supremacy of the legislative body, on

impasse procedures, and on strike penalties (aside from
the decertification penalty), it remained steadfast. Its recommendations call into question the compromises made
by the legislature to get the law passed originally, special
treatment for New York City, and limits on strike penalties. The committee instead called for a return to its earlier proposals on several points. In only one area, that
having to do with the recommendation for an advisory
council, did the 1969 report recommend something different. The idea was John Dunlop's, and it closely resem-
bled a plan later adopted in Massachusetts for police and
fire services. One cannot help but believe that it was included because it was a colleague's favorite idea.

In a political climate prepared for more drastic action,
the Taylor committee report made little impact. Even the
New York Times, ordinarily an enthusiastic booster of
the committee, was restrained in its praise and expressed
reservations. In particular, the *Times* seemed puzzled by
the omission of recommendations relating to unfair labor practices and compulsory arbitration. It added that
"the emphasis . . . on penalties against individual strikers
seems to us to invite a return to the problems that made
Condon-Wadlin unworkable."[24]

For different reasons the report disappointed the governor's office. Marshall recalled:

> That was a terrible disappointment to us. I think it was a
> mistake. . . . They did not seem to recognize, or perhaps they
> thought we were overreacting to, what amounted to a public
> outcry and to an increased number of strikes. . . . It was not
> helpful. . . . They still thought we were going through the
> throes of a big institutional adjustment about how you work
> out labor negotiations. They laid many of the problems,
> probably with some merit, to the fact that upstate boards of
> education just didn't know how to negotiate or were not
> willing to negotiate. And no matter what penalty you had or
> what system you had, if that was their attitude, it was going

to end up in a strike. . . . But what I don't think they had any feel for was this growing concern. The legislature had some; they were feeling the brunt of that.[25]

Some within PERB were disappointed as well, most notably because the report did not recommend that PERB be given authority to regulate unfair labor practices. The anger of one staff member shows in an internal memorandum from Joyner to Helsby in which Joyner is scornful of the report and accuses the committee of "malaise," "ignorance," and the like.[26] While obviously exaggerated, the anger nonetheless reflects agency disenchantment with the committee to some degree. Some of it is doubtless personal pique surviving from the unhappy encounter in Princeton seventeen months earlier. Joyner eludes to it in a postscript: "As you can see, my opinion of the Taylor Committee has decreased since Princeton when it was not notably at high ebb. Some of these people may be great mediators but New York State might benefit if they were retired from any more attempts to revise the Taylor Law."

Besides calling omission of unfair labor practices a "glaring deficiency," Joyner attacks the idea of show cause hearings as "ridiculous," "just plain stupid": "This means, of course, as the *New York Times* pointed out yesterday, that in a school situation the school board would be both negotiator and jury." Likewise, Joyner dismissed the proposal that New York City accord a similar role to its city council as an idea that no mayor "will in his right mind consent to."[27] Joyner also warned that if, as the report recommended, both OCB and PERB were required to report simultaneously on August 1 what they were doing to accomplish substantial equivalence, the result would be conflicting reports and a strain on their relationship.

OCB as the major target for criticism was obviously unenthusiastic about the recommended changes. On the subject of relating negotiations to the budget submission date, for example, Arvid Anderson, looking back, said,

"They identified the problem, but they didn't have the right solution." A solution of sorts came later when the Emergency Financial Control Board was created to monitor city finances.[28] But OCB, like PERB, the governor's office, and finally the state legislature, dealt with the committee's well-intended advice largely by ignoring it rather than by dissenting openly.

OCEAN HILL–BROWNSVILLE: 1968 TEACHERS STRIKE

In terms of the number of workdays lost, the 1968 strike by New York City teachers was by far the largest in the history of the Taylor Law. It also contributed to passage of the 1969 amendments.

The strike was not a labor dispute in the traditional sense of employees versus employer. It was instead a divisive community dispute in which the schools were the battleground in a struggle involving local community control of the schools, racial identity, and due process for teachers. The story is far too complex to recite here. Briefly and far too simply, the controversy grew out of an effort by residents of the community to achieve greater involvement in the schools through decentralization of the city system. A newly established administration in the experimental Ocean Hill–Brownsville School District abruptly dismissed thirteen white teachers in the spring of 1968, setting off a strike. The strike was confined to the Ocean Hill District for the remaining twenty-three days of the school year, but it afflicted the entire school system in the fall, when both the United Federation of Teachers and the Council of Supervisory Organizations, representing principals and assistant principals, struck for thirty-five days. Although the board of education and its employees were clearly within the jurisdiction of PERB, the agency was helpless to do anything to end a dispute that had little or nothing to do with customary terms and conditions of employment. The task of dispute settlement was left to the state commissioner of education.

Labor dispute or not, the school strike prompted further questions about why the board of education, which to a large degree was fiscally dependent on the city, should be outside OCB's ambit. A partial, though incomplete, explanation lies in the strong opposition of the UFT to inclusion, which in turn is traceable to the intense organizational and personal rivalry between the teachers and AFSCME District Council 37, between Shanker and Gotbaum. From the UFT's perspective, OCB and the Municipal Labor Committee were too closely identified with Gotbaum. The UFT's resistance to coverage was reflected in the 1972 revision of the city law, which explicitly excluded pedagogical employees of the board of education, both professional and "paraprofessional employees with teaching functions," the only employees represented by the UFT.[29]

The right to represent the paraprofessionals had resulted in a bitter head-to-head confrontation between the two unions in 1969, further poisoning the Shanker-Gotbaum relationship. District Council 37, already representing other school aides, was well into a campaign to organize the six thousand overwhelmingly black and Hispanic paraprofessionals when the UFT entered the fray. Shanker had to overcome considerable internal resistance from members, what he called "snobbism," to persuade the union that it was in the teachers' own self-interest to bring the paraprofessionals into the UFT fold. Acceptance was even more difficult because the paraprofessionals had worked during the 1968 strike. Shanker recalled that during this period racial feelings ran so deep that he was for a time regarded as the "biggest racist in the country."[30]

Racist or not, the UFT emphasized its ability to get results, its record for delivering benefits for teachers. In a vote supervised by the American Arbitration Association under board of education procedures, the UFT won by the slimmest of margins, something like thirty-five to forty votes. According to Shanker, the victory margin was, paradoxically, attributed to employees from Ocean Hill–Brownsville, whose ballots were the last to be counted and who thoroughly despised district superintendent Rhody McCoy, focus of the earlier strike. Gotbaum laid the defeat to Lillian Roberts being distracted from the campaign by the concurrent state representation election.[31]

The Law Is Amended

It was probably inevitable that the Taylor Law would be changed in 1969 in a direction not to the liking of the unions. Memories of near-catastrophic events like the sanitation strike and the bitter conflict in Ocean Hill–Brownsville were too vivid. Nor were the problems confined to New York City, as evidenced by the strike in the state mental hospitals and a few other stoppages in school districts and municipalities. The number of strikes was not large overall, yet there was enough conflict to suggest widespread unrest. The report of the Select Joint Legislative Committee on Public Employee Relations observed:

The paradox of the Taylor Law is that while it has granted public employees unprecedented rights and has served as a vehicle for substantial economic gains, it seems also to have fostered an extraordinary amount of employee militancy and disaffection. It is arguable that the advantages brought about by the Taylor Law are to a significant degree the actual source of employee discontent. Many public employee leaders are saying that while the door to meaningful negotiations is no longer completely closed, neither has it been completely

opened. The law has provided the means for improving
several aspects of working conditions, but appears to have
had the effect of only raising expectations for even greater
improvement.[32]

The select committee attributed many of these difficulties to the inexperience of the parties and therefore could
conclude its analysis on a more upbeat note, opining
that "time and experience will, no doubt, render [labor-
management difficulties] less abrasive."[33]

The political leadership of the state was unwilling to
wait while the participants acquired experience; it wanted
immediate action. For the governor, strengthening the
"imperfect" Taylor Law ranked high on the legislative
agenda. In his annual legislative message he gave considerable attention to the subject: "I shall make specific legislative proposals in a Special Message when I receive the
recommendations of the Taylor Committee, which I reconvened last year to review problems in this area."[34] The
leaders in both legislative chambers, each now with Republican majorities, shared Rockefeller's resolve to press
for stronger strike sanctions. Thus, when the Taylor committee delivered its report to the governor, he and the
hard-liners were dismayed with the relatively mild recommendations regarding strike penalties.

Disappointment became manifest at the end of January
when Senate Majority Leader Brydges and Speaker Duryea appointed the Select Joint Legislative Committee on
Public Employee Relations, chaired by Senator Thomas
Laverne of Rochester, to undertake its own study of the
law. Although the Laverne committee eventually issued a
valuable report, events were moving too swiftly, and the
report was largely irrelevant to the immediate debate.

On February 17 CSEA declared that it would engage
in a "job action" if the state continued to refuse to negotiate with it in line with PERB's neutrality order. March
13 was set as the deadline. Spurred by the threat, on Feb-

ruary 27 the governor and the legislative leaders announced that they were in agreement on a package of amendments. Their bill was introduced on March 3, passed on March 7, and signed into law by the governor a day or two later. In little more than a week the amendments had moved from the talking stage to final enactment, in "ungodly haste" as one Democrat dubbed it.[35]

With the Republicans commanding a small seventy-eight to seventy-two majority in the Assembly, unionists headed by Victor Gotbaum attempted at the last minute to head off the administration bill with a substitute measure that provided for compulsory arbitration as the final step in impasse. It failed in part because Harry Van Arsdale opposed the idea of compulsory arbitration. As it was, the final vote in the Assembly on the administration bill had to be postponed for six hours to give Speaker Duryea time to bring into line five or six Republicans who had previously declared their intention to vote against the package. The final tally was a slim margin of seventy-six to seventy-one to amend the law.[36]

The 1969 amendments, the most sweeping single revision of the law, contained several important elements, none more controversial than its strike penalty provisions. Here the changes were substantial. Besides removing statutory ceilings on union fines and on the loss of checkoff rights, changes specifically endorsed by the Taylor committee, new penalties were introduced, directed at individual strikers, as distinct from their unions. Henceforth when a strike occurred, the chief fiscal officer of the employer was obliged to deduct from the pay of a striker an amount equal to twice the employee's daily wage for each day on strike.[37] To ease enforcement of the penalty, there was to be a presumption that individuals absent from employment on the day of a strike were themselves engaging in the strike. The burden of overcoming the presumption rested with the employee.

The two-for-one penalty revived a feature of Condon-Wadlin that had been in effect between 1963 and 1965. (Defenders of the penalty are quick to assert that it is a misnomer to call it "two-for-one." They believe a more accurate label is "one-for-one"; since no one should expect to be paid for a day not worked, the penalty assessed is only one day's pay for striking.) The emphasis on individual penalties was an expression of the belief that in many instances, the sanitation strike a prime example, union leaders had lost control over militant membership. This outlook contrasted with the popular view that strikes were often the doing of irresponsible, power-hungry union bosses. The change, according to the *New York Times,* had the private support of some union leaders.[38]

Other arguments were advanced in support of the new penalty. The Taylor committee itself had acknowledged somewhat ruefully the ample evidence that public employers had shown a disinclination to discipline strikers for misconduct through civil service procedures. This being the case, it was necessary to eliminate employer discretion by making the penalties largely automatic. One could also have argued that the earlier two-year experience with the penalty was insufficient to demonstrate that it would not work as a deterrent. Finally, the penalty could be seen as an unmistakable reminder of the government's resolve to prohibit strikes by public workers.

Because it echoed Condon-Wadlin so much and because memories of its futility were still fresh, the new measure was criticized even in quarters where a different reaction might have been expected. Both the New York State School Boards Association and the Conference of Mayors saw it as harsh and unworkable.[39] The *Times* labeled it "Draconian," and on another occasion said, "The forces of repression seem to be in full command."[40] Whether "Dr. Taylor and his colleagues were privately 'amenable' to the new penalties," as the *Times* quoted "sources" as saying, is dubious.[41]

Given the course of events following the issuance of the committee's report, it seems unlikely that any of the political leaders would have had much concern for the opinion of the committee. But even if Taylor had been consulted, his more probable response would have been that the matter was for the legislature to decide. This reaction would have at least been consistent with views he had expressed earlier.[42] Moreover, Dunlop stated that he was personally opposed to the two-for-one penalty, and in this opinion he was probably close to his colleagues.[43] Finally, Alton Marshall recalled a letter from George Taylor in which he "took umbrage" at the administration "coming in with something stronger" after having received the committee's recommendations. As Marshall remembered it, Taylor seemed to be asking, Why did you use us as window dressing?[44]

Helsby and PERB were not sympathetic to the new strike penalty, which is understandable considering that it would have been expected to make settlement of negotiation impasses more difficult. Though some parts of the bill incorporated language drafted by PERB, notably the section on improper practices, the agency had no opportunity to comment on many of the changes, not that its opinion would have been very influential.[45]

IMPROPER PRACTICES

From PERB's perspective, the good news in the 1969 amendments was the addition of section 209-a on improper practices, to take effect September 1. Coupled with changes in section 205.5 that granted the board exclusive and nondelegable authority to prevent improper practices, the amendment clarified and made explicit PERB's power to regulate certain unfair labor practices not unlike the authority possessed by the National Labor Relations Board in the private sector. (In a separate bill OCB was permitted to continue processing improper practice cases until March 1970.)

In adopting the term *improper practice* rather than *unfair labor practice,* the lawmakers were underscoring their view of the difference between the two sectors. The point was further emphasized by the inclusion of an additional sentence in section 209-a: "In applying this section, fundamental distinctions between private and public employment shall be recognized, and no body of federal or state law applicable wholly or in part to private employment, shall be regarded as binding or controlling precedent."

The new section prohibited public employers from (a) interfering with, restraining, or coercing employees in the exercise of their rights under the Taylor Law; (b) dominating or interfering with the formation or administration of public employee organizations; (c) discriminating for the purpose of encouraging or discouraging membership or participation in an employee organization; and (d) refusing to negotiate in good faith. Likewise, the section made it improper for an employee organization to interfere, restrain, or coerce or to refuse to negotiate in good faith.

While PERB had rules that dealt with some of these practices, chiefly in the area of employer reprisals, its intervention had been predicated on implied rights rather than express statutory language. Until September 1, 1969, PERB had received seventy-one claims alleging employer reprisal. In fourteen cases hearings had been held or scheduled, and hearing officers had issued reports in eight of those cases.[46]

One month after enactment of section 209-a, PERB discovered how vulnerable its position on reprisals had been. In the *Gagnier* case a trial court overturned a PERB decision ordering a school district to reinstate a teacher who had been denied reappointment and tenure because of her activities as president of the teacher association. The court held that PERB lacked the authority to hear and determine the complaint.[47]

Of far greater long-term importance to PERB in the realm of improper practices was the authority to enforce the obligation on employers and employee organizations alike to negotiate in good faith. This authority opened the way for active board involvement in defining the duty and scope of collective negotiations.

The 1969 amendments made other important changes. The impasse procedures were modified to incorporate several Taylor committee recommendations. The final step in an impasse was to be a hearing by the legislative body on the factfinding report, after which the legislative body would "take such action as it deems to be in the public interest, including the interest of the public employees involved." The time schedule governing the impasse machinery was also altered, so as to include a five-day delay in the public release of the factfinding report after its receipt by the parties. Fact finders were also expressly authorized to provide assistance to the parties after transmittal of their report. Furthermore, the law now authorized parties to agree on contractual impasse procedures culminating with arbitration, and PERB was empowered to establish a panel of arbitrators.

Another change was the adoption of section 204-a, intended to make clear the ultimate authority of the legislative body when implementation of a negotiated agreement depended on action of the legislature to amend the law or to fund the settlement. Henceforth all agreements were to contain a prescribed statement to that effect "in type not smaller than the largest type used elsewhere in the agreement." Largely symbolic, this section made express what had previously been implied.

NEW YORK CITY PROCEDURES

Addressing the sensitive issue of New York City's compliance with the state law, the central focus of the reconvened Taylor committee, the legislature required that the mayor of New York City submit the following by August 1, 1969:

> a report of the steps taken and a plan designed to bring such practices of the City of New York [under the New York City Collective Bargaining Law] into substantial equivalence with such state [Taylor] law. This report and plan shall, among other things, particularly deal with making effective the jurisdiction of the Office of Collective Bargaining, the need for a specified final step in the impasse procedures, and the relation of negotiations and impasse procedures to budget submission dates.[48]

PERB was to submit its comments and recommendations regarding the mayor's report by December 1.

In his report Mayor Lindsay urged the state legislature to broaden OCB's authority to encompass "all public and quasi-public agencies which provide municipal services." He indicated the city's intent to grant OCB final and binding authority in impasses, thus providing for finality, and argued on grounds of practicality for continued exemption of the city from the requirement regarding the budget submission date. In addition, the mayor asked for restoration of authority in cases of improper practice, for authorization to negotiate on the agency shop, and for changes in the Taylor Law with respect to criteria for excluding managerial and confidential employees.[49]

On several points the views of PERB converged with those expressed by the mayor. PERB voiced reservations, though not disagreement, with the idea of compulsory arbitration and agency shop. On the latter its position was that the right to negotiate on agency shop should be extended statewide. PERB was sympathetic to the mayor's proposal on jurisdiction, but it raised enough difficult

technical and policy questions as to suggest that the legislature ought to tread warily. The most significant point in
PERB's response was its proposal that the statutory presumption of substantial equivalence be repealed. Adopting
the position taken by the Laverne committee, it proposed
that the continued special status enjoyed by the Office of
Collective Bargaining be conditioned on PERB's determination, rather than a court's, that OCB procedures were
substantially equivalent.[50]

The PERB report closed with reference to a subject the
mayor did not mention, forfeiture of dues checkoff. This
matter was to persist as a point of contention between
OCB and PERB. PERB had responsibility for administration of the penalty under section 210.3 except with respect to local governments operating under section 212 of
the law. This distinction presented no special problems
other than in New York City since PERB required all
mini-PERBs to adopt procedures similar to its own as a
condition of approval, although the local boards were far
less assiduous in applying the penalty. With the New York
City law silent on the matter, it was up to the courts
to determine whether the checkoff should be suspended
as part of a criminal contempt proceeding under section
751.2(a) of the Judiciary Law. Since not all strikes resulted in contempt proceedings and not all judges chose
to assess the penalty in cases before them, the enforcement
record was spotty.

There were three possible ways of achieving uniform
application of the law, a principle Helsby felt strongly
about. One was to turn over the responsibility to PERB;
a second was to make OCB adopt PERB procedures; and
a third was to free PERB of any responsibility for applying the penalty. Helsby's preference was for the first of
these options, and PERB recommended that approach in
its response to Mayor Lindsay's report. It was a position
unacceptable to Arvid Anderson and OCB, however, and
when it appeared in a 1970 bill joined with a measure

that Anderson desired—permanent authority for OCB in cases of improper practices—he successfully lobbied for defeat of the bill. Since Harold Newman became chairman, PERB's preference has clearly shifted in favor of the third option.

Throughout these early years relations between PERB and OCB were a delicate matter. The standard of substantial equivalence was an imprecise guide, and the line demarcating their respective spheres of authority was never clear. PERB itself was unsure about what it wanted. Before the December 1969 report, Helsby proposed to the Taylor committee as an alternative to direct PERB jurisdiction that OCB be removed entirely from PERB's oversight. Seemingly, either approach would have been acceptable.[51]

The Taylor committee chose neither alternative, presumably in the hope that persistent prodding and hectoring of the city would accomplish substantial equivalence over time. More than anything, the personal friendship of Anderson and Helsby preserved the peace and maintained a usually cooperative relationship between OCB and PERB. That each of the agencies had essentially different constituencies was potentially divisive. The tripartite character of OCB made it of necessity far more attentive to the views of the unions, whereas pressure from that quarter was more remote at PERB. Nonetheless, from first acquaintance Anderson and Helsby hit it off well and developed genuine respect and trust for each other, thereby facilitating the discussion of mutual problems and curbing any excessive zeal for precedence and turf. The cordiality of the relationship has continued with Newman.

A STRENGTHENED AGENCY

Extensive though the 1969 amendments were in so many respects, the basic principles and structure of the original act were preserved. The amendments could also be read as a ringing endorsement of PERB and as an expression of confidence in the agency. Having survived difficult strikes, some legal setbacks, and almost constant attack from the largest employee organization in the state, PERB emerged with its duties and authority significantly enlarged. The political support of the governor did not waiver even as PERB challenged some of his actions. With Helsby's term on the board soon to expire, Rockefeller invited him to accept reappointment. Helsby conditioned his acceptance on a change in the law to create a statutory term for the chairman coincident with his term as a member of the board, thereby increasing the agency's independence form the executive.[52] The law was amended accordingly.

Two other proposals, both endorsed by the Laverne committee, had to await later enactment. The first was a proposal to permit PERB to retain its own counsel to represent it before the courts rather than having to rely on the state attorney general, who sometimes had clients in conflict with one another. This proposal was adopted in 1970. The other, passed in 1971, afforded mediators protection from being forced to disclose confidential information acquired in their official duties.

During this troublesome early period PERB earned a reputation in the community at large for competence and independence. Even CSEA relented in its hostile criticism once the state representation elections were held. The reasons for this favorable reception were a combination of hard work, solid performance, and attentiveness to the value of public relations. Foremost, PERB operated as a very unbureaucratic part of the state bureaucracy, a refreshing note on the Albany landscape. It responded generously, enthusiastically, and quickly to the flood of inquiries that came from employee groups and governments unfamiliar with labor relations processes. It was prompt in assigning mediators and fact finders where they were needed. Board members and staff blanketed the state, meeting with a variety of groups, conducting conferences, and generally fulfilling PERB's statutory charge to serve as an informational clearinghouse. Helsby himself was peripatetic in spreading the gospel and always ebullient, upbeat, and unflappable even before hostile audiences. The research unit gathered and disseminated data on wages, fringe benefits, and other employment practices useful to negotiators and third parties. The office of public information and education coordinated much of this activity in addition to producing a monthly newsletter and several informational booklets. Press releases were issued regularly with reports on decisions of the board, announcements of appointments of mediators and fact finders, and summaries of factfinding recommendations. PERB was aware that one of its critical audiences was the reporters covering public sector labor stories, often innocents in the field, so it conducted conferences to help inexperienced reporters understand differences between mediation, factfinding, and arbitration and to appreciate why negotiations often are best conducted away from the light of publicity.

Helsby and PERB paid special attention to maintaining cordial relations with A. H. Raskin of the *New York Times,* an effort made easier by the almost total congruence in viewpoint on public sector bargaining. Abe Raskin, long the nation's premier labor journalist and now a member of the *Times* editorial board, wrote the editorials on labor relations matters. In addition, his periodic analyses of labor topics under his own byline were attended to by practitioners and politicians. Consistently the Taylor Law and PERB got strong support from the *Times,* while its critics and detractors, Kheel and some of the union leaders, for example, were often targets of condemnation on the editorial page. The *Times* was a formidable ally for

PERB and useful as well in its running skirmishes with Al Marshall.[53]

An outstanding example of PERB's public relations effort was the Governor's Conference on Public Employment Relations held in New York City in October 1968. Ever the true believer, Helsby was eager to draw attention to the first anniversary of the Taylor Law and convinced Rockefeller to write his fellow governors and invite them to send representatives to the conference. Some thirty-eight states and Canada were represented among the seven hundred–plus attendees who heard from luminaries such as Arthur Goldberg, George Taylor, Jerry Wurf, Al Shanker, John Dunlop, David Cole, Ted Kheel, and Nelson Rockefeller. The correspondent for the *Government Employee Relations Report* opened an account of the event with these words:

> In a confrontation of broad significance for government employee relations throughout the country, the progenitors and administrators of New York State's Taylor Act and their growing band of critics held an extended "talk-in" here this week. As a backdrop for their discussions, New York City provided a teachers' strike, and one of the climatic stages of a triple-decked contract dispute involving sanitationmen, policemen, and firemen.[54]

The conference won enthusiastic approval from the participants and clearly achieved the objective of Helsby and his colleagues in placing PERB and the law in the national spotlight.

NOTES

1. *New York State Governor's Committee on Public Employee Relations, Interim Report* (hereafter *Interim Report*), 17 June 1968.
2. *New York Times*, 3 February 1968, 1.

3. Interview with Richard N. Winfield, 29 April 1985.
4. *New York Times,* 7 February 1968, 35.
5. *New York Times,* 9 February 1968, 22.
6. *New York Times,* 11 February 1968, 1.
7. Ibid.
8. *New York Times,* 1 March 1968, 1.
9. *New York Times,* 23 February 1968, 1.
10. *New York Times,* 18 February 1968, IV:11.
11. PERB press release, 18 February 1968, Cole Papers.
12. Kheel, *Report to Speaker Anthony J. Travia,* 21.
13. Ibid., 13.
14. Cole Papers. Robert E. Doherty called attention to this interesting sidelight in his essay "A Short and Not Entirely Unbiased History of the Taylor Law." Doherty himself suggests an intriguing analogy in an earlier unpublished version of the essay. "It is as though Ben Franklin were responding to the criticism of a draft of the U.S. Constitution by someone who had not been invited to the Constitutional Convention who believed strongly that he should have been."
15. *Government Employee Relations Report,* no. 251, 1 July 1968. George Taylor wrote confidentially to Governor Shafer arguing against the position taken by his advisory commission. A month later he followed up with a more detailed section-by-section critique of the commission's report. Shafer did not endorse his commission's recommendation. Letters from Taylor to Governor Shafer, 3 July 1968 and 2 August 1968, Cole Papers.
16. Memorandum, 14 August 1968, Cole Papers. The questions had been part of a draft press release that was never issued in which reestablishment of the committee was announced.
17. *Interim Report.*
18. Ibid., 10–11.
19. Memorandum, Richard N. Winfield to governor's committee, 25 March 1968, Cole Papers; emphasis added.
20. Memorandum to Helsby, 12 July 1968, PERB Files.
21. *New York State Governor's Committee on Public Employee Relations, Report,* 23 January 1969.
22. On this point, Cole in a marginal note during the drafting stage asks, "Won't this be regarded as a challenge by the Van Arsdale–Paul Hall–Gotbaum axis, and won't they therefore try to sabotage the State law?" Cole Papers.
23. *Report,* 23 January 1969, 8.
24. *New York Times,* 4 February 1969.
25. Interview with Alton G. Marshall, 30 April 1985.

26. Memorandum, Joyner to Helsby, 5 February 1969, PERB Files.

27. According to Arvid Anderson, the city council had a similar reaction. When OCB did draft a proposal that would have given the council final say, its response was, in Anderson's words, "a recommendation for psychiatric care." Interview with Anderson, 23 July 1985. Mayor Lindsay had tried to convince Taylor and Cole that the idea was unsound when he met with them in May 1968, arguing that by their nature legislators are "political cowards" and will inevitably "fold" in the face of union pressure. Memorandum to governor's committee from Richard Winfield, 23 May 1968, Cole Papers.

28. Interview with Anderson.

29. New York City Collective Bargaining Law, Sec. 1173-4.0, as amended 1972.

30. Interviews with Albert Shanker, 11 August 1986, and with Victor Gotbaum, 26 September 1985.

31. Ibid.

32. *New York State Select Committee Report,* 1969, 13.

33. Ibid.

34. New York State, *1969 Legislative Annual,* 500.

35. *Select Committee Report,* 1969, 12; *New York Times,* 3 March 1969, 1; 8 March 1969, 1.

36. *New York Times,* 7 March 1969, 22; 8 March 1969, 1.

37. *New York Times,* 2 March 1969. At one stage of negotiations with the legislative leaders, the governor reportedly favored one and one-half days' penalty for each day of strike.

38. *New York Times,* 3 March 1969, 1.

39. *Select Committee Report,* 12.

40. *New York Times,* 4 March 1969, 42.

41. *New York Times,* 3 March 1969, 1.

42. See chapter 2.

43. Interview with John T. Dunlop, 29 July 1985.

44. Interview with Marshall.

45. Interviews with Robert D. Helsby, 21 June 1985, and with Jerome Lefkowitz, 9 July 1985.

46. Data from records in PERB counsel's office.

47. *Helsby et al. v. Ockawamick Central School District,* 2 PERB 7003; 1 PERB 399.90.

48. Chap. 24, L. 1969.

49. John V. Lindsay, "Report Submitted Pursuant to Chapter 24, Laws of 1969," 1 August 1969, Cole Papers.

50. Public Employment Relations Board, "Comments and Recommendations of PERB," 1 December 1969, Cole Papers.

51. Memorandum, Richard Winfield to governor's committee, 25 March 1968, Cole Papers.

52. Interview with Helsby.

53. Interview with Ralph Vatalaro, 18 November 1986.

54. *Government Employee Relations Report,* no. 267, 21 October 1968, AA-1.

5
COLLECTIVE
NEGOTIATIONS
TAKE HOLD

THE ORGANIZING OF PUBLIC employees to take advantage of the new rights granted by the Taylor Law proceeded quickly so that by the end of 1970 most of it was completed and most negotiating relationships were in place. PERB then estimated that some 900,000 of approximately 1 million public workers in the state were represented in 2,500 negotiating units. Although thirty-eight strikes were recorded in 1970, up from fifteen the year before, it was difficult to dispute PERB's assessment that there had been "steady progress toward a more orderly system of labor relations."[1]

The pace at which collective negotiations spread through New York public employment surprised many knowledgeable observers whose point of reference was the experience of the private sector. The question of why organization for bargaining caught on so quickly is discussed briefly in this chapter, and two exceptions to the general rule are presented. The professoriate of the state university system exhibited far more skepticism toward collective bargaining than other employees. Another exception is the singular example of the city of Albany and its stubborn resistance to unionization. Far from typical, the Albany story illuminates the effects of conflict between public sector bargaining and old-fashioned politics.

The chapter closes with the assertion that 1971 marked a turning point in the history of the Taylor Law. It is argued that the political strength of public employees had reached the stage whereby they were able effectively to veto unacceptable changes in the law.

REASONS FOR THE FAST GROWTH OF BARGAINING

Nothing in the history of private sector labor relations could have predicted the rapid changes that came with the enactment of the Taylor Law. Two factors explain much of the difference in the experiences of the two sectors: employee readiness and the absence of employer resistance. The presence of these two factors also account for why a majority of negotiating relationships came about as a result of voluntary recognition by the employer.

Organizing for bargaining was greatly facilitated by the prior existence at the workplace of a variety of employee organizations—professional, occupational, economic, and social. Practically every school district had teacher associations; most police and paid firefighters belonged to some association; and CSEA, besides its large membership among state workers, was established in most counties and in many other local governments. That members in these organizations may have been attracted for reasons of cheap insurance, social activities, legislative representation, or other objectives seemed to make little difference; organizational adaptation to the bargaining function came relatively easily. Public employees more so than most people were appreciative of the value of politics and collective action in dealing with public officials, and many had experience through their organizations in making presentations to legislative bodies and other officials.

The second fundamental difference in the public sector experience was the absence of any significant opposition to unionization by employers. There was the extreme exception of the city of Albany, to be sure, and there were other scattered instances of employer discrimination or reprisal against employees aimed at discouraging unionization, but these were infrequent events, in sharp contrast to the high incidence of section 8(a)(3) violations under the NLRA.[2] Elected officials had little or no incentive to resist collective negotiations; indeed, some, such as those in New York City and the state of New York, preferred bargaining with all employees once it became clear that there would be bargaining with some employees at least. It did not make sense to officials to risk alienating employees who were an important part of the political constituency. Public employers therefore tended to respond affirmatively and promptly when presented with requests for recognition.

REPRESENTATION OF STATE UNIVERSITY PROFESSIONAL EMPLOYEES

The establishment of a negotiating relationship between the state and the professional employees of the state university, the third unit proposed by the governor in his initial determination of November 1967, was slow to evolve. Beyond disagreement about the appropriate unit configuration or which of several competing organizations possessed majority support, the delay can be traced to the ambivalent attitude of many professionals toward the idea of collective negotiations. Unlike just about every other public employee including public school teachers, the SUNY teaching faculty in particular evinced little enthusiasm for organizing. The concept of collective bargaining seemed at odds with, if not offensive to, their views of a self-governing community of scholars. If it were not for the fact that all other state employee groups were taking advantage of the law, thereby exposing SUNY faculty to the risk that they might be less well treated by the state, the decision to organize might have been even longer in coming. As it was, internal pressure from nonteaching professionals, who as a group had fewer misgivings about collective action, forced the issue.

Not until May 1968 did the State University Federation of Teachers (SUFT) petition for five separate campus units. Soon other organizations entered the fray—the Faculty Association of the State University (it subsequently withdrew), CSEA, the American Association of University Professors, and the Faculty Senate of the State University. The presence of the last organization posed special problems because it was structured in the tradition of an academic senate with representatives of SUNY administration as participating members and financially it was wholly dependent on SUNY. The SUFT challenged that the senate was not an employee organization and was employer dominated. In a decision of August 12, 1969, however, the director of representation found the senate satisfied the act's definition of an employee organization. Given assurances that appropriate changes in structure and financing of the senate would be made, he declined to rule on the question of employer domination, noting that it could be raised later as a separate issue under the improper practice section of the law, due to take effect three weeks hence. On the matter of the structure of the unit, the director accepted the contention of the state, supported by the senate and CSEA, that the unit should be statewide and include all professional personnel exclusive of deans and above.[3]

Without an individual membership base or funds of its

own, the senate struck a deal with CSEA in the course of the proceedings by which they would seek joint representation. When that agreement quickly came undone, the senate forged a new alliance with the New York State Teachers Association (NEA). By the time of the balloting in December 1970, the senate had transformed itself into the Senate Professional Association (SPA), later to become United University Professions. The long interval between the director's decision and certification of the negotiating representative was occupied by appeals to the board and the courts, but, as Jerome Lefkowitz has pointed out, the organizations involved were in no rush since they sought time to win adherents.

> Ultimately it was the employer and PERB which pressed for resolution of the court proceeding. The employer wanted an election in sufficient time to permit negotiations before the expiration of the forthcoming Legislative Session, and PERB sought to avoid embarrassment over the long time between the filing of petitions and the closing of the case.[4]

No organization received a majority of votes in the first balloting. The results were SUFT, 3,287; SPA, 2,974; AAUP, 1,912; CSEA, 705; and no organization, 546. SPA won the run-off election held in January 1971 over the affiliate of the American Federation of Teachers, SUFT. The vote was 5,491 to 4,795.[5]

There is irony in all of this. After the vigorous and costly contest between supporters of SPA and SUFT, much of it couched in ideological or philosophical terms regarding the appropriateness or lack thereof of the trade union model transplanted to an academic setting, the state affiliates of AFT and NEA soon joined together to form the New York State United Teachers. When the NEA tie was dissolved two years later, the connection with AFT survived; thus the losing side in 1970 ultimately prevailed.

ALBANY—A SPECIAL CASE

No other public employer in the state matched the city of Albany for sheer obdurance in its resistance to the Taylor Law and to the proposition that public employees had a right to organize and negotiate collectively with their public employers. In contrast to the acquiescence typical of most public employers, Albany behaved like the most intransigent private employer fighting unionization. The reason had nothing to do with basic ideology and everything to do with preserving the political power of the Democratic party machine, which had controlled public affairs in the city since the early 1920s.

The O'Connell machine, after county chairman Daniel P. O'Connell, dominated city and county politics. Although the old man was still "the boss" until his death in 1977, public leadership of the machine was exercised by Mayor Erastus Corning II. The party organization exerted effective control over all aspects of the city's political and public life, dispensing or withholding favors in the form of jobs, contracts, tax assessments, and various public services. In exchange the party expected and received loyal support for its candidates from employees and citizens. The employment policy of the machine favored a large workforce at meager wages as a way of widening its base of support. The advent of the Taylor Law was understandably a serious threat to the monolith, for unionization would almost surely lead to the creation of new allegiances and to rival power centers no longer under the domination of the politicians. The entire structure of control developed over decades was imperiled.[6]

The city first moved to establish local government procedures sanctioned by section 212, but PERB disapproved of its plan as not substantially equivalent.[7] The city's orientation to labor relations was illustrated by two provisions in the plan that PERB found objectionable. First, the municipal civil service commission, an agency totally controlled by the mayor, was to be designated as the administrative body. Second, the plan included the unusual proviso that the state law would apply "insofar as consistent," a determination the city reserved for itself.

It was not until 1970, well after most public workers in jurisdictions of any size were covered by negotiated agreements, that the first public evidence of organizational activity by city employees surfaced. It was the firefighters who led the way, through the Albany Professional Permanent Firefighters Association (APPFA), which gained PERB certification in May 1970. By then the city had already made plain its intention to fight: a couple of months earlier following APPFA's request for recognition, fire chief Augustus Brophy transferred the president and a vice-president of the union to outlying firehouses and had another vice-president demoted. Although the men were eventually reinstated to their former positions after PERB held that the city had engaged in discriminatory and coercive conduct, the matter was carried all the way to the Court of Appeals.[8]

The troubles of the firefighters were to continue. A few months after filing their first improper practice charge, they lodged yet another. A recitation of the events established through testimony at the hearing reveals much about the methods the city employed to impede and frustrate APPFA.

- Negotiations between APPFA and the city commenced in mid-May 1970. The union submitted its demands and a roster of its membership, 148 out of some 200 firefighters.
- The parties agreed that as of July 1 any firefighter assigned as an acting officer who continued in the position for thirty days would be appointed as a provisional officer and compensated accordingly.

- On May 23 the municipal civil service commission conducted a written promotional exam for the position of fire lieutenant, the first such exam in at least six years.
- A total of 128 firefighters took the exam. Soon afterward APPFA filed a complaint with the state civil service commission alleging that the exam was "rigged." It called the exam "phony."
- On June 11 Mayor Corning reacted by breaking off negotiations. He said he would not resume them until he could complete an investigation into the charges that members of the city administration were crooked.
- On July 1 the mayor ordered that the use of the title "acting lieutenant" be discontinued as of the end of the month.
- On July 10 negotiations resumed with the mayor stating that his investigation of the alleged test rigging had convinced him that there was nothing wrong with the exam.
- On July 14 seven provisional firefighters were notified that they would be dismissed because they had failed the entry exam, which they had taken over a year earlier, in May 1969.
- Six of these men were APPFA members; one was not. The latter was subsequently rehired in August as a provisional employee as were two other new lieutenants.
- APPFA was unsuccessful in finding out who ordered the dismissal of the provisional firefighters. One union official testified that the mayor had said, when charged with having instructed the commissioner of public safety to discharge the men, "I didn't tell him to fire them. I told him to terminate them." Corning denied the allegation.
- On July 16 Mayor Corning announced that he would recommend a one thousand dollar increase for mem-

bers of the police department, a break with the wage parity that had existed between the police and fire departments for twenty-four years.

- The following day Corning told the APPFA negotiating committee, "There's no funds for the firemen. Take it to the fact finders."
- On July 31 the position of acting officer was abolished. Because no one passed the promotional exam, the chief announced the appointment of thirty-one firefighters to the rank of provisional lieutenant; only four were APPFA members. Thirteen union members who had held acting appointments were demoted.[9]
- Beginning September 1 the job of driving police department tow trucks, previously performed by off-duty firefighters at the rate of $3.67 per hour, was assigned to members of the police department at the hourly rate of $6.18.

Despite these "suspicious circumstances" the hearing officer concluded that the union had failed to support its charges of improper practice by a preponderance of the probative evidence, and he therefore recommended dismissal of the complaint. The board agreed.[10]

APPFA also had problems at the bargaining table. The 1970 negotiations ended in a legislative determination, no salary increase, and no contract. In negotiations the next year, the union filed charges that the city had failed to negotiate in good faith when it refused to make a salary proposal until just before the start of the fiscal year. PERB sustained the charge.[11] Altogether it took the firefighters two years to obtain a first contract with the city, hardly an inducement for other city workers to organize.

Indeed, four more years passed before police officers and public works employees formed unions and won certification. They encountered the same hostility as the firefighters had. Two days after the representation election in the police department, the city unilaterally promulgated a new policy on tardiness and began to discipline officers. PERB deemed both actions to be improper practices motivated by anti-union animus.[12] Likewise, PERB and the courts found animus to be the key element in the discharge of George Strokes, president of the local union representing public works employees.[13] The recommendation of PERB hearing officer Harvey Milowe that Strokes be reinstated provoked Mayor Corning to say, "I don't take orders from billy goats." Milowe at the time sported a goatee.[14]

Along the way a more roundabout method was tried in an effort to reduce conflict between PERB and the city. Board member Joseph Crowley was acquainted with the bishop of Albany, who was the son of an old school chum of his. Crowley approached the bishop to ask if he would intercede with the mayor to obtain city compliance with the law. When the matter was raised the mayor responded, "You know, Bishop, I have been thinking that we just may have to levy taxes on a lot of church property."[15]

Throughout these years the city engaged in a kind of guerrilla warfare as it sought to resist unionization. The strategy called for delay, for exhausting all rights of appeal, and for litigating everything. In the cases heard by PERB and the courts, the city often made little effort to produce witnesses or documentation to support its position. Instead it fell back on broad assertions of residual government authority or engaged in sheer sophistry, as when it defended its contention that proposals for paid leaves were not negotiable by arguing that paid leaves "are not terms and conditions of employment, but, in fact, terms and conditions of unemployment. They are not concerned with wages, as wages are compensation for hours worked."[16]

The addition to the Taylor Law of compulsory arbitration for police and firefighters in 1974 provoked a new round of resistance by the city. In a long series of legal maneuvers, it interposed a variety of challenges to forestall arbitration proceedings or, when that failed, to have the awards set aside. Among the issues the city raised were the following:

- Prior PERB determinations concerning the scope of negotiations were no longer applicable inasmuch as compulsory arbitration had replaced legislative determination as the final step of the impasse procedure.[17]
- Awards of arbitrators were subject to judicial review under the broader standards of article 78, Civil Practice Law, rather than the more limited review of article 75.[18]
- The city should have been supplied with a transcript of the arbitration hearing even though it made no timely request for such.[19]
- The city refused to appoint a city member to the arbitration panel, and when PERB twice designated someone to represent the city interest on the panel, each declined to serve. Mayor Corning was one of those named by PERB. His response was "I thought the 13th Amendment prohibited involuntary servitude."[20]
- The city challenged PERB's right to appoint someone as chairman and public member of an arbitration panel whom the city opposed even as it refused to participate in the selection process.[21]
- The city questioned the impartiality and competence of persons PERB nominated as possible public members.

On this latter point a letter to PERB expressed the city's view succinctly and wittily:

July 16, 1975

William E. Spenla
Assistant to the Director of Conciliation
State of New York
Public Employment Relations Board
50 Wolf Road
Albany, New York 12205

Dear Mr. Spenla:

The list provided by you from which the City and its Fire-fighters are charged to pick an arbitrator who will tell the City and the Firefighters how the Albany Fire Department is to be run and what burden shall be incurred by the taxpayers of the city via increased wages and fringe benefits is unacceptable to the City.

The resumes of four of the people on the list include among their qualifications the fact that they have each had a hand in solving the labor problems of New York City. It should be noted that these resumes were apparently submitted approximately one year ago, before it became common knowledge that the public employee unions were a major cause of New York City's state of bankruptcy.

The remaining three are all College Professors from the western part of the State. If they are typical representatives of their profession they work short hours at an attractive salary scale.

What all of the people proposed have in common is the fact that no matter what deterioration of fire service the arbitrator's fiat may visit upon the City of Albany, no matter what the added financial burden he or she may place upon the Albany taxpayer—it will be of no concern to the arbitrator who will be back in Ithaca, or Syracuse, or Rochester or New York City.

The arbitration provision of the Taylor Law is an albatross which removes Municipal Police and Fire Departments from the democratic process and instead provides that they be governed by someone from West 86th Street in New York City.

We will face the gallows if we must but from the nooses you offer there is none which seems more attractive than the others.

Very truly yours,

Vincent J. McArdle, Jr.
Executive Deputy Corporation Counsel[22]

The courts rebuffed the city of Albany on all significant points of law, and its efforts to evade compulsory arbitration were for naught. The constitutionality of the 1974 amendment had been upheld by the Court of Appeals in the *City of Amsterdam* in June 1975, and the Albany cases sustained PERB's implementation of the arbitration provision.[23] Still the city kept up the pretense that it was somehow beyond the reach of the Taylor Law. The Albany Common Council adopted a local ordinance in August 1976 to exempt itself from compulsory arbitration, the rationale being that since New York City was excepted, the Taylor Law was not a general law. Never invoked, the ordinance remains on the books.

Total resistance came to an end after a December 1976 ruling by the Court of Appeals that confirmed the arbitration award in the firefighters' case.[24] Thus about one and a half years after the award was issued, the city paid up and the average firefighter collected $3,400 in back pay. Even more surprising, in May 1977, the city accepted a fact finder's salary recommendation in an impasse with the firefighters. This turn of events seemed related to the expected opposition to the mayor in the Democratic primary.

Since 1977 labor relations in Albany have gradually come to resemble those of other jurisdictions in that they are far from harmonious but nonetheless within the normal range. The Democratic party organization is still strong, even without Erastus Corning, yet it is hardly the unchallenged powerhouse it was before the Taylor Law.

Several events contributed to the declining power of the machine, but surely one of them was the unionization of the city workforce.

A WATERSHED YEAR—1971

The year 1971 was the last in which a concerted effort was mounted in the legislature to restrict employee and union rights under the Taylor Law. Although the legislature acted to exclude managerial and confidential employees from coverage, a setback for the unions, at the same time it rebuffed an attempt to write management rights language into the statute. The legislature made two other changes as well. The term *budget submission date* was replaced by *end of fiscal year* in describing the impasse procedures, a relatively noncontroversial modification intended to bring procedures in line with the realities of negotiations. A second change provoked protest by all municipal employer associations and led them to urge a veto of the entire bill; it reduced from four months to thirty days the time within which a party could seek judicial review of a PERB decision.

A management rights amendment was part of an omnibus bill proposed by the governor and identified with its Assembly sponsor, Charles Jerebek.[25] The measure itself was not particularly exceptional; analogs could be found in the management rights sections of the federal executive order and of New York City law. Yet, from the perspective of the unions, the bill threatened to circumscribe seriously the scope of collective negotiations. The teacher unions were especially concerned because so many of the issues they typically sought to negotiate could be regarded as infringing on management prerogatives. The NEA-affiliated New York State Teachers Association and affiliates of AFT therefore set aside their usual rivalry to work cooperatively for the defeat of the measure, an important way station to their merger the following year. Whether the management rights proposal would have had the baleful consequences feared by the unions is uncertain; that it would have significantly increased the amount of disputation and litigation, there can be no doubt. PERB opposed it for that reason.[26]

Defeat of the Jerebek bill marked a fundamental political shift in New York. Public sector unions had now become a dominant power, and there was no effective challenge from employer interest. Future changes in the Taylor Law would essentially expand the rights of employees and unions. The one exception to this trend was the 1973 exclusion of retirement benefits from negotiations, but the full force of that amendment was immediately mitigated by temporarily allowing certain pension negotiations to continue, a proviso that has been renewed annually ever since.

NOTES

1. *PERB News* 4 (May 1971):1.

2. Paul Weiler calculated the odds that a union supporter in an NLRB representation election in 1980 would be fired for union activity as twenty to one. Paul Weiler, "Promises to Keep," 1781.

3. *State of New York (State University of New York)*, 2 PERB 4010.

4. Lefkowitz, *The Legal Basis of Employee Relations*, 18.

5. Ibid., 18–19.

6. Robinson, *Machine Politics.*

7. *City of Albany,* 1 PERB 307. The county government submitted an almost identical plan that was rejected. *County of Albany,* 1 PERB 309.

8. *City of Albany and Fire Chief Augustus Brophy,* 3 PERB 4507; 3 PERB 3096; 4 PERB 7008; 5 PERB 7000. Besides ordering reinstatement, PERB required the city to post notice that it would cease and desist from engaging in discriminatory conduct. The appellate division modified the order to eliminate the notice requirement on the grounds that it compelled the employer to admit in writing what it had consis-

tently denied. The Court of Appeals reinstated the notice remedy minus the phrase *cease and desist.*

9. Jack Ginsburg of PERB's research unit analyzed statistically the relationship between nonmembership and promotion or the converse. Ginsburg concluded that the probability of the correlation being purely coincidental was less than one in a thousand. Memorandum from Jack Ginsburg to Harvey Milowe, 13 January 1971, PERB Files, ILR Documentation Center, Cornell University.

10. *City of Albany et al.,* 4 PERB 4502; 4 PERB 3056.

11. *City of Albany,* 5 PERB 4509; 5 PERB 3035.

12. *City of Albany,* 8 PERB 4553; 9 PERB 3009; 10 PERB 7006.

13. The lengthy report of hearing officer Harvey Milowe is again instructive because of the glimpse it offers of the city's mode of operation, even though the decision was ultimately limited to a finding of improper practices by a single supervisor. *City of Albany and Harry Maikels, Commissioner of the Department of Public Works,* 9 PERB 4512; 9 PERB 3055; 10 PERB 7012; 11 PERB 7007.

14. Interview with Harvey Milowe, 24 June 1986. PERB staff members all have their favorite Mayor Corning story. Counsel Martin Barr remembers the mayor's reply when Barr was quoted in a newspaper as saying that Mayor Corning was on strike against the Taylor Law. Corning quipped, "I agree. This is the first time I have ever agreed with PERB on anything." Interview with Martin Barr, 24 June 1986.

15. Interview with Joseph R. Crowley, 23 July 1985.

16. *City of Albany,* 7 PERB 3078.

17. 7 PERB 3078; 7 PERB 3079; 8 PERB 7012; 9 PERB 7005.

18. 9 PERB 7006; 9 PERB 7007; 9 PERB 7008; 9 PERB 7026.

19. 9 PERB 7008.

20. 9 PERB 7009.

21. 9 PERB 7009.

22. PERB Files, ILR Documentation Center, Cornell University.

23. 8 PERB 7011.

24. *Albany Permanent Professional Firefighters Association, Local 2007, IAFF,* 9 PERB 7026.

25. Intro. A. 7796 (1971).

26. Interview with Jerome Lefkowitz, 25 June 1985.

6
ADMINISTERING
THE LAW

THE FOCUS OF THE rest of this book is on administration of the law, which rests largely with PERB. As discussed previously, the statute does, however, accord a high degree of autonomy to New York City. Moreover, it allows other local governments some measure of self-regulation through the device of a mini-PERB. After a brief look at mini-PERBs, attention centers on the board, its membership, and its decision-making processes.

MINI-PERBS

The inclusion of section 212, entitled "Local Government Procedures," was instrumental in winning passage of the Taylor Law in 1967. While it served primarily as a concession to New York City and its supporters, it also made the law somewhat more palatable to local governments elsewhere in the state. Section 212 permitted local governments to establish their own procedures for dealing with representation matters and negotiation impasses so long as the procedures adopted and their continuing implementation met the test of substantial equivalence with the state law as interpreted by PERB. Prior approval from PERB was needed to implement these procedures.

151

The appeal for a local government of having its own mini-PERB, as it soon came to be called, was associated with prized values of home rule and an abiding belief that local procedures would be more attuned to local circumstances and needs than anything emanating from Albany. Furthermore, local regulations held promise of being more expeditious in coping with the anticipated rush of activity. In a few instances, however, darker motives may have been at work: the notion that through local procedures the political leadership would be able to control, if not altogether frustrate, employee efforts to organize and negotiate. The prime example, the city of Albany, was discussed in the previous chapter.

In a burst of enthusiasm for home rule, PERB was deluged with section 212 applications. In December 1967 and January 1968, the board formally acted on forty-two applications. Only two, from Nassau County and Oswego County, were approved, the latter, the second time around. Disapproval was often based on failure to assure impartiality in local administration as well as a host of technical shortcomings in the plans. It soon became apparent that the criteria the board applied allowed little deviation from the state pattern. Though some jurisdictions reapplied after an initial turndown, a number abandoned the effort. By the end of 1970, thirty-four local enactments had been approved.[1] A few were never implemented, and some were disbanded after a brief existence; over the years the number of mini-PERBs has steadily dwindled, so that only eight remained in 1987. Of these only three or four are active.[2]

Several circumstances aside from the tough standards imposed by PERB helped chill enthusiasm for mini-PERBs. The presumed greater efficiency of having a locally based administrative apparatus turned out to be largely a mirage. In many communities it was difficult to find individuals who were both impartial and qualified to deal with representation matters or to act as mediators and fact finders. During impasses mini-PERBs tended to employ the same persons who appeared on PERB's roster, the only difference being that the cost was borne locally rather than by the state. There were additional costs to absorb as well. Thus the virtues of home rule gave way to the realities of cost and efficiency. Although one could argue that mini-PERBs served a useful purpose during the start-up period of the Taylor Law by facilitating the establishment of collective bargaining relationships, they soon became largely anachronistic. The 1969 report of the select joint legislative committee urged that mini-PERBs, other than New York City's, be abolished on the ground that they did not always give the appearance of neutrality in relation to the employer because they were usually dependent on the employer for financial and administrative support.[3] That proposition had PERB's full support.

BOARD MEMBERSHIP OVER THE YEARS

The three-member public employment relations board has had only two chairmen in twenty-plus years, Robert Helsby for the first ten years and Harold Newman since then. Besides his duties as member of the tribunal, the chairman is also the chief executive officer of the agency. Seven other persons have sat as part-time members on the board. Because the board customarily meets only a few days each month, and then often under pressure to turn out decisions, the part-timers lack the luxury of time. They are thus at a disadvantage in dealings with full-time staff and consequently have less influence on the shape and direction of policy. A clear exception to this generalization was Joseph Crowley, who left his mark during PERB's formative period. His influence was attributable to a combination of competence, personality, timing, and his close relationship with the chairman.

Whereas observers of the National Labor Relations Board often speak of the Eisenhower, Kennedy, or Reagan Board as a shorthand way of indicating a particular labor policy orientation associated with the political views of the incumbent president, the policies of PERB have been remarkably constant over its history, irrespective of state administration, agency leadership, or board composition. Under both Helsby and Newman the board's approach has been pragmatic and largely unaffected by ideology, even though Newman stands to the left of Helsby in his general political outlook. Some suggest that the Newman board is more sympathetic to the concerns of unions, as in its decisions related to the restoration of dues deduction privileges, but this may be as much a pragmatic response to altered political power relationships as it is a reflection of political bias.

The first change in board membership occurred with the resignation of George Fowler and the appointment of Fred L. Denson in his place almost a year and a half later, in December 1973. Delays in filling board vacancies have become increasingly common in recent years, a sign of declining interest in PERB on the part of the executive chamber once the state's own employee relations stabilized. (As of the end of 1989 the board has operated for two and one-half years without a third member.) An episode recounted by Harold Newman underscores the degree of inattentiveness displayed by the governor's office. Only when Denson's term ended in May 1976 did Governor Hugh Carey's appointments office become aware that Denson was black.[4]

Ida Klaus joined the board in 1976 and served for the next eight years. A formidable intellectual presence, Klaus possessed an impressive background in private and public labor relations. She had been with the National Labor Relations Board for many years and had been its solicitor. In the 1950s she was the principal author of Mayor Wagner's executive orders governing employee relations policies for New York City and later took part in putting together President Kennedy's Executive Order 10988 on federal employee relations. For more than a decade before her retirement, Klaus was in charge of labor relations for the New York City Board of Education, where she established its labor relations system and negotiated on its behalf. Her relations with Albert Shanker and the UFT were good, but it was to Donald Wollett, director of the Governor's Office of Employee Relations, and David Burke, Carey's secretary, that Klaus attributed her initial appointment to PERB. Shanker supported her reappointment two years later, however.[5]

In a way Ida Klaus never felt fully comfortable, emotionally or intellectually, in her association with PERB. Some of this discomfort stemmed from her own personality. She was the prototypical self-assured New Yorker who on occasion could be prickly in contacts with others. She felt excluded from the family feeling that seemed characteristic of the small agency, in contrast to colleague David Randles, who appeared to be accepted. Beyond that, Klaus had a view of labor relations that sometimes was at odds with that of her colleagues. In her estimation the agency placed far too much emphasis on dispute intervention and not enough on ways to encourage the parties to bargain out their differences. She had a strong commitment to "free collective bargaining," meaning a minimum of intrusion by PERB, a reflection of her time with the NLRB and the city school board. PERB, she thought, did not make a "sufficient effort to liberalize the statute in favor of collective bargaining." These beliefs found expression in some of her dissenting opinions. In addition, she perceived too strong a "disposition toward consensus" and with it a tendency to pay inadequate attention to developing a rationale for decisions, that is, to applying a theory of labor relations.[6]

Helsby announced his resignation from the board in mid-1977. He had contemplated leaving for some time because he believed that one ought not to stay too long in any job and also because he was unhappy about working for Hugh Carey, but it was the opportunity to embark on a new and interesting assignment that tipped the scales. The Carnegie Foundation was prepared to fund a study of state public sector labor relations commissions around the country with the idea of possibly creating a national clearinghouse for the exchange of information and technical assistance. It was a job ideally suited to someone with Helsby's missionary instincts.[7]

For nine months after Helsby's departure, the board operated with less than full membership, some of that time without a chairman. Harold Newman took over as chairman in late January 1978. The appointment seemed a natural succession in that Newman had for so long been director of conciliation, the position that next to that of chairman commanded the most public attention. He had acquired wide acquaintance and acceptance among practitioners and political folk alike in carrying out his duties and in appearances on public platforms, where he could display his considerable gift for witty rhetoric.

When David C. Randles was appointed in June 1978, the board was back to full strength. To conform to statutory dictates, it was essential that the nominee not be a Democrat, a not insignificant obstacle within the labor relations fraternity. Randles was a Republican and also an Episcopalian priest (he was a canon) from the Albany area. He had gained public sector exposure as a sometime mediator and arbitrator on PERB panels. Although he was relatively inexperienced to begin with, not long after leaving PERB almost eight years later, he quit his church position to devote full time to labor arbitration.

Two other names complete the list of persons who served on the board during its first twenty-two years.

Walter L. Eisenberg, a former professor of economics at Hunter College and an impartial member of the New York City Board of Collective Bargaining, succeeded Ida Klaus one year after her term had expired. In contrast to Randles, Eisenberg was an experienced hand.

Finally, in mid-1986 Jerome Lefkowitz, after so many years as the chief legal adviser to the board, resigned as deputy chairman to become one of its members. His tenure was brief, however, for a year later he quit PERB to join CSEA as its deputy counsel, an irony if ever there was one, recalling not so ancient history when Lefkowitz was CSEA's arch villain in its war with PERB.

BOARD DECISION MAKING

Early on the board had developed a routine for handling cases that gave its deputy chairman, Jerry Lefkowitz, a major role. The routine has remained essentially unchanged.[8] As attorney to the board, Lefkowitz prepared memoranda on the cases to be heard and often prepared draft decisions. In so doing he significantly affected the course of discussion and the eventual outcome, although his own opinion did not necessarily prevail. One such example was the important *West Irondequoit Board of Education* decision in which Lefkowitz shared the dissenting view of George Fowler that class size was a mandatory subject of negotiations.[9]

Within the first board (Helsby, Crowley, and Fowler), Crowley on occasion wrote opinions. Helsby did little or no decision writing, although he was fully engaged in deciding cases. In contrast, Fowler had less interest in decision making and would have preferred a more active role in administration and dispute settlement. Indeed, when he joined the board he suggested that he be placed in charge of the New York City office, an idea Helsby found unacceptable. Fowler was assigned as a mediator in the 1968 mental health workers strike, but that did not go well and thereafter the board adopted a policy that its members should not become directly involved in impasses lest they be called upon later to decide on strike penalties.[10]

The influence of staff, Lefkowitz in particular, did not sit well with Ida Klaus. She differed in her view on the role of staff in the business of the board and in her philosophy of labor relations, differences exacerbated by a clash of strong personalities. Nonetheless, the procedures for decision making remained intact.

Formal dissents to decisions of the board have been infrequent, thirty-eight in twenty years. Although dissents could and did arise for reason of irreconcilable differences in outlook or in interpretation of facts, they sometimes reflected a desire to save time rather than prolong internal debate in an attempt to reach consensus. Dissent was also a device for signaling to the outside community the closeness of a particular call that might very well have gone the other way. These several elements came into play in the landmark *West Irondequoit* decision. Fowler kept changing his opinion during the discussion on whether class size was a mandatory bargaining issue, and it was therefore proposed that a dissent be recorded.[11] Overall, what is surprising is the infrequency with which dissents have been recorded in thousands of board decisions. One major reason is that the board has been forced to operate at less than full strength for much of the time in recent years and there has been no opportunity to dissent formally.

Klaus dissented on nine occasions, Crowley and Denson on eight each. Ida Klaus's core beliefs about collective bargaining found expression in the sharp criticism of the majority's conclusion that a wage parity clause was a prohibited subject of bargaining; that it was an improper practice for a party to carry to factfinding a permissive subject over the objection of the other party; and that an employer was not obligated to negotiate concerning unemployment insurance for certain school employees.[12] A second theme sounded in her opinions favored a narrower reading of the board's statutory authority. It is most clearly stated in her dissent in the wage parity case and in *Niagara County*, which dealt with the interpretation of the Triborough amendment.[13]

Like Klaus, Fred Denson would have limited PERB's role in determining what the parties could properly negotiate, for example, a parity clause.[14] He also differed with the majority's approach to unit determination, displaying a greater willingness to approve petitions for unit severence.[15]

In Crowley's case, several of his dissenting opinions show the orientation of a law professor who is perhaps more sensitive than others to fine legal distinctions. This is evidenced particularly in his disagreement with the majority's holding that the county and the sheriff are joint employers and in *New York Public Library*, which raised similar questions and in which Crowley wrote a lengthy concurring opinion.[16] Only once did a minority opinion later get adopted as the majority view, that in Crowley's dissent in *Town of Orangetown* with respect to the role of PERB in contract enforcement.[17]

CONCLUSION

Continuity more than any other characteristic has been the hallmark of PERB's administration of the law in the first two decades. The turnover in membership of the board has not been excessive, and, more important, the agency has had only two chairmen, the second of whom, Harold Newman, has generally been faithful to the policies and procedures developed during the Helsby administration.

Only infrequently have any differences in outlook among board members appeared in the form of split decisions.

The broad area of consensus that has existed among them is reflective of wide agreement within the state public labor-management community on basic matters of labor relations policy. This is far from the case in private industry, where the fundamental ideological conflict between employers and unions is reflected in politics and ultimately in appointments to the NLRB and in NLRB policies.

Finally, the continuity in administration is also due to the stability within PERB's top professional staff. Persons such as Ralph Vatalaro, Martin Barr, Harvey Milowe, Erwin Kelly, and, until fairly recently, Jerry Lefkowitz have been with the agency from the beginning or soon thereafter. Their presence has been an important stabilizing force.

Notes

1. *PERB News* 4 (May 1976):3.
2. Records of PERB counsel's office, Albany.
3. *Select Committee Report,* 25–26.
4. Interview with Harold R. Newman, 19 December 1986. Whether the fact would have made a difference is beside the point. One could hardly imagine the same thing happening in the Cuomo administration. See chapter 3 on the Erwin Kelly appointment.
5. Interview with Ida Klaus, 20 November 1985.
6. Ibid.
7. Interview with Helsby, 21 June 1985. In 1972, Helsby had been a major figure in founding the Society of Professionals in Dispute Resolution (SPIDR), and he served as its first president.
8. Pauline R. Kinsella joined the agency in mid-1987 as special counsel to the board and performs some of the duties Lefkowitz previously handled.
9. 4 PERB 3070; interview with Jerome Lefkowitz, 25 June 1986.
10. Interviews with Lefkowitz; with Ralph Vatalaro, 18 November 1986.
11. Interview with Lefkowitz, 18 November 1986. An interesting example of a case in which all three members read the evidence quite differently is *Fashion Institute of Technology,* 5 PERB 3018.

12. *New York City and Patrolmen's Benevolent Association of the City of New York,* 10 PERB 3003; *Monroe-Woodbury Teachers Association,* 10 PERB 3029; and *Greater Amsterdam School District,* 12 PERB 3074.

13. 16 PERB 3071.

14. *City of Albany and Albany Permanent Professional Firefighters Association,* 7 PERB 3079; also *Buffalo Patrolmen's Benevolent Association,* 9 PERB 3024.

15. *Town of Smithtown,* 8 PERB 3015.

16. *County of Ulster,* 3 PERB 3032; *New York Public Library,* 5 PERB 3045.

17. 8 PERB 3042. See chapter 8.

7
REPRESENTATION MATTERS

As a PRELIMINARY TO collective negotiations, it is necessary to determine which employees are to be represented and what organization shall negotiate on their behalf. Although PERB's authority in this realm is not exclusive, the agency carries important responsibilities in answering questions such as, Which employees are eligible for representation? What is the appropriate grouping of employees for purposes of negotiations? How shall the desires of employees regarding representation be ascertained?

We saw in the example of the state representation case in chapter 3 just how troublesome the issue of unit determination can be. In general, PERB has applied the criterion of the most appropriate unit in deciding cases. That concept is discussed in this chapter, as is the issue of unit proliferation. The chapter closes with an extended account of the representation battle between CSEA and the Public Employee Federation, which ultimately led to the affiliation of CSEA with AFSCME. Once again the customary routine of the representation function was upset as PERB was caught in the midst of political cross currents.

The Statutory Scheme

Absent a contesting employee organization, local governments have usually been quick to grant recognition on request. When a dispute over representation did arise because of the presence of a competing organization or because a public employer denied recognition on grounds of differences concerning the dimensions of a claimed negotiating unit or for some other reason, the Taylor Law specified the manner in which the dispute would be resolved. Three possible mechanisms were provided for in the statute. First, where an approved mini-PERB existed, the responsibility lay with it. Second, section 206 of the law offered local governments without mini-PERBs the option of adopting their own procedures to handle representation cases. By no means were they given a free hand, however; they were constrained, just as the mini-PERBs and PERB were, by the three unit determination standards of section 207 and, moreover, by a PERB requirement that an impartial agent be used to determine the dispute. The latter condition effectively discouraged extensive use of the option. Finally, if neither section 206 nor 212 was applicable, PERB had the authority to resolve representation matters.

Section 207.2 speaks of ascertaining employee wishes regarding representation "on the basis of dues deduction authorizations or other evidences, or, if necessary, by conducting an election." Because of this seeming preference for a mechanism other than an election, PERB initially promulgated in its rules a schedule for certification without an election. If an organization was able to offer proof of 55 percent membership in an appropriate unit, it would be certified unless a competing organization was able to show similar evidence of support from at least 10 percent of the employees. At the other end of the sched-

ule, a showing of 25 percent was required to prevent certification of an organization that could demonstrate 70
percent membership.

Experience soon indicated that membership was less
than a perfect guide to employee preference, and in a
1969 revision of its rules PERB mandated elections in
all cases involving more than one employee organization.
The use of certification on the basis of membership was
reserved for uncontested cases. This latter practice came
under fire from a few employers who contended that a
secret ballot election should be held in all representation
cases. As a way of expressing displeasure with the PERB
rule, the employers withheld their agreement to exclusive
status for the majority employee organization. Without
such a stipulation, the certification issued by PERB was
for members only.[1] In 1989 the legislature, at PERB's request, changed the language of section 204 to read that a
certified or recognized employee organization shall be the
exclusive representative.

THE MOST APPROPRIATE UNIT

PERB's unit determination decisions have greatly affected
the shape and content of labor relations in New York
State. By adopting the standard of "most appropriate
unit" as its touchstone rather than following the NLRB
approach of "an appropriate unit," PERB made clear its
preference for large as opposed to small negotiating units
and for a few units, as opposed to many. This point of
view received its clearest and most visible expression in
the huge state representation case in which none of the
petitioners sought the units that were established.[2] The
decision was described many years later by R. Theodore
Clark, a nationally prominent management attorney, as
"without question the most important unit decision decided in the public sector nationally."[3]

The concept of "most appropriate unit" is traceable to the three criteria set forth in section 207.1 of the law. The first of these states the customary standard that there be a community of interest among employees; the next two need to be read as qualifiers of that criterion. One provides that the public employer at the level of the unit possess the authority to agree to or to make effective recommendations with respect to the terms and conditions to be negotiated. The second states that "the unit shall be compatible with the joint responsibilities of the public employer and public employees to serve the public." The latter in particular introduces the notion of administrative convenience, and it has been construed as an admonishment to avoid excessive fragmentation of units. Member Crowley summed up PERB's policy in a law review article:

> In brief, the PERB's policy is that fragmentation of a public employer's employees into small units is to be avoided unless there is present such a conflict of interest as to preclude effective and meaningful negotiations. To avoid such fragmentation, the Board has adopted the "most appropriate unit" policy.[4]

A finding of community interest, or conversely a conflict of interest, turned on issues such as the structure of the compensation plan, hours of work, retirement and other fringe benefits, applicable personnel policies, work location and supervision, negotiating history, and the like. On occasion PERB supported separate units for blue- and white-collar workers,[5] for professional and nonprofessional employees,[6] and for supervisory and nonsupervisory personnel, as in the case of school principals. Overall, however, the preference for large units and for the avoidance of proliferation was the dominant theme. In contrast to the private sector, the desires of the employer were given weight as one aspect of the standard of administrative convenience. This outlook also reflected an unarticulated assumption that public employers, because of their presumed commitment to serving the public, were less likely to take a position on unit determination for the sole purpose of frustrating free employee choice. This assumption has generally proved to be correct.

Once basic unit lines were fixed, most unit decisions have consisted of minor modifications involving accretions to or subtractions from those units. Only infrequently has PERB approved a petition to split off part of the original unit. In such instances it was up to the petitioning group to demonstrate that the incumbent organization had neglected to represent effectively the petitioner's interests, a most difficult test. *County of Sullivan* is one of those few cases in which the board granted severance to a large group of public works employees. The employer's preference for a separate unit was decisive in this case.[7] During his tenure board member Fred Denson on several occasions questioned the concept of "most appropriate unit" and the majority's tendency not to disturb an existing unit. Denson believed that his colleagues gave too much weight to administrative convenience.[8]

The most common exception to PERB's reluctance to approve fragmentation of units occurred with respect to deputy sheriffs, and it was slow in evolving. Early on deputies were usually included within an overall unit of county employees, and the sheriff was regarded as a joint employer with the county.[9] As an increasing sense of exceptionalism took hold among all law enforcement personnel, deputies began to press for separate units across the state. The many requests for separate representation brought to PERB from 1975 on produced inconsistent outcomes, however, sometimes approval of a separate unit, more often denial.[10] A kind of catch-22 quality appears in the PERB rationale. In *County of Cayuga* the petition was dismissed in part because the sheriff was not involved in any way in the county's labor relations, a situation that presumably would have been remedied if severance was granted. Beginning with *County of Montgomery,* however, the board altered its view, giving considerable weight to the preference expressed by the sheriff, despite opposition from the county.[11] Separate units for employees of the sheriff's department have since become the norm.

THE MULTIPLICITY OF UNITS

Despite PERB's commitment to the avoidance of unit proliferation, the actual number of negotiating units in the state has swelled to 3,695 according to the 1988–89 annual report.[12] The number of units is, of course, a result of the very large number of government entities in the state but also of the readiness of public employers, unmindful of the consequences, to extend recognition to small occupational groupings. Thus it is not uncommon to find five or six separate negotiating units in a small school district. To be sure, consolidations have occurred, yet many small units remain.

For a brief period in the early 1970s, PERB participated in a test of the feasibility of multiemployer bargaining in the schools. The undertaking was triggered by the report of a state commission examining the public schools that recommended a state takeover of financing.[13] The report proposed that collective bargaining, at least on the major economic issues, be conducted on a statewide basis. It saw advantages in the saving of time spent in negotiations; in the quality of negotiations by virtue of greater knowledge and expertise; in the elimination of interdistrict whipsawing by the unions; and in a more workable impasse procedure because the final step would be a determination by the state legislature rather than by a local school board. With his customary enthusiasm for innovation, Robert Helsby involved PERB with the state education department and the New York State United Teachers (NYSUT) in an attempt at multidistrict bargaining among a half-dozen Oneida County school districts. It was hoped that with the substantial assistance of consultants and mediators, the parties in Oneida would develop a model approach. But even with the best efforts, the parties were unable to overcome the problems associated with disparate employment conditions and practices in the districts and with the parochial interests of individual boards of education and teacher associations. To a degree the later emergence of a number of boards of cooperative educational services (BOCES) as a major source for negotiation assistance to local school districts served some of the purposes envisioned by the Oneida project. The BOCES usually supplied more skilled negotiators and greater uniformity in bargaining outcomes.

EXCLUSION OF MANAGERIAL AND CONFIDENTIAL EMPLOYEES

In 1971 the legislature redefined the term *public employee* so as to exclude managerial and confidential employees from the protection of the act. Heretofore a public employee was "any person holding a position by appointment or employment in the service of a public employer," the sole exception being members of the state organized militia. The Taylor committee had finessed the issue of whether managers and supervisors ought to have the same negotiating rights as other employees because, it reasoned, the answer would depend on how employees chose to exercise their new rights, still an unknown. Very quickly, however, reality began to intrude. For example, the state as an employer initially contemplated the exclusion of only very top officials from its proposed negotiating units, but it soon came to realize that it depended on the loyalty of a much larger cadre to carry out its responsibilities in a collective negotiation context. Thus its list of proposed exclusions in the hearing before PERB grew to seven thousand five hundred persons.

Tompkins County illustrated the problem at the extreme. There the county board of supervisors extended recognition to CSEA for a unit that encompassed all employees of the county so that there existed the anomaly of at least two members of the employer's negotiating team, the principal budget officer and the commissioner of personnel, negotiating terms and conditions of employment that would apply to themselves.

In making unit determinations in cases brought before it, PERB was perforce excluding persons on the basis of managerial functions without having to address the logical next question of whether managers themselves could constitute an appropriate unit for negotiations. Prompted by the suggestion of the select joint legislative committee, PERB commissioned Melvin K. Bers, a professor at SUNY, Albany, to examine the issue. His report, *The Status of Managerial, Supervisory and Confidential Employees in Government Employment Relations,* was published in January 1970. Though Bers made no recommendations, his belief that some statutory change was needed was implicit in his conclusion.

The amendment excluded from the definition of public employee "persons who may reasonably be designated from time to time as managerial or confidential." The test of managerial status, as outlined in section 201, was to be those

> (i) who formulate policy or (ii) who may reasonably be required on behalf of the public employer to assist directly in the preparation for and conduct of collective negotiations or in personnel administration provided that such role is not of a routine or clerical nature and requires the exercise of independent judgment.

A confidential employee was defined as one who had a confidential relationship to a manager. In an entirely new section 214 of the law, managerial and confidential employees were barred from holding membership in an employee organization. The designation of managerial or confidential status was to reside with PERB (or a mini-PERB) on application from the public employer.

After a period of almost universal coverage, the new restrictions in coverage threatened established arrangements, particularly within the police and fire services and among school principals and administrators. It was not uncommon for a negotiating unit in a fire department, say, to include everyone from the chief on down. This was, after all, merely a continuation of traditional relationships. Immediately after it adopted the managerial exclusion, the legislature added a statement of intent that stands out as a masterful example of linguistic ambiguity. In circuitous fashion the legislature seemed to exempt existing negotiating units of school principals and administrators from the reach of the new amendment.

Several CSEA members and officers who were excluded from negotiating units challenged the amendment on constitutional grounds. They claimed that the statute denied freedom of association and equal protection and that it impaired the contractual benefits of the insurance program available only to CSEA members. The Court of Appeals rejected their claim.[14]

Since then, administration of these provisions of the law have presented few problems. The numbers of petitions from managerial and confidential employees have remained fairly substantial, but most cases are resolved at the level of the director of representation on the basis of stipulation by the parties; few require review by the board itself.

PERB FEELS POLITICAL HEAT

Robert Helsby recalls the 1972 representation election in which SEIU challenged CSEA in two large state negotiating units as one of the rare occasions when he was subjected to overt, intense political pressure.[15] In 1972 SEIU petitioned to displace CSEA in the forty-four thousand–member institutional services unit and in the professional, scientific, and technical (PST) services unit of thirty-four thousand members. The controversy in the institutional unit was whether the election should be conducted by mail ballot, as favored by CSEA and originally by the employer, or by on-site, in-person voting, as urged by SEIU. Each organization offered an appropriate rationale in support of its position. The decision of the board hints at some unusual happenings:

> Because of the great size of the unit and the unusual interest in the question, we departed from our normal procedure of having the Director of Public Employment Practices and Representation rule on questions involving the mechanics of an election and invited the parties to submit argument before the Chairman of the Board. After consultation with his colleague [Crowley was at the time the only other member of the board], the Chairman wrote to the parties on September 15, 1972, advising them of the determination to hold a mail ballot. Thereafter, the employer reversed its position and, on October 13, 1972, wrote a letter to us which was in the nature of a motion to reconsider our determination to hold a mail ballot. In support of this request, the employer advised that it had just become aware of the experience of the Commonwealth of Pennsylvania in holding on-site elections in statewide units of employees of the Commonwealth.[16]

What the decision did not say was that the chairman was being pressed to accommodate to SEIU's position. Governor Rockefeller had received calls on behalf of SEIU from George Meany and from persons closely identified with President Richard Nixon.[17] Helsby was summoned to the governor's mansion, where he explained that for the board to consider altering its initial determination favoring a mail ballot, the Office of Employee Relations would have to change its position and support the change with persuasive argument. Although the Pennsylvania experience was incomplete, controversial, and, because it was so recent, undocumented and unevaluated, all duly noted in its discussion, the board nonetheless concluded that the information from Pennsylvania was sufficient to justify backing off from its first position. In a Solomon-like approach to the dispute, the board decided to conduct half the election by mail and the other half by on-site voting and to regard it as a test of the relative merits of the two methods. Institutions were paired according to size and location. In the end, voting method made no difference and CSEA decisively defeated SEIU. Of the eligibles in the institutional services unit, only 52 percent voted, close to three-quarters for CSEA. In the PST unit, where voting was completely by mail ballot, 70 percent of the eligibles voted and CSEA won by a two-to-one margin.[18]

Outside political interference eased, but a resumption of the bruising battle for representation rights among PST unit members presented PERB with fresh difficulties. SEIU mounted another campaign in the PST unit in 1975, this time as part of a newly formed coalition of unions, the Public Employee Federation (PEF). As initially put together, the coalition consisted of SEIU, NYSUT, the state Building Trades Council, the Laborers, and Local 237, Teamsters. The objections of AFSCME caused the Teamsters to withdraw even as AFSCME was deciding it would not join the alliance; instead AFSCME opted for a strategy of trying to persuade CSEA to affiliate with it, very much a long shot given the strong antipathy of CSEA leadership.[19] As part of an "AFSCME/CSEA Unity campaign," AFSCME urged support for CSEA in the election. The Public Employee Federation failed to win, but it did force a runoff election.

Two years later, reconstituted as a two-union alliance of SEIU and NYSUT, PEF petitioned once more. The ensuing dispute was not resolved until the Court of Appeals pronounced judgment on several charges of irregularities brought by CSEA. When the ballots were counted on April 12, 1978, the tally gave PEF a majority of 15,062 to 12,259 for CSEA in a unit that by then had 45,000 employees. CSEA promptly moved to have the election set aside, alleging among other things that PEF had engaged in fraud by forging authorization cards in order to meet the requisite 30 percent showing of interest for an election. It also alleged that state management officials in the labor department had improperly aided PEF in the campaign.[20]

The charge by CSEA that PEF's original showing of interest had been tainted by fraud was a serious matter indeed, calling into question customary representation practices. Was an administrative agency obliged to scrutinize each and every signature on an authorization card or petition whenever an allegation of fraud was made? If so, the cost in time and money might effectively frustrate the fundamental right of employees to be represented by organizations of their own choosing. On the other hand, could an agency tolerate abuse of its processes through wholesale fraud? These were underlying concerns in the lengthy, complex hearing conducted by Harvey Milowe, the director of representation.

Relying on the findings of a handwriting expert engaged by PERB, Milowe concluded there was insufficient evidence of fraud to warrant setting aside the election. Likewise, he dismissed the charge that management favoritism toward PEF had affected the outcome of the election. His decision that the results of the election should stand was affirmed by the board.[21]

At the appellate division a divided court faulted the

method used to investigate the alleged forgeries and re-
mitted the matter to PERB for further proceedings. In all
other particulars the court affirmed the decision of the
board. In very strong language it castigated a cozy arrangement countenanced by the labor department for several years that had permitted John Kraemer, the first
president of PEF, to function as a full-time SEIU representative while retaining a "no-show" job in the department. The court referred to "this pattern of shameless
conduct ... [that] strikes at the very heart of the governmental process."[22] On appeal by PERB, the Court of
Appeals reinstated the decision of the board, holding
that the method used by the director of representation
to detect possible forgery was reasonable.[23] In the estimate of PERB counsel Martin Barr, the decision was
of great importance because a contrary result would
have required fundamental revisions in representation
procedures.[24]

In the meantime, the representation proceeding had
become hopelessly entwined with a fierce intramural
struggle between PEF and AFSCME. Two days after objections to the election had been filed but before PERB
could certify the results, AFSCME president Jerry Wurf
announced the affiliation of CSEA with AFSCME. Wurf
also immediately invoked article XX of the AFL-CIO constitution designed to protect established bargaining relationships from raids by other AFL-CIO affiliates. Thus,
while appeals to PERB and the courts were running
their course, the claims and counterclaims of AFSCME
and PEF were being aired through the machinery of the
AFL-CIO Internal Disputes Plan. The impartial umpire,
Daniel Quinn Mills, first held for AFSCME but was reversed by the AFL-CIO Executive Council. After a second
hearing Mills concluded that neither affiliate had an established collective bargaining relationship and therefore
there could be no violation under article XX.[25]

CONCLUSION

Since 1967 close to three-quarters of a million public employees have been eligible to vote in PERB-conducted elections. Not surprisingly, there has been a long-term decline in the agency's workload in resolving representation matters because most employees are already placed in bargaining units. The majority of certifications issued by PERB are done without an election on the basis of authorization cards. In the five-year period 1984–88, the number of elections conducted annually averaged about thirty. Few of these involved brand-new organizing situations or units of any real size. More commonly, the elections pit an independent union wishing to break away against the incumbent bargaining representative.[26]

Recently, more consequential representation proceedings have taken place under the auspices of mini-PERBs in Suffolk, Nassau, and Westchester counties. In each of these counties very large CSEA units have been or are in the process of being challenged by an independent movement from within their ranks. The defection succeeded in Suffolk and failed in Nassau; the ultimate outcome in Westchester County is unknown.

NOTES

1. See *Town of Penfield,* 21 PERB 3019; *Village of Webster,* 21 PERB 7015.
2. *State of New York v. Council 50, AFSCME, et al.,* 1 PERB 399.85. See chapter 3.
3. Clark noted that the New York decision directly affected unit determination in some ten other states. He suggested that it also was reflected in the *St. Francis II* decision of the NLRB. *Government Employee Relations Report* 24 (1986):1496.
4. Crowley, "The Resolution of Representation Status Disputes under the Taylor Law," 520.
5. *County of Rockland,* 1 PERB 430.
6. *County of Ulster,* 3 PERB 3032; 4 PERB 7015.

7. *County of Sullivan,* 7 PERB 3069.

8. *Town of Smithtown,* 8 PERB 3015; *Town of Ramapo,* 8 PERB 3057.

9. *County of Ulster,* 3 PERB 3032; 4 PERB 7015.

10. PERB supported a separate unit for deputies in *County of Monroe,* 10 PERB 4031; it denied it in *County of Clinton,* 8 PERB 4044; *County of Ontario,* 9 PERB 4038; *County of Wyoming,* 9 PERB 4039; *County of Rockland,* 11 PERB 3050; and *County of Cayuga,* 12 PERB 3126.

11. *County of Montgomery,* 12 PERB 3126.

12. *PERB News* 22 (April 1989):1. The figure is an informed estimate. PERB rules require public employers to file with it a copy of all contracts entered into, but obtaining full compliance is another matter. The purpose of the rule was to enable the agency to perform its statutory function as a clearinghouse for information.

13. The New York State Commission on the Quality, Cost and Financing of Elementary and Secondary Education, chaired by Manly Fleischman. Its three-volume report was published in October 1972.

14. *Shelofsky v. Helsby,* 6 PERB 7005.

15. Interview with Robert D. Helsby, 21 June 1985.

16. *State of New York and Service Employees International Union, New York State Employees Division,* 5 PERB 3056.

17. Jerry Lefkowitz believed the Committee to Re-elect the President was involved. Interview, 25 June 1986.

18. *State of New York and Service Employees International Union,* 5 PERB 3056; interview with Helsby.

19. *Civil Service Leader,* 9 September 1975, 1. President Wenzl warned the members of the direct attack being made by PEF and "in many ways, much more insidious" attack by AFSCME.

20. *State of New York and Public Employees Federation,* 11 PERB 4053.

21. Ibid.

22. *CSEA and Thomas H. McDonough v. Harvey Milowe,* 12 PERB 7001.

23. 12 PERB 7005. Months after the decision, CSEA attempted to reopen the entire case on the basis of a report by the New York State Commission on Investigation on "Personnel Abuses at the Department of Labor." The board denied the motion. 12 PERB 3110.

24. *PERB News* 12 (April 1979):2.

25. *Government Employee Relations Report* 771 (7 August 1978):41, and 798 (19 February 1979):14.

26. PERB annual reports; telephone conversation with Harvey Milowe, 6 June 1989.

8

REGULATING THE BARGAINING PROCESS

PERB REGULATES FACETS OF the negotiation process primarily through its power to prevent and remedy improper practices. It helps to define the rights and obligations of individuals and negotiating parties; to determine the substantive boundaries of what is negotiable; and to establish procedural requirements of acceptable negotiating behavior. How PERB has carried out its responsibilities in this area is the subject of this chapter. Major attention is given to the scope of the duty to bargain and how that has developed, including the evolution of the policy embodied in the 1982 Triborough amendment. The chapter closes with a review of the controversy surrounding the issue of the agency fee and the appropriate role of PERB in its regulation.

ADMINISTRATION OF IMPROPER PRACTICE CASES

Since 1969 improper practice cases have accounted for a substantial portion of PERB's workload. Table 8.1 provides data on case volume. (The agency does not report cases by type of charge.) The bulk of the cases arise from allegations of a refusal to negotiate; very few are related to

Table 8.1. PERB's Caseload for Improper Practice Charges

Reporting Period	Charges Filed	Hearing Officer (ALJ) Decisions	Board Decisions	Settled by Agreement, Withdrawn, or Closed[a]
1970	156	N.A.	13	N.A.
1971	227	N.A.	23	165
1972	297	N.A.	21	245
1973	307	N.A.	38	280
1974	352	40	30	296
1975	541	46	26	373
1976	509	62	59	372
1977–78[b]	751	121	52	610
1978–79	697	61	29	463
1979–80	704	134	61	607
1980–81	686	147	87	567
1981–82	691	153	66	526
1982–83	707	178	80	330
1983–84	657	208	49	434
1984–85	662	185	87	508
1985–86	590	127	59	409
1986–87	688	167	57	512
1987–88	710	139	56	448
1988–89	643	92	55	407

Source: PERB annual reports for various years.

[a] Before 1977–78, the figures on charges settled referred only to charges settled by agreement.

[b] PERB changed to fiscal year for statistics. Data for 1977–78 are for fifteen months, January 1977 to March 31, 1978.

claims of employer interference or discrimination, which loom so large in the private sector. Complaints concerning the agency fee have constituted a small but steady source of improper practice charges.

Table 8.1 shows that the number of charges filed has remained fairly constant since 1977, on the order of 650 to 700 each year. Output as measured by the number of hearing officer (now called administrative law judges or ALJs) and board decisions has also been stable during that period, although there was a sharp rise in 1988–89 in the volume of cases pending and carried over to the next year. The backlog may be attributable in part to the unsettled membership of the board, just as the falloff in decision making during 1978–79 was associated with a period of change in the board's composition.

The processing of improper practice charges is the responsibility of the director of public employment practices and representation and the staff of administrative law judges, who investigate, hear, and decide charges. From the beginning PERB chose not to follow the NLRB model, under which the agency, through its general counsel, undertakes a prosecutorial role in unfair labor practice cases. Instead, for reasons of cost, expeditious handling, and some concern that a separate general counsel's office might diminish the authority of the board, PERB leaves responsibility for presenting a case to the charging party.[1] To speed the handling of scope of negotiation cases, an expedited procedure was established to permit the board to decide directly, without an intermediate decision by a hearing officer.

SCOPE OF THE DUTY TO BARGAIN

When the Taylor Law was passed, there was already a body of law and regulation in place that governed many aspects of employment in the public sector, often in minute detail.

The imposition on public employers of a requirement to negotiate, however, immediately raised questions of precedence about the relationship of negotiations to preexisting law. To what extent could parties negotiate on matters hitherto controlled by civil service, education, or other law? Furthermore, did the obligation to negotiate also extend to a host of other matters not specifically addressed by law but traditionally determined by public employers exercising their policy-making functions?

The Taylor Law provided only limited guidance on such questions. To be sure, it required collective negotiations on terms and conditions of employment, implying some form of bilateral determination beyond a mere meet and confer requirement. Yet it was ambiguous, albeit flexible, in defining the phrase *terms and conditions of employment* as "salaries, wages, hours and other terms and conditions of employment." In this respect it was similar to the National Labor Relations Act. The Taylor committee had not attempted to delineate the bounds of the scope of bargaining, preferring instead to leave disputes over negotiability for the appropriate legislative body, which in a no-strike system possessed the final word.[2] The committee recommended that PERB conduct studies of what should or should not be open to negotiation, anticipating that these might provide the basis for later statutory clarification.[3]

Clarification of the scope of the duty to bargain was to come largely through decisional law, however, rather than through statutory refinement. When the law was amended in 1969 to include language on improper practices, PERB gained statutory authority to decide disputes over allegations of a refusal to negotiate by one party or another (see chapter 4). This in turn enabled PERB to address questions of negotiability and to order an offending party to negotiate in good faith.

THE MISSION DOCTRINE

Although the Taylor Law explicitly stated that private sector law was not controlling, PERB did not ignore the wealth of experience represented in the federal law. It adopted the classification of bargaining subjects enunciated by the U.S. Supreme Court in *Borg-Warner* as either mandatory, permissive, or illegal.[4] As formulated by PERB, a mandatory subject must be a term and condition of employment; must be within the discretion of the employer; and may not go to the mission of the employer. The "mission doctrine" was first expressed in *New Rochelle City School District* in the following terms:

> A public employer exists to provide certain services to its constituents, be it police protection, sanitation or, as in the case of the employer herein, education. Of necessity, the public employer, acting through its executive or legislative body, must determine the manner and means by which such services are to be rendered and the extent thereof, subject to the approval or disapproval of the public so served, as manifested in the electoral process. Decisions of a public employer with respect to the carrying out of its mission, such as a decision to eliminate or curtail a service, are matters that a public employer should not be compelled to negotiate with its employees.[5]

New Rochelle was but one example of many difficult cases to come in which the subject of a negotiating proposal could be regarded at one and the same time as a condition of employment and as a matter of public policy or management prerogative. In this instance the school district, because of budgetary considerations, acted to eliminate a large number of jobs without prior discussion with the teacher organization. PERB noted that, although the employer's decision would obviously affect "conditions of employment," it "does not follow that every decision of a public employer which may affect job security is a mandatory subject of negotiations."[6]

A similar conclusion was reached in *West Irondequoit Board of Education,* later affirmed by the Court of Appeals, in which the issue was the school board's refusal to negotiate numerical limitations on class size.[7] Finding class size to be a matter of educational policy, the board majority elaborated on its rationale in *New Rochelle:*

> Underlying [*New Rochelle*] was the concept that basic decisions as to public policy should not be made in the isolation of a negotiation table, but rather should be made by those having direct and sole responsibility therefor, and whose actions in this regard are subject to review in the electoral process.[8]

Applying a balancing standard, the board concluded that the interests of the employer as guardian of the legitimate claims of other interest groups to participate in shaping educational policy outweighed those of teachers concerned with their workloads. Dissenting member George Fowler saw it quite differently: "In my judgment, the impact of numerical limitations of class size upon teaching loads is so direct as to make a line of demarcation impossible."

Important though *New Rochelle* and *West Irondequoit* were in providing some basis for distinguishing between mandatory and nonmandatory subjects of bargaining, they proved a less than perfect guide. What is the duty to bargain with respect to a demand that combines an element that is unquestionably a matter of management prerogative with elements that are equally clearly mandatory? What about a proposal to establish an upper limit on the number of weighted student contact minutes required of a teacher during the week, when one part of the formula is derived from class size? Or, to take another example, what about firefighters who wish to negotiate the minimum number of personnel assigned to a piece of fire apparatus on grounds of safety? In the latter case the determination of staffing requirements is a public policy matter to be decided by the employer, whereas employee safety is a basic condition of employment subject to negotiation. Both situations were presented to PERB, and in each case the board held the union demands to be mandatory subjects.[9]

The board's efforts to grapple with the troublesome concept of mission in these and other decisions provoked criticism from the management camp. William H. Englander, a management advocate, sharply scored PERB in an article published in early 1975 subtitled "The Fog-Bound 'Mission' of the Public Employer." He took the agency to task for failing "to reflect a consistent and shared understanding of the goals of the 'mission doctrine,'" thereby leaving the parties adrift, "unable to predict the legal consequences of their conduct." He criticized PERB decisions for encouraging "artful repackaging" of union bargaining demands as in *Yorktown* and *White Plains* in order to reach nonmandatory subjects. Moreover, he questioned the logic of having a permissive category of bargaining subjects and a policy that required an employer to negotiate the impact of its decision on a nonmandatory subject: "If it disserves public policy to allow basic decisions to be made in the 'isolation of a negotiation table', shouldn't such basic decisions be prohibited subjects of bargaining?"[10]

Whether in reaction to outside critics or not, the board retreated from its earlier position that sanctioned combining mandatory and nonmandatory elements in a single proposal or demand. Thus, in *White Plains Police Benevolent Association* decided in 1976, it held that a police demand for two-man patrol cars was nonmandatory, even though it might relate to safety. The board acknowledged "inherent inconsistency" in some prior holdings such as the White Plains firefighter case and in *City of Albany and Albany Police Officers,* which also presented the issue of two-man patrol cars. Eventually, the board took the position that it would not impose the duty to bargain on demands that incorporated nonmandatory elements.[11]

COURT RULINGS ON THE DUTY TO BARGAIN

The decisions of the courts, usually in disputes arising over enforcement of collective agreements, gave a relatively broad reading to the scope of negotiations and to the duty to bargain. Public employers, of course, were free to enter into agreements on permissive subjects, and they often did. Some of these agreements occurred because many of them were less well prepared for the early rounds of negotiations than the unions were. Also, during the period when federal wage and price controls were in effect, 1971–74, the unions placed greater emphasis on nonmonetary gains, given the difficulty of achieving substantial economic benefits.[12]

At the other extreme were employers who were unshakable in their belief that many employee demands were illegal incursions on management rights. In their opinion the refusal to negotiate a particular demand was justified on the grounds of lack of specific statutory authorization or, alternatively, the existence of a law bearing on the topic in dispute. Most commonly, refusal to negotiate occurred in negotiations involving teachers and in part was attributable to advice, frequently mistaken as it turned out, emanating from the New York State School Boards Association, which took a very narrow view in those first years on how far the duty to negotiate extended. For example, the association counseled that it was unlawful to agree to binding grievance arbitration and that once the school district budget was adopted, it established the ceiling on expenditures for the year. The Court of Appeals ruling in *Huntington* in 1972 helped clear the air.[13] The court employed broad language in confirming the validity of a disputed collective agreement:

> Under the Taylor Law, the obligation to bargain as to all terms and conditions of employment is a broad and unqualified one, and there is no reason why the mandatory provision of that act should be limited, in any way, except in cases where some other applicable statutory provision explicitly and definitively prohibits the public employer from making an agreement as to a particular term or condition of employment.[14]

Subsequent court decisions elaborated on the language of *Huntington*. Although a public employer's power to bargain was not unlimited, the employer was free to negotiate on nonmandatory matters "in the absence of 'plain and clear' prohibitions in statute or controlling decisional law, or restrictive public policy."[15]

THE TRIBOROUGH DOCTRINE

What came to be called the Triborough doctrine, after *Triborough Bridge and Tunnel Authority* decided by the board in July 1972, represented a major PERB pronouncement regarding the nature of the duty to bargain.[16] Although the courts later limited its reach, the doctrine essentially survived intact until 1982, when the legislature incorporated the idea in an amendment to the law.

Triborough dealt with the question of whether an employer could unilaterally alter terms and conditions of employment, in this case by refusing to follow the longstanding practice of paying increments, after an agreement had expired but before a successor agreement had been negotiated. PERB said that it could not alter a term of employment if it involved a mandatory subject of bargaining and the employee organization did not disturb the status quo by striking. It reasoned that, as a quid pro quo for the denial of a right to strike, the union was entitled to the maintenance of the status quo. An exception was made if the employer action was essential to the continued operation of the public enterprise. In this case unilateral change was permissible so long as the employer stood ready to continue good faith negotiations on the issue.

A different rule applied with respect to nonmandatory subjects in a contract; they did not survive after the agreement expired. The parties could mutually agree to negotiate such items, but carrying a nonmandatory subject to factfinding over the objections of the other side was a violation of the duty to negotiate.[17] PERB distinguished *Triborough* from decisions of the court that had held that contract rights did not survive the expiration of a contract, as in *Poughkeepsie Board of Education,* in which the court stayed arbitration under a grievance procedure contained in an expired agreement.[18] Jerome Lefkowitz explained:

> PERB does not disagree with these decisions. It reasons that the *Triborough* doctrine is based not upon contract rights, but upon statutory language prohibiting unilateral changes in terms and conditions of employment. This statutory right sounds in improper practice and not in contract law. As such, it is within the exclusive jurisdiction of PERB. It is PERB's contention that a court could neither enforce an expired contract nor impose a duty upon an employer not to alter a previously existing term and condition of employment unilaterally. Court action could only follow action by PERB in an improper practice case.[19]

When the 1974 legislature amended the impasse procedure affecting educational employees by eliminating legislative determination as the final step (see chapter 9), PERB saw the amendment as an endorsement of its Triborough doctrine.[20] This was probably a fair assessment; however, the courts were still to present some obstacles. In *Jefferson County Board of Supervisors,* PERB suffered a setback when the Court of Appeals stated that PERB's re-

medial power was limited to entering an order to negotiate in good faith.[21] The decision temporarily foreclosed
the one substantive remedy the board had used on occasion in the past. The law was subsequently changed in
1977 to empower the board to direct "an offending party
to cease and desist from any improper practice, and to
take such affirmative action as will effectuate the policies"
of the law.[22]

Application of the Triborough doctrine was further
hedged by *Rockland County BOCES,* wherein the Court
of Appeals, "without expressing complete disapproval of
the 'Triborough Doctrine,'" nonetheless held that PERB
erred in interpreting status quo as requiring an employer
to pay customary salary increments while negotiations on
a new contract were unresolved: "To say that the status
quo must be maintained during negotiations is one thing;
to say that the status quo included a change and means an
automatic increase in salary is another."[23]

THE "TRIBOROUGH" AMENDMENT

From the perspective of the unions, PERB's status quo
policy toward expired agreements, modified at the edges
by the courts, was inadequate protection against aggressive employers. The unions claimed that employers delib-
erately prolonged negotiations beyond the term of the
contract in order to rid themselves of unwanted contract
provisions and to increase the pressure on employee negotiators. Some of the loudest complaints came from teacher
organizations that encountered school districts determined
to purge their agreements of language dealing with nonmandatory subjects such as class size or teacher evaluation
standards. Arguing that the negotiating process would be
strengthened and that equity would be served, the unions
urged legislation that would "merely" preserve the status
quo, a condition they defined differently than did PERB

and the courts. The amendment on its face was simple. It would make it an improper practice for an employer "to refuse to continue all the terms of an expired agreement until a new agreement is negotiated." Status quo would thus apply not just to mandatory subjects but also to non-mandatory subjects, arbitration clauses, increment schedules, and some other benefits.

The amendment was adopted by the legislature on the last day of the 1982 session, to the surprise of many who believed it had no chance of passage. The question remained whether Governor Carey would sign it. After all, only five years earlier, Carey had proposed major changes in the Taylor Law, at the urging of his then director of employee relations, Donald Wollett. Included in those changes was one that would have permitted a public employer to modify benefits after bargaining in good faith to a genuine impasse (see chapter 9).[24]

Invited to comment on the bill, PERB called attention to "a number of questions relating to its impact on existing legal principles enunciated by PERB and the courts and on various sections of the Taylor Law."[25] What effect would the amendment have on statutory impasse procedures that provided for final determination by the legislative body? Is a binding arbitration award in the case of police or firefighters a "negotiated agreement"? In the past PERB had held it was not; nor had it permitted nonmandatory issues to be brought to interest arbitration. Would the consequence therefore be that prior agreements on nonmandatory subjects would continue in effect indefinitely? These concerns were echoed by others such as the New York State School Boards Association, which declared that the amendment "would apparently repeal *sub silencio* some of the Taylor Law's carefully developed impasse resolution procedures."[26]

Governor Carey referred to these points in his memorandum on the bill. He also observed that it would require employers to continue all terms of an expired agreement even if employees should engage in a strike, thereby undercutting a fundamental justification for the preservation of the status quo. The memorandum itself is interesting because until the very end it reads as though it were a preamble to a veto. Yet Carey decided to approve the measure despite obvious misgivings. He explained: "Prior to my taking action on this bill, assurances were sought and received that the Senate and the Assembly will later this year pass a chapter amendment which addresses these important concerns.[27]

When the legislature convened in December in an extraordinary session, it had before it two bills amending section 209-a.1(e). The administration bill, which in addition to permitting an employer to change terms and conditions if employees struck, treated a legislative determination or an interest arbitration award as having the same effect as a negotiated agreement. The alternative, supported by the unions, dealt only with the situation of a strike. This was the measure that was adopted. Against the recommendation of Meyer Frucher, successor to Wollett, the governor approved the bill.

The Triborough amendment as it finally emerged did alter the impasse resolution procedures of the act. This became clear in *Niagara County*. Negotiations and factfinding having failed to end an impasse with CSEA, the county legislature in accordance with section 209.3(e) imposed a settlement that changed some of the terms of the expired agreement. The board found the action violative of the plain meaning of the new amendment, although Ida Klaus dissented, unpersuaded by her colleagues' reading of the legislative history. The appellate division affirmed the decision.[28]

City of Kingston offered additional evidence of the impact of the amendment, this time as it bore on interest arbitration.[29] PERB declined to process the city's petition for interest arbitration, reasoning that it would be futile to do so given that the firefighters objected to having an arbitration panel consider issues that could result in a loss of current benefits. Moreover, it was unlikely that the firefighters would participate in the proceedings lest such an action would be regarded as a waiver of objections. Finally, PERB stated that to proceed ex parte would afford the union the unfair advantage of deciding whether to be bound by an award after it was issued.

In summary, the Triborough amendment has altered to a degree the dispute resolution procedures of the Taylor Law and the power relations these procedures reflect. Tactically, the amendment has strengthened the ability of unions to resist employer demands for concessions and givebacks. But this is a short-run phenomenon. In the long run, the amendment has probably had little or no strategic effect on bargaining power relationships. After all, one assumes that over time employees desire many things of which improved wages are only the most evident. If so, tradeoffs are possible. Conceivably, the situation could change in a period of severe economic decline like the Great Depression. Short of that, however, the law does not provide an ironclad guarantee that past employee gains will be retained.

ASSESSMENT OF THE SCOPE OF BARGAINING

In judging the breadth or narrowness of the scope of the duty to bargain in the public sector, it is customary to use the private sector as a standard for comparison. On that test it can be fairly said that scope under the Taylor Law as it has evolved is also broad. To be sure, certain legislative mandates limit the scope, such as the unfettered authority of a school board to grant tenure or civil service rules regulating promotion in the competitive service. There have proved to be relatively few such rules, however. The concept of mission, which has been likened to "the core of entrepreneurial control" applied by the NLRB and courts in the private sector, has also imposed some limits, but this is an elusive and not an insurmountable standard.

Decisions bearing on subcontracting and the transfer of bargaining unit work to nonunit employees are particularly troublesome. In cases of this kind it is extremely difficult to disentangle public policy and mission concerns from terms and conditions of employment. To introduce change, an employer must demonstrate that a genuine deadlock in negotiation exists, not always easy given the Triborough amendment and the general inconclusiveness of the law's impasse procedures. Furthermore, the employer must establish that there is a "compelling need" for change. Ordinarily that has nothing to do with a judgment about relative economic efficiency but rather turns on a showing that the continued functioning of the government enterprise is at risk. Failing to meet these tests, an employer is obliged to negotiate the decision as well as the impact of the decision on terms and conditions of employment. In contrast, a private employer is free to implement a decision to subcontract after having bargained in good faith to the point of impasse. The argument has been made that the Taylor Law and the decisions of PERB reflect an acceptance of the notion that the public expects less in the way of economic efficiency from government employers.[30]

ENFORCEMENT OF CONTRACTS

The addition of improper practices to the law presented PERB with the question of what its role should be in the interpretation and enforcement of contracts. Should a breach of contract be treated as a violation of section 209.a1(d), as a refusal to negotiate in good faith? Or should the matter be deferred to grievance arbitration or to whatever other processes might be available? Conceding that it lacked general authority to enforce agreements, the board nonetheless took an interventionist position, a view most fully explicated in *Town of Orangetown*.[31] The majority of Helsby and Denson, emphasizing the disruptiveness to labor relations harmony caused by disregard for negotiated agreements, concluded that contract violations "almost invariably" constituted a unilateral change in the terms of employment and therefore a refusal to negotiate. That being so, the board would take jurisdiction except where an employer charged with unilateral action defended its conduct on a claim of contractual right and binding arbitration was available. In those circumstances PERB would defer to arbitration.

Crowley said that he would intervene only in situations in which an employer instituted a term of employment or withdrew a benefit not expressly provided for in the agreement without negotiation; otherwise, enforcement of the contract ought to be left to arbitration under the contract or to the courts. Crowley's position obtained legislative endorsement in 1977. With respect to the powers of the board, the legislature added the following proviso: "The board shall not have authority to enforce an agreement between an employer and an employee organization and shall not exercise jurisdiction over an alleged violation of such an agreement that would not otherwise constitute an improper employer or employee organization practice."[32] The later Triborough amendment was to create the anomaly of giving PERB authority to enforce expired agreements while continuing to deny it such power during the life of a contract.[33]

AGENCY FEE

The only form of union security provided for in the original Taylor Law was the dues checkoff that accompanied recognition or certification of an employee organization.

The issue of the negotiability of the agency shop was presented to PERB in *Monroe-Woodbury Teachers Association*.[34] PERB concluded that because employees were protected by statute in the right to refrain from participating in an employee organization, the agency shop was a prohibited subject of negotiation, a decision affirmed at the appellate division.[35] By the same reasoning, a maintenance of membership clause was also illegal.[36] Consequently, the agency shop became a high-priority issue on the legislative agenda of the unions.

The agency shop had been endorsed by study committees such as the joint select legislative committee in 1969 and the Fleischmann Commission on Education in 1973 as a device for stabilizing labor relations and deterring strikes. Nonetheless, it remained too controversial an issue. By 1977 the climate had changed and Governor Carey announced support for making the agency shop subject to negotiation, as one part of a package of changes. But because several elements in his omnibus measure were totally unacceptable to the unions, the entire package was suspect. The unions in the meantime had acquired some new friends on the Republican side, notably Warren Anderson, the majority leader of the Senate. AFSCME District Council 37 for one had conscientiously tried to cultivate the Republicans through occasional legislative endorsements and campaign contributions, and Anderson appreciated the favors.[37] A result was a separate bill sponsored by the Republican leadership that went further than the governor's proposal by making the agency fee mandatory for state employees. It passed both chambers by a comfortable margin, and Carey approved it.

The new section 208.3 imposed conditions regulating the collection and use of the agency fee that were in keeping with the constitutional limitations set forth by the U.S. Supreme Court in *Abood v. Detroit Board of Education* decided the same year.[38] Employee organizations were required to have a procedure in place for refunding to an objecting nonmember any part of the agency fee "which represents the employee's pro rata share of expenditures by the organization in aid of activities or causes of a political or ideological nature only incidentally related to terms and conditions of employment."

Ever since the addition of section 208.3, a steady stream of improper practice charges challenging agency fee arrangements has been directed to PERB, most of them originating with disaffected professional employees in SUNY or the public schools. Two very determined SUNY professors, Thomas Barry and Morris Eson, have alone accounted for a sizable portion of the case filings.[39]

In deciding agency fee cases, PERB has confined itself to a review of the adequacy of the procedures established and maintained by unions in processing claims for refunds. It has studiously avoided passing on the propriety of union expenditures or on the proper amount of a refund, on the grounds that it lacked jurisdiction. PERB explained its stance in *Hampton Bays Teachers Association*:

> There is logic to the distinction made by the Legislature between the structure of the refund process which is subject to PERB's jurisdiction and the precise amount of a refund which is not. The latter involves a question of civil liability of the type that is traditionally resolved by courts in civil litigation while the former involves the area of organizational conduct that is traditionally committed to the jurisdiction of labor relations agencies. The right to a refund in a particular amount is analogous to the right to a particular benefit in a collectively negotiated agreement. The Legislature has distinguished between the duty to negotiate in good faith, which is a process, and the obligation to comply with the terms of an agreement, which involves substantive rights. Failure to participate in the process is an improper practice that is subject to the jurisdiction of this Board, but, to prevent this Board from going further than inquiring into the process, in L. 1977, c.429, the Legislature provided that this Board:

"shall not exercise jurisdiction over an alleged violation of such an agreement that would not otherwise constitute an improper . . . practice."[40]

The courts have deferred to PERB's interpretation of its jurisdiction.[41]

PERB's conservative reading of its jurisdiction in agency fee matters contrasts with its assertiveness on other subjects. *Realpolitik* would seem to dictate restraint. An enlarged, more vigorous role would almost certainly bring PERB into conflict with the unions but without offsetting benefits in that public employers in general have no great stake in the dispute. Recent decisions by the U.S. Supreme Court in *Ellis* and *Hudson,* which articulated additional standards if an agency fee arrangement was to survive constitutional challenge, have presented PERB with fresh problems.[42]

As part of a reexamination of the matter, PERB asked Richard Briffault of Columbia University Law School to prepare an analysis of the New York law in light of the Supreme Court decisions. Although he did not advise a particular course of action, Briffault did question PERB's approach.

> PERB has hitherto taken the position that while it may pass on the structure of a union's internal refund procedures it lacks jurisdiction to review the accuracy of the refund itself. However, in this area substance and procedure are closely intertwined. *Hudson*'s procedures flow directly from the substantive rights at stake, and part of the procedure required by the Constitution is an independent substantive determination by an impartial decision-maker prior to a union's use of contested fee payments. A contested agency fee payment is not really analogous to a contested benefit under a collective agreement—the analogy PERB has drawn in justifying its non-involvement in the review of the correctness of refunds. There is neither a statutory nor a constitutional interest in determining whether a particular benefit is paid or not paid;

it is entirely a matter of private agreement between the employee and the union. By contrast, as *Ellis* and *Hudson* demonstrate there is a significant constitutional interest in whether a particular expense is properly charged to a non-member and in the procedures for considering a non-member's refund claim.[43]

Briffault concluded:

> *Ellis* and *Hudson* remind us that the agency shop fee deduction cannot be considered an internal union matter. . . . [They] put the burden on the state to develop and implement effectively substantive standards and procedures for notice and hearing which adequately vindicate non-members' constitutional rights.[44]

The paper served as a focus for a symposium held by the board in September 1986. Any interested party wishing to be heard (or to hear) was invited. The message coming from the union contingent, the largest segment of the attendees, was almost without exception that PERB should not get involved in the substantive issues of agency fee. To date that is the course the board continues to follow.

DUTY OF FAIR REPRESENTATION

Conflict between individual and collective rights and interests so evident in agency fee disputes also arises in cases concerning the duty of fair representation. The close link between the two was noted by Harold Newman, who observed that the increase in duty of fair representation litigation coincided with the 1977 authorization of the agency fee. Newman wrote,

> Persons who do not pay for services rendered may content themselves to accept contractual benefits without question. The imposition of a charge for that service, however, has a natural tendency to increase the level of expectation, and that which may have been acceptable when free is satisfactory no longer.[45]

PERB has in its rulings generally followed private sector standards in defining the duty of fair representation.

CONCLUSION

PERB has displayed a predilection for active involvement in regulating collective negotiations, an exception being in the area of agency fee matters. In general, it has come down on the side of an enlarged scope of bargaining and of closer regulation of the negotiating process. PERB's interventionist tendencies have usually received support from the courts and, if not there, from the legislature. The evolution of the Triborough concept from board decision through legislative amendment is a case in point. On balance, the performance of PERB as a regulator of the bargaining process has been more widely approved within the labor community than by public management.

NOTES

1. Interview with Martin L. Barr, 24 June 1986. Data on the timeliness of PERB's handling of improper practice charges are reported in a study conducted by two academic researchers, Norma Riccucci and Carolyn Ban, in "The Unfair Labor Practice Process in Dispute-Resolution Technique in the Public Sector," 64–65.
2. *Final Report,* 31 March 1966, 18, 45–46.
3. The recommendation was included in sec. 205.5(g) of the law, and PERB did commission two reports, one by Irving Sabghir of SUNY, Albany, entitled *The Scope of Bargaining in the Public Sector* (1970), the other, *Determining the Scope of Negotiations under Public Employment Relations Statutes* (1971), done by two Cornell University law professors, Kurt L. Hanslowe and Walter E. Oberer.
4. *Borg-Warner Corp. v. NLRB,* 356 U.S. 342 (1958).
5. 4 PERB 3060.
6. Ibid.
7. 4 PERB 3070; 6 PERB 7010.
8. 4 PERB 3070.

9. *Yorktown Faculty Association*, 7 PERB 3030; *City of White Plains*, 5 PERB 3008.

10. Englander, "Scope of the Duty to Bargain under the Taylor Law," 4.

11. *White Plains Police Benevolent Association*, 9 PERB 3007; *City of Albany and Albany Police Officers*, 7 PERB 3132; see, for example, *Town of Haverstraw*, 11 PERB 3109.

12. Helsby, "Scope of Bargaining under the Taylor Law," 15.

13. *Board of Education, Union Free School District No. 3 of Town of Huntington*, 5 PERB 7507.

14. Ibid.

15. *Yonkers City School District*, 9 PERB 7519.

16. 5 PERB 3037.

17. *Board of Higher Education of the City of New York*, 7 PERB 3028. In a similar case a few years later, member Ida Klaus dissented. For her, it was not enough that the union continued to press its demand; rather, it had to be established that the union made acceptance of its demand a precondition for any agreement before the improper practice could be sustained. *Monroe-Woodbury Teachers*, 10 PERB 3029.

18. 6 PERB 7518.

19. Lefkowitz, "The Duty to Negotiate under the Taylor Law," 5.

20. *PERB News* (July–August 1974).

21. 8 PERB 7008.

22. Sec. 205.5(d), amended chap. 429, L. 1977.

23. 10 PERB 7010. The original *Triborough* case had also revolved around the payment of increments but was never challenged in court.

24. Memorandum on governor's program bill, 10 March 1977.

25. Memorandum to John G. McGoldrick, counsel to the governor, 16 July 1982, PERB Files.

26. Quoted in *Niagara County Legislature*, 16 PERB 3071.

27. Governor's memorandum of approval, 29 July 1982.

28. 16 PERB 3071; 17 PERB 7021.

29. 18 PERB 3036.

30. The argument is developed in greater detail in Donovan and Orr, *Subcontracting in the Public Sector.* A recent expression of PERB's policy can be found in *West Irondequoit Teachers Association*, 20 PERB 3064.

31. 8 PERB 3042.

32. Sec. 205.5(d).

33. See, for example, *Fulton-Montgomery Community College*, 16 PERB 4561.

34. 3 PERB 3104.

35. 6 PERB 7009.
36. 5 PERB 3021.
37. Bellush and Bellush, *Union Power and New York,* 264–65.
38. 431 U.S. 209 (1977).
39. Their negotiating representative, United University Professions, initially calculated the rebate due protesting agency fee payers at 76 cents on annual dues that ran as high as $250. More recently, the UUP rebate has been approximately 3 percent of dues.
40. 14 PERB 3018.
41. *Bodanza v. PERB,* 19 PERB 7010.
42. *Ellis v. Railway Clerks,* 466 U.S. 435 (1984); *Chicago Teachers Union v. Hudson,* 106 S. Ct. 1066 (1986).
43. Briffault, *The New York Agency Shop Fee and the Constitution,* 50–51.
44. Ibid.
45. Newman, "The Duty in the Public Sector," 87–88.

9
DISPUTE RESOLUTION
AND STRIKES

WITH THE STRIKE OUTLAWED, alternative procedures for resolving negotiation disputes assume extra importance. In the original design the Taylor Law emphasized mediation and factfinding as the chief tools for achieving negotiated settlements, leaving undisturbed the ultimate authority of the legislative body to act as final arbiter in the event a dispute persisted. The hope of the framers of the law was that legislative intervention would be needed only infrequently and that when it was required it would be exercised in a fair, evenhanded fashion. The role of the legislative body has since been significantly diminished by statutory amendments. In the case of school disputes, the legislative hearing was eliminated; for impasses involving police and fire personnel, interest arbitration became the terminal step in the procedure. These changes came in 1974. Moreover, the Triborough amendment of 1982 made further inroads on legislative authority where other public employees were at impasse. What was at the beginning a single, undifferentiated impasse procedure has therefore become three distinct procedures. Furthermore, other changes in dispute resolution procedures have occurred as a result of PERB's administration of the law.

RECORD ON DISPUTE SETTLEMENT

How well has the Taylor Law fared in achieving one of its · major goals—the resolution of bargaining stalemates without strikes? Before attempting an answer, it is necessary to point to some inadequacies in the basic data. Although PERB has probably done as much if not more than any other state labor relations agency in the nation in collecting and reporting on its activities, the data still present problems. For one, no accurate figures exist on the size of the New York public sector universe. The U.S. Census Bureau figure on state and local government employment (full and part time) in New York in October 1986 was 1.2 million workers, exceeded only by California.[1] What proportion of these workers are actually represented in negotiating units is unknown, although an estimate of 1 million seems not unreasonable. PERB has made a conscientious effort in recent years to develop estimates of the number of negotiating units and of the number of contracts open for negotiation in any given year. For 1988–89, the respective figures were 3,695 and 2,497.[2] Another complication in data analysis stems from changes made by PERB in reporting periods and in its reporting methods. These cautions noted, we examine the available data.

Table 9.1 shows data on the number of impasses brought to PERB and their disposition. The peak—972 cases—came in 1975. Since then, the number has been in the 500-plus range. In three years—1975, 1976, and 1978—half of all negotiations went to impasse, in contrast to 30 percent or less in most other years. The time lag between the intake and disposition of cases is especially notable in the figures for 1977. Clearly the mid- to late 1970s was a difficult period for bargainers, who had to confront severe financial problems at state and local government levels coupled with sharply rising inflation.

TABLE 9.1. Impasse Cases Received and Closed by PERB and Method of Settlement, 1967–1989

Reporting Period	New Cases	Cases Closed	Method of Settlement				
			Mediation or Factfinding without Report	Factfinding Report Accepted or Modified	Post-Factfinding Conciliation	Arbitration	Other Reasons[a]
1967–68	300	300 (est.)	n/a				
1968–69 (15 mos.)	665	635	309	286[b]	n/a		40 (6%)
1970	758	630	434 (69%)	196 (31%)	n/a		
1971	755	777	463 (60%)	314 (40%)	n/a		
1972	839	828	517 (62%)	311 (38%)	n/a		
1973	743	801	533 (67%)	268 (33%)	n/a		
1974	788	711	459 (65%)	192 (27%)	55 (8%)		
1975	972	892	514 (58%)	277 (31%)	69 (8%)	29 (3%)	
1976	859	693	370 (53%)	236 (34%)	57 (7%)	40 (6%)	
1977–78 (15 mos.)	817	1024	567 (55%)	341 (33%)	77 (8%)	44 (4%)	

1978–79	788	843	468 (56%)	246 (29%)	97 (12%)	32 (4%)	
1979–80	583	651	380 (58%)	159 (14%)	64 (10%)	48 (7%)	
1980–81	700	567	328 (58%)	154 (27%)	35 (6%)	18 (3%)	
1981–82	608	692	431 (62%)	171 (25%)	53 (8%)	37 (5%)	
1982–83	645	631	422 (67%)	154 (24%)	35 (6%)	20 (3%)	
1983–84	651	684	424 (62%)	178 (26%)	50 (7%)	24 (4%)	
1984–85	566	541	365 (67%)	105 (19%)	37 (7%)	22 (4%)	12 (2%)
1985–86	540	610	373 (61%)	130 (21%)	39 (6%)	23 (4%)	45 (7%)
1986–87	580	534	325 (61%)	115 (22%)	22 (4%)	15 (3%)	57 (11%)
1987–88	511	547	371 (68%)	85 (15%)	25 (5%)	24 (4%)	42 (8%)
1988–89	566	476	322 (68%)	78 (16%)	19 (4%)	12 (3%)	45 (9%)

Source: PERB annual reports.

Note: PERB has altered the manner in which it records the disposition of impasses. Since 1974, however, the system has remained essentially the same.

[a]Includes cases in which the parties filed a declaration of impasse but settled without third-party assistance and arbitration cases that were settled without an award.

[b]A fact finder was appointed; not known whether report was issued.

These difficulties were mirrored in the decline in the proportion of disputes settled short of the issuance of a fact-finding report. More recent data disclose not only less reliance on PERB for assistance but also, as in the earliest period, the renewed effectiveness of less intrusive methods of dispute settlement. Whether this is a sign of growing labor-management maturity or of an improved economic climate remains to be seen.

THE STRIKE RECORD

Between September 1967 and January 1989, there were 313 strikes by New York public employees (see table 9.2). The dramatic falloff in the number of strikes since 1981 corresponds with a return to a more robust state economy. A comparison of New York's experience with that of other states is difficult because of fundamental differences among the states. On the one hand, New York probably has many more bargaining units than any other state and therefore a greater potential for bargaining disputes. Further, when strikes do occur in New York the number of workers involved tends to be higher. On the other hand, state public policies toward the strike vary significantly. For example, most Pennsylvania public employees may legally strike, and that they do so often should surprise no one. Other states, Michigan being the best example, have followed what in effect is a policy of a de facto right to strike.[3]

Qualifications aside, New York accounted for approximately 5 percent or 279 of the 5,410 work stoppages occurring among state and local government employees in the period from 1968 through 1980, the last year the Bureau of Labor Statistics (BLS) compiled such data. The year 1980 may be taken as fairly representative of the period. In that year New York ranked seventh in strike frequency with 21 stoppages, according to BLS. (PERB

TABLE 9.2. Summary of Work Stoppages by Public Employees and Penalties, New York State, 1967–1988

| Year | Strikes | Approx. No. of Workers | Approx. Workdays | Approx. Worker-Days Idle | Penalties | | |
					2 Days' Pay for Each Strike Day[a]	Dues Checkoff Suspension[b]	Penalties for Contempt of Court[c]
1967	2	49,527	33	644,040	—	1	1
1968	26	72,778	142	1,997,519	—	12	6
1969	13	2,138	50	6,722	5	5	1
1970	31	7,103	109	29,631	17	22	6
1971	22	45,055	96	207,282	15	13	1
1972	27	15,815	141	60,426	19	15	7
1973	17	4,494	110	28,213	8	7	4
1974	17	4,181	82	19,462	14	11	2
1975	33	77,755	222	394,423	28	24	7
1976	15	25,549	149	139,448	15	14	8
1977	16	5,702	106	56,301	15	16	4
1978	18	3,930	82	33,441	17	13	3
1979	21	12,979	115	90,000	17	11	2
1980	23	41,000	89	400,000	18	15	3
1981	16	2,032	103	16,033	13	10	2

(continued on next page)

TABLE 9.2. Summary of Work Stoppages by Public Employees and Penalties, New York State, 1967–1988 *(continued)*

					Penalties		
Year	Strikes	Approx. No. of Workers	Approx. Workdays	Approx. Worker-Days Idle	2 Days' Pay for Each Strike Day[a]	Dues Checkoff Suspension[b]	Penalties for Contempt of Court[c]
1982	4	1,350	26	10,733	4	4	1
1983	0	0	0	0	0	0	0
1984	2	83	40	765	0	2	0
1985	1	296	4	1,183	1	1	1
1986	3	209	5	359	3	2	0
1987	2	180	2	180	1	0	0
1988	4	345	3	95	0	0	0
22	313	372,501	1,709	4,136,256	210	198	59

[a]Once in 1974 and again in 1975, a lump sum fine against the union was accepted as the sole penalty for the strike. The amounts of the fines were $35,000 and $60,000. During the entire period, there was "information not available" in seventeen cases.
[b]There was "information not available" in four cases.
[c]There was "information not available" in three cases.

reported 23 for the year. It was surpassed by Pennsylvania (82), Michigan (75), Ohio (60), Illinois (51), California (51), and New Jersey (50). The first four states almost always outranked New York during the 1970s. On workdays lost to strikes, however, New York typically ranked higher because of its larger bargaining units. In 1980 it was fourth in lost time, primarily because of a lengthy strike by subway workers.[4]

STRIKE PENALTIES

The relatively low number of strikes in New York is clearly attributable to the statutory penalties of the Taylor Law, which have generally been enforced. A comparative study by Craig Olson has provided strong statistical evidence to support that conclusion.[5] The 1969 requirement that public employers deduct two days' pay for each day an employee has engaged in a strike acts as a powerful deterrent to the extent that a prospective striker can anticipate that the penalty will be applied. PERB data indicate that the two-for-one penalty has been enforced about 80 percent of the time. The exceptions have most commonly occurred in situations in which the stoppage was brief or partial, often wildcat strikes. On a few occasions the penalty was set aside because of procedural defects in its application or because there was a question that a strike actually occurred. Municipalities have tended to be more lax in enforcement than school districts. On balance, however, the two-for-one penalty has been applied with sufficient regularity to give it real meaning.

One aspect of the two-for-one penalty that has drawn special criticism has to do with the allocation of the fines collected from strikers. For example, a school district might actually "profit" from a strike: tax revenues and state aid continue to flow in, fines are collected, and meanwhile salary expenditures are reduced. Some neutral observers believe that in some instances this anomaly has contributed to prolonging strikes. But despite some complaints, there has been no concerted effort to change the law.

Enforcement of a second strike penalty, the suspension of dues deduction privileges, presents a somewhat different picture. Since 1967 the penalty has been applied in two-thirds of all strike situations. Matters are complicated because responsibility for its enforcement lies with PERB except where a local government has established a mini-PERB. In these circumstances the courts have authority in the first instance to order dues forfeiture if a union is found in contempt of a court order brought under section 211. In the case of New York City and the Office of Collective Bargaining, no such penalty will result should the court decline to impose the sanction because OCB lacks that authority under its law. Among the other mini-PERBs few have chosen to impose forfeiture, whereas PERB has generally been consistent in its application of the penalty. PERB has not suspended dues in instances when there was doubt concerning union responsibility, as in wildcat or unauthorized stoppages, or when there were mitigating factors, such as an employer's extreme provocation. Suspensions have been for anywhere from three months to an indefinite period (ordinarily eighteen to twenty-four months) depending on such considerations as the length of the stoppage, its impact on the public health and safety, and whether the union had previously struck.

Disparity in enforcement of the penalty between organizations under PERB jurisdiction and those within the orbit of a mini-PERB has resulted in extensive litigation. The issue first surfaced in 1976 in a case involving the United Federation of Teachers.[6] In a footnote the board stated its concern "that the administrative machinery provided by the law does not insure a standard of evenhandedness in the imposition of the statutory penalty of forfeiture of dues deduction privileges." Nonetheless, the board concluded that it lacked discretion to correct the inequity and that the problem needed to be addressed by the legislature. At the same time, the board left the door open to early restoration of the checkoff. In reargument of the case a month later, the UFT raised the constitutional claim of denial of equal protection under the law, a position not fully resolved until the U.S. Court of Appeals rejected it in *Shanker v. Helsby,* decided in 1982.[7]

The Buffalo Teachers Federation employed the same argument when it went into U.S. District Court to obtain an order against imposition of dues forfeiture.[8] Judge Marvin Frankel, after comparing the enforcement record of PERB and OCB, found that there was sufficient merit in the claim to justify a preliminary injunction. A few months later another judge of the same court faced with a parallel claim reached the contrary conclusion.[9] As with the UFT, the Buffalo teachers lost at the U.S. Court of Appeals.[10] The Frankel decision, however, was enough to cause PERB to initiate a court challenge of the substantial equivalence of OCB's procedures, much to the dismay of Arvid Anderson, who urged Helsby to drop the case. It was not dropped, but PERB chose not to press for a decision.[11]

The administration of the dues forfeiture penalty has presented another question for PERB: are there circumstances that would warrant the restoration of the checkoff privilege before the period of forfeiture has run its course? That issue was brought to the board by District Council 82, AFSCME, following a long strike by state corrections personnel.[12] The union argued that the criterion of financial resources should substantially mitigate the length of any suspension. The geographic dispersion of the bargaining unit and the multiple work shifts made direct collection of dues extraordinarily difficult. Further, some officers of the local were of the opinion that only 10 to 20 percent of unit members would pay dues if there were no checkoff. The board rejected the argument as conjecture and premature, and it imposed an eighteen-month suspension. At the same time, the board indicated that it would consider a petition for resumption of the checkoff should the union experience financial incapacity to perform its statutory duty of representing unit employees after having made good faith efforts to collect dues by alternative methods. The board reasoned that if the union was so impoverished as to be unable to fulfill its statutory duty, the result would be de facto deauthorization, a penalty specifically rejected by the legislature when it adopted the Taylor Law.[13]

The UFT case was the first in which PERB restored the checkoff ahead of time.[14] There the union was able to demonstrate that its income had declined by 30 percent despite attempts at alternative ways of collecting dues and in consequence it had been compelled to reduce substantially its level of service to unit members. Similar outcomes occurred in cases affecting the Transport Workers Union and the Amalgamated Transit Union.[15]

Criticism of the board's position on dues restoration has generally been muted, although an editorial writer from the *New York Daily News* referred to the "weepy-eyed Board." Still one senses some discomfort with a seemingly contradictory application of the penalty. Harold Newman defends the decisions: "I realize that's a hard sell. It takes more time and attention before a person's finally persuaded than most people are able to give to the issue. All they know is that the big fish got away and the little fish didn't. But that's not true."[16]

Indeed, if Newman were to have his way, PERB would have no role whatsoever in administering the checkoff penalty and the matter would be left to the courts. He has frequently expressed his opinion that an agency that depends heavily on its reputation for impartiality in labor-management affairs should not be saddled with responsibility for punishing unions. Any such relief is unlikely to come. Instead, PERB has sought a more modest change that would relieve it of the prosecutorial function it now has. It has sponsored a bill that would make it the duty of the chief legal officer of the affected public employer to bring charges to the board instead of requiring PERB's counsel to do so. Even if that measure were to be adopted, the issue of disparate treatment would remain.

Strikers are also exposed to possible individual fines and jail sentences of up to thirty days and their organizations to fines should they defy court orders against striking. Data compiled by PERB show that penalties for contempt of court have been assessed in about one of every five strikes, most often in the form of organizational fines. Accurate information is lacking on the extent to which the contempt penalties initially levied were in fact ultimately applied. It has not been uncommon for judges to impose fines and jail sentences only to modify or suspend them later. For example, the fine against Council 82, AFSCME, for the 1979 prison guard strike exceeded $4 million by strike's end but was eventually reduced to $150,000.[17] Even though the law mandates that the chief legal officer of the government employer apply forthwith for injunctive relief, frequently this has not been done because the employers believed that an injunction would only delay getting the workers back on the job. For similar reasons, judges, at least in some instances, have chosen to move slowly on motions for injunctive relief. Overall, among the array of sanctions available to deal with illegal work stoppages, recourse to judicial processes has proven to be of lesser importance.

ADMINISTERING SECTION 209

The Taylor committee was mindful of the "pitfalls" of a statutorily prescribed impasse procedure that was unlikely to be appropriate to all circumstances and that also might induce overreliance to the point of discouraging genuine give and take among the parties.[18] Accordingly, the committee urged parties to create their own systems, advice that went largely unheeded. Instead, the parties came to rely on the statutory procedures of section 209, even though they tended to approach disputes mechanistically by setting forth precise time limits for each impasse step in order to coordinate collective negotiations with the budget-making process of government. The law defined an impasse as the absence of an agreement 60 days before the budget submission date (later changed to 120 days before the end of the fiscal year) and prescribed the timing of mediation, factfinding, and each successive step in the procedure.

It was not long before the exigencies of administering the dispute settlement scheme made it apparent that adherence to the formal requirements of the law was often impractical. The heavy volume of disputes, seasonal variations in caseload, and, above all, its own pragmatism resulted in PERB paying less attention to the time limits specified in the statute. Substance was to triumph over form, an approach supported by the court in an early test. In 1968, when the city of Schenectady challenged PERB's authority to enter a dispute after the budget submission date, the judge sustained PERB's action, stating that section 209 "must be given a construction which does not render PERB powerless when an impasse does in fact exist."[19]

Another significant procedural modification came a few years later when PERB discontinued its practice of first appointing a mediator in all impasse situations in favor of combining the mediation and factfinding functions in a single appointment of a fact finder or mediator/fact finder. The change was motivated in part by budgetary considerations, but primarily it reflected the belief that mediation as a separate step was declining in effectiveness. Although other issues were also involved, one measure of the change was the reduction in the ratio of appointments per impasse from 1.7 to 1.2.[20] Thus the Taylor committee's concerns about the inflexibility of statutory procedures were less of a problem in practice.

Responsibility for administering the dispute settlement procedures rests with PERB's conciliation division, composed of ten or so full-time professionals. This staff is used mostly in mediation, in strike or potential strike situations, and in special projects such as fostering of labor-management committees. Permanent staff occasionally do factfinding, but such assignments are chosen carefully insofar as fact finders leave a trail of written recommendations that in time may diminish their acceptability.[21] Moreover, a factfinding report issued by a PERB staff mediator may be construed by some to be the "official" position of the agency.

The bulk of PERB's third-party assistance to disputants is provided by members of its panel of mediators and fact finders or by its separate panel of arbitrators. From the beginning PERB recognized that the volume of requests for assistance would overwhelm the capacity of its small staff, especially during periods such as the summer when school negotiations are at their peak. Initially, PERB drew from existing lists of arbitrators for its panel. Soon individuals from widely varying backgrounds were recruited, few of whom possessed firsthand experience in mediating labor disputes. Academics were the single largest source of new panel members, but lawyers, private sector employee relations people, retired government employees, and others were also enlisted. The inexperience of many of these individuals was partially mitigated in that they were frequently dealing with parties who themselves were novices. As the advocates acquired a measure of sophistication, so too did the new panelists. Through a winnowing process of trial and error and accumulating experience, the level of professionalism among the panelists has increased. Currently there are about 250 persons on the active roster. Erwin Kelly classifies them roughly as "reliables," "now and thens," and "names" or "superstars." The last group, numbering about forty, includes individuals who only occasionally are willing to take on a case and whom PERB tends to use in more difficult or visible disputes. Most of the assignments go to the "reliables," the 160 or so panelists who usually are available and do a creditable job.[22]

PERB makes use of ad hoc mediators much more extensively than does any other state labor relations agency, a circumstance that has occasioned some questioning and mild criticism within the professional community. In the early days Robert Howlett, venerable chairman of the Michigan Public Employment Relations Commission, would get after his friend Bob Helsby for using per diem mediators and for allowing fact finders to mediate. Howlett firmly believed that the distinction between mediation and factfinding and between the respective province of staff mediators and ad hoc neutrals had to be maintained. There are also critics who believe that mediation in New York has always been less effective than in other jurisdictions because of the reliance on less experienced part-timers. In that no useful comparative data exist, this conclusion seems to rest more on intuition than on empirical evidence. A lower settlement rate at mediation, if it does exist, can be more plausibly explained by the statutory mandate of factfinding (with few exceptions) and consequently the diminished importance of the mediation step and that the cost of both dispute procedures are borne by the state, which places New York in a class by itself. Moreover, one would expect the effectiveness of mediation to be related directly to the final step in the impasse procedure and most effective when the alternative is costly, as with either a de jure or a de facto right to strike.

PERB has devoted considerable effort to developing the understanding, skills, and loyalty of the ad hoc panel through regular communications and annual training sessions. For many years a major vehicle was the monthly newsletter *PERB Bulletin,* which reported changes in the law and recent bargaining settlements. The lead item in each issue was a message from the director of conciliation, Harold Newman, under the heading "The Cloudy Crystal Ball." Besides affording him an opportunity to indulge his wit and penchant for literary allusion, from the Greeks and Romans to the moderns, Newman in avuncular style would exhort panel members to keep in mind that the primary objective was to fashion a settlement acceptable to the parties.

As another example of PERB's professional development activity, the agency has conscientiously sought to recruit women and minority mediators and fact finders. In 1974 and again on two other occasions, PERB conducted extensive training programs for that purpose. Affirmative action in recruiting has not been limited to these formal programs, although the programs have yielded twenty minority members for the active roster.[23]

In the first few years more than half of the impasses brought to PERB were settled at mediation. Some of that success is explainable by the newness of negotiations and a corresponding innocence on the part of some of the negotiators which often led them to accord special deference to the mediator, "the outside expert." Fact finders too tended to benefit from these attitudes. Neutrals oftentimes performed a valuable missionary function in educating the parties to the procedures and practice of collective negotiations. But the age of innocence passed and economic conditions changed, and with these changes the relationship between negotiators and outsiders was altered.

When mediation and factfinding failed to achieve settlement, PERB was empowered "to take whatever steps it deems appropriate to resolve the dispute," a step that came to be called "superconciliation." Though foreclosed from imposing a settlement, PERB could conduct further mediation, hold public hearings, or do just about anything else that might in its judgment move the parties closer to agreement. For PERB, superconciliation presents a formidable test of its understanding of the dynamics of a dispute, its own imagination, and its persuasive powers. A variety of techniques have been employed, some of them unavailing, others marvelously successful. A 1975 strike by Orchard Park teachers provides an example of the latter.

The strike had gone on for three weeks and negotiations had come to a halt as the school board refused to meet unless the teachers returned to work. PERB convened a public meeting at the local Catholic Church that attracted an overflow crowd in excess of one thousand two hundred persons. With Jerry Lefkowitz of PERB presiding, the audience heard from spokesmen for both sides and from five representatives of the community. The *Buffalo Evening News* reported, "If either side had hoped for an overwhelming community endorsement of their stand, they did not appear to get it, judging from the applause and the words of five speakers." Faced with this show of community anger at the continuing stalemate, the parties were forced to resume negotiations immediately following the meeting, this time, in ecumenical fashion, at the Presbyterian Church under the supervision of staff mediator Mark Beecher. Talks continued until 8:00 P.M. the next day and again over the weekend before an agreement was reached.[24] Public hearings have not always been so successful; on occasion no one has shown up.

THE IMPASSE PROCEDURES ARE CHANGED

In 1974 the state legislature made two important changes in the law's procedures for dispute resolution. The first change applied to employees in school districts and other educational institutions. It eliminated the authority of a legislative body to resolve an impasse, substituting instead a proviso that "the legislative body may take such action as is necessary and appropriate to reach an agreement." The second change established compulsory arbitration as the final step for impasses involving local government police officers and firefighters.

It was about this time, 1974, that Robert Helsby was actively promoting what he labeled the "three-choice system" of arbitration in teacher disputes under which, when factfinding failed, a tripartite panel would be empowered to choose among the final offers of the employer, the teachers, or the recommendation of the fact finder. The concept found no favor among unions or employers and thus went nowhere. According to Helsby, however, it was his testimony before the New York Legislature that persuaded the state of Iowa to adopt the idea for its own law.[25]

The amendment affecting educational employees came as a recommendation from a task force appointed by Governor Malcolm Wilson that included representation from NYSUT and the New York State School Boards Association. It addressed a problem long complained about by teachers and other school employees, namely, that in school settings the presumed separation of powers between the executive and legislative branches was pure fiction. The superintendent of schools, as chief executive officer and public employer for purposes of negotiations under the law, was in fact an employee of the board of education and served as its agent in negotiations. Furthermore, board members often sat on the negotiating team for the employer. Consequently, employees were indirectly, or even directly, negotiating with the legislative body that also acted as final arbiter in the event of a stalemate.

Also, some school boards were none too keen about exercising the power given them in the Taylor Law, a conclusion supported by a study conducted by PERB of legislative hearings in the schools during 1970 and 1971. The study identified 103 cases in which a legislative hearing was held, in 72 of which a decision was issued. What those bald facts did not disclose was that negotiations usually continued before, during, and after the hearings, whether or not employees had struck or threatened to do so, and that a negotiated agreement had been reached in more than 90 percent of all the cases taken to hearing.[26]

Although some might puzzle over the vagueness of the new section 209.3(f), PERB had no such difficulties. In *PERB News* Jerome Lefkowitz and Harold Newman wrote, "Whatever ambiguities there are in the statutory language, we believe that any reading and careful analysis of the amendment makes unmistakably clear that the legislature wished to insure *bilateral* agreement."[27] They went on to caution school negotiators not to expect PERB to engage in post-factfinding conciliation in each and every case. Rather, they emphasized that the agency would continue to exercise flexibility in dispute settlement.

Governor Wilson's aspirations were a factor in the enactment of both the school and police and fire amendments. Having recently succeeded Nelson Rockefeller, who had resigned to become the nation's vice-president, Wilson very much wanted to be elected governor in his own right in the 1974 election. To bolster his relations with the unions and to overcome a reputation as an arch-conservative, he gave full support to the amendments, and they passed easily. Whatever appreciation NYSUT may have felt for the governor's assistance, it did not last until the election, for NYSUT in a surprise move endorsed Hugh Carey. The police and fire unions, however, remained loyal to Wilson.

COMPULSORY ARBITRATION IS ADOPTED

Achievement of compulsory arbitration for police and fire personnel culminated a continuing campaign by the state firefighters. Since 1968 they had annually submitted bills calling for last best offer arbitration but had been stymied by Ray Corbett and the state AFL-CIO, which viewed compulsory arbitration as anathema.[28] Corbett finally relented and approved a draft prepared by Ludwig Jaffe, the research director of the state federation, that provided for arbitration by a tripartite panel, a method that could be portrayed as a mere continuation of collective bargaining. With AFL-CIO opposition withdrawn, the firefighters' bill was adopted unanimously by the legislature late in the 1974 session. According to Robert Gollnick, president of the New York State Firefighters' Association, the measure passed so quickly that "legislators didn't know what they were voting for," testimony to the political clout of fire and police unions.[29] The New York State Police Conference immediately followed suit with a bill of its own. The speed of these actions caught the Conference of Mayors completely off guard so that strong employer opposition was not communicated until the bill was on the governor's desk. Wilson, in disregard of the advice of his Office of Employee Relations and Division of the Budget, both of which had recommended a veto, approved the measures.

The separate bills, one covering firefighters, the other police, were identical in all other respects. Due to expire in three years, each was "experimental." Arbitration could be invoked by either negotiating party after mediation and factfinding. The arbitration panel was to consist of one member chosen by each side plus a mutually selected public member who would act as chairman. PERB would provide a list of qualified public members if the parties could not agree on a public member and would bear the cost for a public member chosen from its list; otherwise, the cost was the responsibility of the parties. An award by a majority of the panel was binding. Although the law enumerated criteria, arbitrators were not obliged to consider them; judicial review of awards was not mentioned.

Compulsory arbitration was a significant departure from two fundamental principles expressed by the Taylor committee, the belief that all public services were by definition essential and the conviction that the supremacy of the legislative body must be preserved. The first principle was undercut by singling out police and fire services for different treatment. The second more profound change, however, was the acknowledgment of an exception to the overriding principle of legislative supremacy, that there were circumstances when the authority of elected representatives should give way to the determination of public policy by private parties.

Several municipalities challenged the constitutionality of the law, asserting inter alia that it constituted an infringement on home rule principles, that it improperly delegated legislative power to private persons, including the power to tax, and that it violated the principle of one person, one vote. All of these arguments were rejected by the Court of Appeals in June 1975 when it upheld the constitutionality of the amendments. In brief, the court held that the statutory standards of the law and the possibility of judicial review were sufficient to meet the charge of improper delegation.[30]

With arbitration on trial for a three-year period, Thomas Kochan and colleagues from Cornell University initiated an extensive evaluative study with a grant from the National Science Foundation and the full cooperation of PERB. The findings and recommendations of the study became the focal point for the ensuing debate over continuation. In brief, the Kochan report favored continuation even though it found some evidence that the availability of arbitration may have had both a chilling and a narcotic effect on the negotiation process. The report recommended that the intermediate step of factfinding be eliminated as unproductive and time-consuming. Later Kochan accurately observed that the report probably did little to influence positions of the interest groups but that because of its wide dissemination, it compelled the parties to rationalize their positions in light of the report's findings.[31]

When the 1977 legislature convened, the police and firefighters pressed for making the amendments permanent, while the municipalities urged that they be allowed to lapse. PERB took a middle position, suggesting that further experimentation was needed. Governor Carey weighed in with yet a different proposal, one that reflected the skepticism toward compulsory arbitration of his director of employee relations, Donald Wollett. The governor's bill would retain arbitration but would permit the municipal legislative body to reject an arbitration award. Moreover, it set forth explicit criteria that were to guide the arbitration panel and provided for judicial review.[32]

When the time for action arrived, the legislature was not prepared to go against the wishes of the uniformed services. Minor adjustments were made: factfinding was eliminated; the costs of arbitration would be shared; the criteria were modified and made obligatory; and judicial review was included. Essentially, however, the fundamental process remained intact. The bill extended arbitration for an additional two years, a practice the legislature has continued ever since. By so doing, the legislature, the Senate Republicans in particular, could be assured that the unions would have to return regularly to seek new favors and would not be likely to be too demanding.[33] Governor Carey in signing the bill tried to put the best face on a less than perfect outcome by emphasizing that it clarified the standards for judicial review and further that as a two-year extension it offered additional time for experimentation. Despite continued reference to experimentation, few if any close observers could have believed other than that arbitration had become a permanent feature of the Taylor Law.

The experience with police and firefighter arbitration has been analyzed periodically since 1977. Robert Doherty and Mary Gallo of Cornell University conducted one such analysis in 1979, and PERB staff have conducted studies since then.[34] In general, the number of negotiations reaching impasse has declined markedly so that it now is in line with the proportions recorded by other employee groups, in the 20 to 30 percent range. More than half the cases are settled at mediation, and another quarter are settled after filing for arbitration but before an award is issued. The median time from declaration of impasse to settlement continues to be long, on the order of 250 days. Approximately 60 percent of the awards are unanimous, and there is usually a close correspondence between negotiated salary adjustments in other units or cities and arbitrated salary increases.

Compulsory interest arbitration has not completely eliminated work stoppages by police and firefighters. Since 1974 there have been ten recorded strikes, the last six against the city of Yonkers. The most recent and most serious of these strikes occurred in 1981 when members of the city fire department and high-ranking police officers were out for three days. Except for the troubled city of Yonkers, the special procedures for police and firefighters have functioned well.

GOVERNOR CAREY SEEKS MAJOR CHANGES

For a brief time in 1977, PERB had to contend with two proposals emanating from the governor's office, one of which threatened PERB's hegemony, the other of which would have fundamentally altered the Taylor Law. The proposals were the work of Donald Wollett and were a reflection of his strong preference for applying the private sector model of labor relations in the public sector. Years earlier he had said of the Taylor committee report, "While one hesitates to attack the work product of such a prestigious group, it seems irresponsible not to do so lest the luster of the authors blind their readers to the intrinsic inadequacies of what they have written."[35] The proposals also demonstrated a high degree of political naiveté on Wollett's part in that both seemed designed to alienate just about every possible constituency. The result was that the bills were essentially dead on arrival in the legislature.[36]

A budget bill submitted by the governor would have consolidated the administration of labor relations in the state by combining the functions of PERB, the state labor relations board (SLRB), and the state mediation board into two agencies, a state employment relations board (SERB) and a state mediation service.[37] Representation and unfair labor practice procedures for both the private and public sectors would be the responsibility of the new SERB, while the state mediation service would be responsible for all mediation, factfinding, and arbitration. The state labor relations board, whose jurisdiction had virtually disappeared as the NLRB expanded coverage to private, nonprofit health care facilities and to colleges and universities, would be discontinued. Free factfinding offered by PERB and free grievance arbitration provided by the mediation board would have both been dispensed with.

The plan might have produced some cost savings, but Wollett defended it largely on programmatic grounds. In his view, the reorganization would give primary emphasis to mediation by restoring the two-step procedure of mediation and factfinding mandated by the law in place of PERB's increased reliance on one-step intervention (factfinding). Moreover, mediation would become the responsibility of career staff professionals instead of per diem panel members. As Wollett said, "Mediation takes specialized skills developed through experience, is the best hope of achieving settlements by agreement, and is most effective when done by career staff personnel. I believe there is national consensus on this among experts." Wollett cited the experience of the Wisconsin and Michigan commissions in support of this point as well as on the desirability of having a single agency handle both public and private sector disputes: "The New York pattern of separation is not the norm; it is the exception."[38]

Lack of support for the reorganization plan, if not downright opposition to it, was universal. PERB's employer and union clientele, who were generally satisfied with PERB's performance, saw no advantage to change, and certainly the agency did not. Even the mediation board, which presumably would have gained from an expanded jurisdiction, was unenthusiastic, and some of the unions that benefited from its free grievance arbitration were vigorous in criticizing the scheme. The plan has not resurfaced since.

The governor's program bill, a package of "improvements" deemed warranted after ten years' experience, would have resulted in far-ranging changes in the conduct of public sector labor relations.[39] Some elements of the bill were relatively unexceptional at least from the perspective of PERB, such as plans to strengthen its remedial power in improper practice cases; to abolish mini-PERBs outside New York City; and to authorize agency shop negotiations. More fundamental changes addressed the questions of duty to bargain and strike penalties. Regarding the former, the bill would have adopted the approach of the NLRA whereby an employer would be free to make unilateral changes after having negotiated in good faith to the point of genuine impasse. In effect it did away with PERB's Triborough doctrine.

Regarding strikes, the bill would have allowed courts to issue injunctions only when a strike threatened substantial and irreparable injury to the public health, safety, or welfare. Those accused of violating a court order enjoining a strike could obtain a jury trial. The matter of strike penalties for employee organizations, including the loss of dues deduction privileges, would be left to the courts. Further, PERB would be allowed to reduce penalties against individual strikers upon a finding that the strike was caused by an improper practice of the employer. A final element in the bill would have required that supervisors be in separate negotiating units.

All together, the governor's bill represented a radical change, erasing to a large degree the distinctions between public and private sector bargaining that the Taylor Law had stressed and moving toward a de facto acceptance of the right to strike. Although the unions might have applauded easing the strike prohibition, the entire package lost its attractiveness when that change was coupled with the change in an employer's duty to bargain.

ARBITRATION IN THE METROPOLITAN TRANSPORTATION AUTHORITY

The state legislature has extended compulsory interest arbitration to one other group of public employees, those of the Metropolitan Transportation Authority (MTA). Strikes in the New York City transit system in 1966 and 1980 dramatically illustrated the city's vulnerability to a shutdown of such a vital service. Paradoxically, it was the principal union, Local 100 of the Transport Workers Union, that pressed the legislature in 1982 and again in 1985 to pass special bills imposing arbitration in the event negotiations did not result in a voluntary agreement.

The legislation in effect established impasse procedures akin to those applicable to city employees who came under the Office of Collective Bargaining, thereby recognizing the existence of pattern bargaining in city labor relations. Still recovering from the fines and loss of dues deduction as a result of its 1980 strike, the leadership of TWU was prepared to abandon a longstanding policy of no contract, no work in return for protection from a rambunctious, militant rank and file that compulsory arbitration provided. The 1985 bill was vigorously opposed by the chairman of the MTA, Robert Kiley, who viewed it as totally undercutting his efforts to obtain significant concessions on work rules through negotiations. Mayor Koch also opposed the measure, preferring instead final offer rather than conventional arbitration. With Governor Mario Cuomo's support, however, the union version passed.[40] These earlier ad hoc arrangements were followed in 1987 by an amendment establishing procedures for the MTA similar to those applying to police and fire negotiations. Although scheduled to expire in 1989, it was renewed, and there is little reason to believe that it will not be renewed periodically.

Throughout the debates PERB favored the extension of arbitration to the MTA not only because it gave greater assurance that city transportation services would not be interrupted but also because it spared the agency from the awkward role it had had in previous transit negotiations. Over the years PERB had learned that the labor relations culture of New York City was significantly different from what it was elsewhere and that "outsiders" from Albany were little attended to either by city unions or employers.

Conclusion

In its first two decades the Taylor Law has provided effective machinery for the resolution of collective bargaining disputes and has discouraged, though not eliminated, work stoppages. That the strike prohibition has not been universally honored is a surprise to no one; that it has been obeyed to the degree that it has is quite a different matter. New Yorkers have reason to feel satisfied considering the difficulties of the Condon-Wadlin years and the experience in many other states.

Notes

1. *Government Employee Relations Report,* Reference File 71:2114.
2. *PERB News* 22 (April 1989):1.
3. Kearney, *Labor Relations in the Public Sector,* 205–44.
4. *Government Employee Relations Report,* Reference File 71:1014, 1019.
5. Olson, "Strikes, Strike Penalties, and Arbitration in Six States."
6. 9 PERB 3071.
7. 15 PERB 7008. Because of appeals, the UFT forfeiture did not commence until May 1982. Checkoff rights were restored four months later. 15 PERB 3091.
8. *Buffalo Teachers Federation v. Helsby,* 10 PERB 7015.
9. *Civil Service Employees Association, Columbia County v. Helsby,* 10 PERB 7018.
10. 15 PERB 7009.
11. Interview with Jerome Lefkowitz, 15 June 1986.
12. 14 PERB 3069.
13. The checkoff privileges of District Council 82 were not actually withdrawn until February 1986, almost seven years after the guards strike, and they were restored six months later. 19 PERB 3042. The delay was largely the result of a suit brought by the union in federal court alleging a violation of due process. Besides contending that there had been improper ex parte communication between PERB attorneys prosecuting the case and the board members responsible for deciding the matter, District Council 82 also asserted ironically that the members of the board were biased in part because of the verbal abuse

heaped upon them by union members during the strike, when they were publicly accused of "lying, of not being neutral, of being incompetent, immoral, unethical, and degenerate." The court was unpersuaded. *New York Inspection, Security and Law Enforcement Employees, District Council 82, AFSCME, AFL-CIO v. New York State Public Employment Relations Board et al.*, 19 PERB 7020.

14. 15 PERB 3091.
15. 16 PERB 3020; 16 PERB 3033; 16 PERB 3078.
16. Interview with Harold R. Newman, 19 December 1986.
17. Zimmer and Jacobs, "Challenging the Taylor Law," 543.
18. *Final Report,* 31 March 1966, 33.
19. 1 PERB 704.
20. Interview with Erwin J. Kelly, 18 November 1986.
21. Ibid.
22. Ibid.
23. *PERB News* 19 (April 1986):5.
24. PERB Files, ILR Documentation Center, Cornell University.
25. Benjamin and Hurd, *Rockefeller in Retrospect,* 169–70.
26. Ginsburg, *Legislative Hearings in School Districts.*
27. *PERB News* 7 (July-August 1974):4.
28. In last best offer arbitration, the discretion of the arbitrator is limited to choosing between the last offers of either the union or the management. Few public employee unions showed much interest in obtaining compulsory arbitration. For a brief time in the mid-1970s, CSEA was an exception as it sought to promote what it called LOBA, or last best offer binding arbitration, presumably similar to that proposed by the firefighters.
29. Interview with Robert Gollnick, 25 June 1986.
30. *City of Amsterdam v. Helsby* and *City of Buffalo v. NYS Public Employment Relations Board,* 8 PERB 7011.
31. Kochan et al., *Dispute Resolution under Fact-Finding and Arbitration,* 157–77; Kochan, "The Politics of Interest Arbitration."
32. Memorandum on governor's program bill, 10 March 1977.
33. The legislature has followed the same strategy on the subject of the agency fee, renewing authorization two years at a time.
34. Doherty and Gallo, "Compulsory Interest Arbitration in New York State"; memorandum, Thomas Joyner to Harold Newman, 26 January 1982; memorandum, Erwin Kelly to Harold Newman, 5 March 1985, PERB Files.
35. "The Taylor Law and the Strike Ban," lecture delivered 20 August 1968, Cole Papers.

36. Wollett's temperament—independent, outspoken, and iconoclastic—seemed ill suited to the job of director of employee relations. The point is illustrated by an episode in the midst of difficult negotiations with CSEA when Wollett referred publicly to CSEA and its president Ted Wenzl: "The outfit has no head; it's as though the neck grew long and haired over." Cited by Robert E. Doherty in "A Short and Not Entirely Unbiased History of the First Fifteen Years of New York's Taylor Law." Relations between Governor Carey and the unions improved in later years when the more political Meyer "Sandy" Frucher took over OER.

37. S. Intro. no. 1337 (1977).

38. Letter, Wollett to Robert Helsby, 4 March 1977, PERB Files.

39. Memorandum on governor's program bill, 10 March 1977.

40. *New York Times,* 1 April 1985, I:1; 2 April 1985, II:1.

10
THE TAYLOR LAW:
AN APPRAISAL

THE TAYLOR LAW HAS transformed relations between government employers and their employees. After more than two decades collective bargaining has largely replaced civil service procedures as the primary method for defining the terms and conditions of employment for New York's public employees. In the statement of policy that serves as the preamble to the act, the legislature announced its purposes as "to promote harmonious and cooperative relationships between government and its employees and to protect the public by assuring, at all times, the orderly and uninterrupted operations and functions of government." Harmony and cooperation are elusive concepts, neither easily described nor easily achieved. Probably few existing bargaining relationships merit such a description. Yet open conflict between the parties has gradually declined, and strikes have become something of a rarity in recent years as antagonisms have generally yielded to acceptance of the negotiation process. These recent hopeful signs carry no assurance that the future will follow a similar pattern.

This final chapter records some of the changes that have taken place in the twenty-plus years of the Taylor Law. Special attention is paid to labor relations at the state government level. The chapter closes with an appraisal of PERB and its administration of the law.

SOME CHANGES

The most striking change on the employment scene has been the phenomenal increase in collective negotiations. While the demand for bargaining rights by public employees was bound to grow whether sanctioned by law or not, the results were immediate once those rights were given statutory protection and encouragement in the Taylor Law. The terms of employment, including not only wages, hours, and benefits but also many other critical aspects of work life, for nine out of ten nonfederal public workers in New York are now established through collective negotiations. Although it may be impossible to demonstrate conclusively that government employees in New York are compensated more generously or are treated more fairly as a direct consequence of collective negotiations, few close observers would challenge either assertion.[1]

Because personnel costs are such a large component of total public expenditures, what happens at the bargaining table bears critically on political decisions regarding taxes, budgets, and levels of service. Thus, in a very immediate way, the organizations representing government employees are influential players in the political life of the community. Beyond that, like any powerful interest group, they also employ the customary methods of pressure politics—lobbying, endorsements, and contributions of money and campaign workers. The public sector unions have acquired further political muscle as a consequence of the 1977 authorization of the agency fee (mandated in the case of state employees), which has swelled their treasuries. The growing preeminence of public employee unions relative to private industry unions became increasingly visible in the 1970s as public employee leaders such as Got-

baum, Shanker, and Feinstein overshadowed Corbett and
Van Arsdale as representatives of labor in the state.

That public sector unions have become significantly
more influential in shaping public policy is hardly arguable. Acknowledging such a power shift, however, is
not to share the apocalyptic vision of Harry Wellington
and Ralph Winter, Jr., of public unions acquiring so much
power as to lead to a distortion of the "normal political
process."[2] That has not happened in New York; nor is it
likely to occur. Looking back, it seems that Wellington
and Winter's analysis underestimated the adaptability of
government and its capacity to resist.

CHANGE IN STATE GOVERNMENT

As an employer, the state of New York is large and very
visible. State workers make up close to one-fourth of the
nonfederal public workforce and are scattered across the
state. The outcome of state negotiations therefore affects
local bargaining, not necessarily in that it establishes
a pattern or level of settlement but rather in that it inevitably becomes a reference point for local negotiators.
Equally interesting, even if much less influential, have
been the changes in what might be called the collective
bargaining culture of the state. The approach to labor relations taken by the Governor's Office of Employee Relations is markedly different since the arrival in 1978 of
Meyer ("Sandy") Frucher as director.

In its first decade OER maintained an arm's-length relationship in its dealings with the unions representing
state workers. Melvin Osterman described the strategy followed by Abe Lavine and himself, and to some degree by
his successor, Donald Wollett.

> It was important to us not to be in the debt of our unions
> and to be able to make our decisions on the basis of what was
> in the best interest of the State. . . . Our commitment was to

the long run, not to merely surviving the next four years until the next gubernatorial election. In part that resulted in our
giving up CSEA as an ally, not only in support for the Governor for reelection but their assistance in obtaining support
for the Governor's other programs.[3]

Frucher's style was openly political. Sandy Frucher made
skillful use of labor-management committees to promote
alliances and to assure continued support from union leadership. Even Council 82, which Frucher had bested in the
painful, bitter guards strike of 1979, came around, so that
among its top leadership at least the relationship with
OER was cordial.[4]

Joint committees generously financed by the state were
established to address quality of work life issues, health
and safety matters, pay equity, employee assistance programs, and the like. A great deal of the effort and funds of
the joint committees was directed toward education and
training, investments that Frucher regarded as fundamental to achieving long-term improvements in state service.
There were important advantages in channeling training
through the joint committees: first, it offered protection
from the risk of the traditional legislative gauntlet and
oversight because training expenditures comprised but a
small part of a complex negotiated settlement; and second, the method permitted OER to control the training
function directly and thus to rely less on the cooperation
of others, particularly the Department of Civil Service.

The magnitude of the change in OER strategy is illustrated by a few numbers. Betweeen 1975 and 1983, the
core staff of OER expanded threefold, from seventeen to
fifty persons. A portion of that growth is accounted for
by new responsibilities with respect to managerial and
confidential employees. Beyond this group, however, a far
larger number of employees was attached to the joint
committees that were created by OER with each of its major bargaining partners. In the 1985–86 fiscal year, the

joint labor-management committees had more than $16 million for distribution.[5]

Inexorably, OER has expanded its role and its say in areas that previously were the charge of the civil service department such as health insurance, classification, and workforce planning. Karen Burstein, president of the civil service commission and head of the department, observed that what were once seen as necessary elements in a merit system of personnel administration "have slowly, but inevitably, shifted to OER, because they concern questions which are increasingly answerable only in a labor-management context."[6]

PROGRAM INITIATIVES

In relative terms public sector labor relations in New York have been extraordinarily placid since 1982. Conflict as measured by the number of impasses is down; few workers remain to be organized; existing bargaining structures are stable; and there are no outstanding fundamental issues agitating the labor-management community. Consequently, PERB less often provides a battleground for contending forces or a forum for critical decisions. Instead, public sector labor relations have achieved what some might call "maturity." Mature or not, for PERB this has meant that routine has replaced much of the excitement of an earlier time. Indeed, the slower pace caused the chairman to voice concern that the agency not become "just another stodgy bureaucracy with civil servicitis," and it has prompted a search for opportunities to be "relevant."[7] PERB's 1985–86 annual report quotes Newman as saying, "We seek always to be relevant—(involved with new issues arising in labor-management relations)—and we hope, never bureaucratic."[8]

In its search for relevance and, not incidentally, for activities to occupy the time and talents of its staff, PERB initiated a program in 1984 to promote the establishment of labor-management committees within existing bargaining relationships. The objective was to develop effective vehicles for continuing communication and problem solving outside regular negotiations, which tend to stress competitive rather than cooperative issues. PERB drew upon its conciliation staff and panel members for assistance in starting up more than forty such committees.

The initiative has had considerable success, according to participants, and frequently the labor-management committee has become a permanent, vital structure. One spectacular example of cooperation between a union and a management is that of the Rochester city schools and the Rochester Teachers' Association. In 1987 the parties captured national attention when they jointly announced plans for a major restructuring of the teacher-administration relationship in an effort to breathe new life into public education. While PERB can hardly claim major credit for what transpired in Rochester, it did assist early on in the creation of a labor-management forum that provided a hospitable environment for far-reaching change.

Another new service was launched in 1988 when PERB announced that it would make its staff available for settling grievances through the process of med-arb.[9] At the request of the parties, PERB assigns a staff member, who attempts to settle the grievance by mediation. Failing that, the parties agree to be bound by the mediator's decision. PERB charges a nominal fee for its assistance. Initially the program was to be limited to the Albany area for reasons of cost, but soon it was extended to the entire upstate region. Still modest in scope, the new endeavor has been successful: twenty-two of the first twenty-four cases were settled by mediation.[10] The service has provoked mild complaints from a few private arbitrators who are concerned about incursions onto their turf.

Educational activities have always been given high priority in PERB's overall program. In addition to their strong personal commitment to education, both Robert Helsby and Harold Newman believed that the educational and training function was integral to the achievement of the agency's mission. Examples of several educational efforts have been cited earlier: national and international conferences, training programs for members of minority groups, workshops for ad hoc panel members, internships for university undergraduates, and frequent conferences to update its clientele.

Overall, there has been no letup in PERB's training efforts. A new generation of negotiators seems to replenish constantly the potential audience for the agency's programs. Likewise, PERB's receptivity to the novel, to experimentation, has not flagged, as evidenced by its collaboration with Rockefeller College of Public Affairs and Policy in a project to assess the application of automated decision-making techniques to impasse resolution. Despite the temptation to relax into a semisomnolent state during these quieter times, PERB has strived to find new, worthwhile ways of serving its constituency.

A FINAL WORD

In anticipation of its twentieth anniversary, PERB gave itself a birthday party of sorts in October 1986. It was an occasion to reflect on its journey over the years. Among the invitees were many of the prominent users of PERB's services from both unions and the government. The observations of one participant are worth noting. Bill Scott, a close associate of Al Shanker, has been a staff member of the United Federation of Teachers for a long time. Speaking from the floor, Scott stated that even after twenty years the Taylor Law was still a bad law, made tolerable only by the good administration of PERB. Indeed, were it

not for that saving grace, he said, outraged New York
public workers would eagerly fill Shea Stadium to protest
the law's fundamental unfairness, easily dwarfing the dramatic Madison Square Garden rally of 1967. Allowing for
the expected rhetorical extravagance associated with such
occasions and the fact that exaggerated criticism of any
law prohibiting strikes is almost obligatory for trade
union leaders, Scott's complimentary appraisal of the administration of PERB is nonetheless a fair representation
of opinion within union ranks.

Victor Gotbaum is another articulate unionist who
finds it difficult to speak of the Taylor Law without
sharply criticizing it for its failure to deliver evenhanded
justice. He regards the law's impasse procedures as woe-
fully inadequate, especially when faced with employer
unfair labor practices, in contrast to the impasse arrangements under OCB in New York City. In his opinion only
the presence of two sympathetic (and Democratic) governors, Carey and Cuomo, has served to ameliorate the basic unfairness of the Taylor Law.[11]

From the management side, an assessment of PERB
and how well it has executed its statutory responsibilities
is bound to be less generous. By nature of its function
alone, PERB will inevitably be identified with some loss
of managerial prerogative. Further, there are employer
representatives who believe that PERB has acquired a
pro-union tilt in recent years. They see bias in the quick
restoration of dues deduction privileges to unions that
struck; in the line of decisions on work assignment and
subcontracting; and in the Triborough doctrine and ultimately the Triborough amendment, even though PERB
recommended rejection of the latter in the form in which
it was presented to Governor Carey. For some management critics, the acceptance by Jerry Lefkowitz of a job
with CSEA symbolized the agency's loss of neutrality.

The forgoing critical perception can hardly be said to represent majority opinion on the employer side. The great number of public managers and the diversity in their interests and circumstance make it especially difficult to characterize attitudes in the "management community." That diversity has indeed prevented public managers from coalescing effectively to express unified positions on labor relations issues in the way the unions have through their Public Employee Conference. The two largest public employers, New York City and state government, are much more self-regulating or self-contained and therefore little affected by PERB decisions. Their sophistication and political clout probably make PERB more circumspect in dealing with them.

In sum, PERB has provided high-quality administration of the statute over the years and has in the process earned the respect of practitioners from both sides in spite of occasional outbursts, periodic complaints, and the general grousing often directed at the referee. CSEA's vituperative assaults on the agency during the 1960s illustrate this point. Operating in a field in which considerations of power are often at least as important as economic or legal concerns, PERB has been politically sensitive without permitting politics to control its behavior.

In one respect Bill Scott was correct in attributing whatever success has been achieved in public sector labor relations to the intelligent administration of PERB. Scott was wrong, however, in his dismissal of the Taylor Law as bad law. George Taylor and his colleagues can also claim responsibility for the success of public bargaining in New York. The legal framework they designed has supplied guidance while preserving the possibility of adjustment and accommodation. It was because of this blend of firm principle and flexibility that the Taylor Law was able to survive its early trials and to hold up remarkably well for more than two decades.

NOTES

1. Freeman, "Unionism Comes to the Public Sector," 53–61. Estimates by economists of the union wage effect vary widely. There is a consensus of sorts that at minimum unionization in the public sector raises wage levels on the order of 5 percent. Freeman presents a summary of research on the topic.

2. Wellington and Winter, *The Unions and the Cities*, 25.

3. Osterman, "Two Strikes and You're Out" (unpublished speech).

4. An excellent account of that strike is in Zimmer and Jacobs, "Challenging the Taylor Law."

5. Burstein, *Report to the Governor on Civil Service Revitalization*, 42.

6. Ibid., 36. Burstein recommended a total restructuring of state personnel functions. Most of the functions of the present Department of Civil Service would be combined with those of OER in a new human resources division or department. A small, independent civil service commission would serve as an appellate body for merit system matters.

7. Interview with Harold R. Newman, 19 December 1986.

8. *PERB News* 9 (April 1986):2.

9. PERB news release, 11 January 1988.

10. Richard Curreri, speech at PERB training conference, 18 November 1988.

11. Interview with Victor Gotbaum, 25 September 1985.

BIBLIOGRAPHY

Public Reports and Documents

Bers, Melvin K. *The Status of Managerial, Supervisory and Confidential Government Employment Relations*. Albany: Public Employment Relations Board, January 1970.

Briffault, Richard. *The New York Agency Shop Fee and the Constitution*. Albany: Public Employment Relations Board, 8 August 1986.

Burstein, Karen S. *Report to the Governor on Civil Service Revitalization*. Albany: Department of Civil Service, January 1986.

Cole, David L. Papers. Catherwood Library, Cornell University, Ithaca, New York.

Dewey, Thomas E. Public papers, 1947. Albany.

Doherty, Robert E., and Mary E. Gallo. *Compulsory Interest Arbitration in New York State: Experience under the 1977 Amendments*. Ithaca, N.Y.: School of Industrial and Labor Relations, Cornell University, February 1979.

Ginsburg, Jack A. *Legislative Hearings in School Districts*. Albany: Public Employment Relations Board, May 1972.

Hanslowe, Kurt L., and Walter E. Oberer. *Determining the Scope of Negotiations under Public Employment Relations Statutes*. Albany: Public Employment Relations Board, 1971.

Kheel, Theodore W. *Report to Speaker Anthony J. Travia on the Taylor Law*. Privately published, 21 February 1968.

New York City. *Report of the Mayor's Advisory Committee*. 9 September 1946.

241

New York State. *Commission on the Quality, Cost and Financing of Elementary and Secondary Education, Report.* Albany, October 1972.

———. *Governor's Committee on Public Employee Relations, Final Report.* Albany, 31 March 1966.

———. *Governor's Committee on Public Employee Relations, Interim Report.* Albany, 17 June 1968.

———. *Governor's Committee on Public Employee Relations, Report.* Albany, 23 January 1969.

———. *Joint Legislative Committee on Industrial and Labor Conditions, Report.* Legislative Document no. 32, 1960; no. 17, 1961; no. 26, 1962; no. 38, 1963; no. 17, 1964. Albany.

———. *Legislative Annual.* Albany, 1965, 1969.

———. Public Employment Relations Board. Files. Albany.

———. Public Employment Relations Board. *Official Decisions, Opinions and Related Matters.* Washington, Penn.: Labor Relations Press, 1967–.

———. Public Employment Relations Board. *Record of Proceedings in the Matter of State of New York.* Case no. C-0002 et al., 1967–69. Albany.

———. Public Employment Relations Board. *Year One of the Taylor Law, September 1, 1967–August 31, 1968.* Albany.

———. *Select Joint Legislative Committee on Public Employee Relations, Report.* Legislative Document no. 14, 1969. Albany.

New York State School of Industrial and Labor Relations, Cornell University. *Report and Findings: Conference on Employee-Management Relations in the Public Service.* Ithaca, N.Y., October 1964.

Sabghir, Irving. *The Scope of Bargaining in the Public Sector.* Albany: Public Employment Relations Board, 1970.

U.S. Bureau of Labor Statistics. *The Dimensions of Major Work Stoppages, 1947–59.* Bulletin 1298. Washington, D.C.: Government Printing Office, 1961.

BOOKS AND MONOGRAPHS

Bellush, Jewell, and Bernard Bellush. *Union Power and New York: Victor Gotbaum and District Council 37.* New York: Praeger, 1984.

Benjamin, Gerald, and T. Norman Hurd, eds. *Making Experience Count: Managing Modern New York in the Carey Era.* Albany: Nelson A. Rockefeller Institute of Government, 1985.

———. *Rockefeller in Retrospect: The Governor's New York Legacy.* Albany: Nelson A. Rockefeller Institute of Government, 1984.

Committee for Economic Development. *The Public Interest in National Labor Policy.* New York, 1961.

Donovan, Ronald, and Marsha J. Orr. *Subcontracting in the Public Sector: The New York Experience.* Ithaca, N.Y.: Institute of Public Employment, Cornell University, 1982.

Dulles, Foster Rhea. *Labor in America.* 2d rev. ed. New York: Thomas Y. Crowell, 1960.

Eddison, John Corbin. "Teacher Strikes in the United States." Master's thesis, New York State School of Industrial and Labor Relations, Cornell University, 1947.

Finkelman, Jacob, and Shirley B. Goldenberg. *Collective Bargaining in the Public Service: The Federal Experience in Canada.* Ottawa: Institute for Research on Public Policy, 1983.

Goulden, Joseph C. *Jerry Wurf: Labor's Last Angry Man.* New York: Atheneum, 1982.

Hanslowe, Kurt L. *The Emerging Law of Labor Relations in Public Employment.* Ithaca, N.Y.: New York State School of Industrial and Labor Relations, Cornell University, 1967.

Hardisky, David L. "The Rochester General Strike of 1946." Ph.D. diss., University of Rochester, 1983.

Horton, Raymond D. *Municipal Labor Relations in New York City: Lessons of the Lindsay-Wagner Years.* New York: Praeger, 1973.

Kearney, Richard C. *Labor Relations in the Public Sector.* New York: Marcel Dekker, 1984.

Kheel, Theodore W., and J. K. Turcott. *Transit and Arbitration.* Englewood Cliffs, N.J.: Prentice-Hall, 1960.

Kochan, Thomas A., Mordehai Moroni, Ronald G. Ehrenberg, Jean Baderschneider, and Todd Jick. *Dispute Resolution under Fact-Finding and Arbitration: An Empirical Analysis.* New York: American Arbitration Association, 1978.

Kramer, Milton, and Sam Roberts. *I Never Wanted to Be Vice President of Anything!: An Investigative Biography of Nelson Rockefeller.* New York: Basic Books, 1976.

Lefkowitz, Jerome. *The Legal Basis of Employee Relations of New York State Employees.* Association of Labor Mediation Agencies, 1973.

Mackell, Thomas J., Jr. "David L. Cole: An Analysis of His Philosophy of Labor Relations and Its Impact on the Development of the New York State Taylor Law." Ed.D. thesis, Rutgers University, 1981.

Moskow, Michael H., and Myron Lieberman. *Collective Negotiations for Teachers: An Approach to School Administration.* Chicago: Rand McNally, 1966.

Oberer, Walter E., Kurt L. Hanslowe, and Robert E. Doherty. *The Taylor Act: A Primer for School Personnel (and Other Beginners at Collective Negotiations).* Ithaca, N.Y.: New York State School of Industrial and Labor Relations, Cornell University, 1968.

Persico, Joseph. *The Imperial Rockefeller.* New York: Simon and Schuster, 1982.

Quill, Shirley. *Mike Quill, Himself—A Memoir.* Greenwich, Conn.: Devin-Adair, 1985.

Robinson, Frank S. *Machine Politics: A Study of Albany's O'Connells.* New Brunswick, N.J.: Transaction Books, 1977.

Salz, Arthur Eliot. "The Growth of Teacher Unionism in New York City, 1945–1962." Ed.D. thesis, Columbia University, 1968.

Spero, Sterling D. *Government as Employer.* New York: Remsen Press, 1948.

Wellington, Harry H., and Ralph K. Winter, Jr. *The Unions and the Cities.* Washington, D.C.: Brookings Institution, 1971.

Ziskind, David. *One Thousand Strikes of Government Employees.* New York: Columbia University Press, 1940.

ARTICLES

Crowley, Joseph R. "The Resolution of Representation Status Disputes under the Taylor Law." *Fordham Law Review* 37 (May 1969):517–34.

Doherty, Robert E. "A Short and Not Entirely Unbiased History of the First Fifteen Years of New York's Taylor Law." *Journal of Collective Negotiations* 13 (1984):361–72.

Englander, William H. "Scope of the Duty to Bargain under the Taylor Law: The Fog-Bound 'Mission' of the Public Employer." *New York Law Journal* 173 (6 February 1975):1,4.

Freeman, Richard B. "Unionism Comes to the Public Sector." *Journal of Economic Literature* 24 (March 1986):41–86.

Kochan, Thomas A. "The Politics of Interest Arbitration." *Arbitration Journal* 33 (March 1978):5–9.

Lincoln, Albert L. "The New York City Transit Strike: An Explanatory Approach." In *Public Policy*, edited by John D. Montgomery and Albert O. Hirschman. Cambridge, Mass.: Harvard University Press, 1967.

McKelvey, Jean T. "The Role of State Agencies in Public Employee Labor Relations." *Industrial and Labor Relations Review* 20 (January 1967):179–97.

Newman, Harold R. "The Duty in the Public Sector." In *The Changing Law of Fair Representation*, edited by Jean T. McKelvey. Ithaca, N.Y.: ILR Press, 1985.

Olson, Craig A. "Strikes, Strike Penalties, and Arbitration in Six States." *Industrial and Labor Relations Review* 39 (July 1986):539–51.

Raskin, A. H. "Politics Up-Ends the Bargaining Table." In *Public Workers and Public Unions*, edited by Sam Zagoria. Englewood Cliffs, N.J.: American Assembly, 1972.

Riccucci, Norma, and Carolyn Ban. "The Unfair Labor Practice Process in Dispute-Resolution Technique in the Public Sector: The Case of New York." *Review of Public Personnel Administration* 9 (Spring 1989):51–67.

Rosenzweig, Stefan. "The Condon-Wadlin Act Re-examined." *ILR Research* 11 (1):3–8.

Taylor, George W. "Collective Bargaining in the Public Sector." In *The Next Twenty-Five Years of Industrial Relations*, edited by Gerald G. Somers. Madison, Wisc.: Industrial Relations Research Association, 1973.

Weiler, Paul. "Promises to Keep: Securing Workers' Rights to Self Organization under the NLRA." *Harvard Law Review* 96 (1983):1769–1827.

Zimmer, Lynn, and James B. Jacobs. "Challenging the Taylor Law: Prison Guards on Strike." *Industrial and Labor Relations Review* 34 (July 1981):531–44.

PAPERS AND SPEECHES

Helsby, Robert D. "Scope of Bargaining under New York's Taylor Law." Paper presented at Temple University, Philadelphia, 3 September 1975.

Lefkowitz, Jerome. "The Duty to Negotiate under the Taylor Law." Speech delivered at conference, New Paltz, New York, 4 August 1975.

Osterman, Melvin H., Jr. "Two Strikes and You're Out—The Taylor Law: The First Ten Years." Remarks delivered at Hidden Valley, New York, 15 November 1983.

INDEX

About the Author

Ronald Donovan is a professor emeritus in the School of Industrial and Labor Relations at Cornell University, where he has taught since 1955. His teaching and research have focused on public sector collective bargaining. Beginning in 1966, he was responsible for a statewide educational program to familiarize state and local employees and managers with ways to prepare for collective bargaining. Subsequently, he developed one of the first courses on collective bargaining in the public sector. A member of the PERB panel of mediators and fact finders, he has continued to work closely with public unions and public managers in New York and elsewhere. He is the coauthor of *Subcontracting in the Public Sector: The New York State Experience*.